BRITISH SUBMARINES AT WAR
1939-1945

KU-679-327

BRITISH
SUBMARINES
AT WAR
1939-1945

ALASTAIR MARS

Foreword by
Vice-Admiral J.C.Y. Roxburgh
CB CBE DSO DSC
Flag Officer Submarines

WILLIAM KIMBER
LONDON

First published in 1971 by
WILLIAM KIMBER & CO. LIMITED
Godolphin House, 22a Queen Anne's Gate,
London, S.W.1

© Alastair Mars, 1971

SBN 7183 0202 8

*This book is copyright. No part of it may be
reproduced in any form without permission in
writing from the publishers except by a reviewer
who wishes to quote brief passages in connection
with a review written for inclusion in a magazine
or newspaper or a radio broadcast.*

PRINTED IN GREAT BRITAIN BY W. & J. MACKAY, LTD.
CHATHAM, KENT

CONTENTS

ILLUSTRATIONS

(Photographs are reproduced by permission of the Imperial War Museum unless otherwise noted)

MAPS

ACKNOWLEDGEMENTS

First and foremost, I am most deeply indebted to Rosabel Menzies and her sons Gavin and Robin for permission to use, and quote extensively from, the diaries of the late Captain Menzies, without which this book could not have been written in its present form. When Captain Menzies was at the very hub of submarine operations at home, I myself was far away and much too junior to have his close and intimate knowledge of the situation. These meticulously kept diaries therefore close an otherwise unbridgeable gap.

In the book, Captain Menzies is last seen operating his Second Flotilla out of Halifax, late in 1941. On 11th February 1942, he took command of the cruiser *Orion* and drove her long and arduously through the hottest of Mediterranean convoy fire, later to bombard the invasion beaches at Salerno and to be awarded the Distinguished Service Order.

I am grateful also to Captain G.A.W. Voelcker, Royal Navy who, early in 1942 at Gibraltar, ensured *Unbroken's* war efficiency before unleashing her into the Mediterranean with myself in command. Captain Voelcker later commanded the cruiser *Charybdis* in which he was to die close to the home of his ancestors when that ship was sunk by torpedo-boat night attack, off the Channel Islands in 1944.

Although the main body of the book is comprised of material within my own knowledge, my memory has been much refreshed by quite recent conversations with many of those appearing in the text who are not therefore mentioned here. But I would particularly like to thank Rear-Admiral Ben Bryant CB DSO DSC for supplying the names of his officers in *Safari*, some of which I had forgotten. Additionally, Commander E.T. Stanley DSO DSC, Royal Navy, has kindly confirmed some details regarding the Italian October 1942 convoy to Tripoli which he, in *Unbending*, attacked shortly before *Unbroken* did so.

I also owe thanks to Lieutenant-Commander Matthew Todd, Royal Navy, once my sturdy navigator in *Thule*, who is now the Navy's expert and record holder for deep submarine escapes; for he has supplied me with an expert opinion regarding the lost submarine *Perseus*.

I must also record my appreciation of the distinguished foreword which to even an author of the greatest renown would be something to preserve for his grandchildren. Its writer, Vice-Admiral J.C.Y. Roxburgh CB CBE DSO DSC, the present Flag Officer Submarines, states that he does not agree with all my opinions; but this I could hardly expect from any man!

For details of military activity at Hong Kong, I am grateful for the assistance of Colonel Frank Walden MBE DL, Majors Henry Marsh and Max Langley of the Middlesex Regiment and for that of Major R.W.J. Smith MBE of the Middlesex Regimental Association.

My first book, *Unbroken*, is still appearing in an 'Evergreen' edition from William Collins, Sons & Company Limited, having been published in its original edition by Frederick Muller Limited. I am indebted to both these publishers for permission to quote one paragraph verbatim and to use the work as a centre-piece around which to construct the pattern of some operations and episodes in the Mediterranean during 1942 and 1943.

As regards research facilities, I would like to thank the Staff of the British Museum Reading Room and particularly that of the State Paper Room, all of whom have been most helpful. My thanks are also due to the Chief Librarian of the Royal Borough of Kensington & Chelsea Central Library, and to the Daily Telegraph Information Bureau of which the Staff have painstakingly answered many telephoned enquiries and some written ones.

A short list of informative, and sometimes prodigious, works and documents consulted will be found in the Bibliography which constitutes Appendix III.

With its many unfamiliar names of personalities, ships and far distant places, the typescript has not been an easy one to produce. I therefore feel it fitting that I should credit the Peter Coxson Typing Service with a most difficult job well and truly done.

Finally, although of the utmost importance, are the maps and diagrams which have been prepared with great clarity by Mr Leslie Perry, with some helpful suggestions from the Curator of the Submarine Museum at Gosport. I am delighted that Leslie Perry, a Member of the Submarine Chief and Petty Officers' Mess at Fort Blockhouse, should have devoted his spare time in helping to produce a work which is, I trust, a tribute to all Submariners. I am also grateful to the President of the Mess* and others in that select company whose friendly entertainment has inspired me to greater efforts.

* Chief (CMEA(P)) R.G. Maddern R.N.

DEDICATION

With admiration and deep affection for the late Captain George Menzies, D.S.O., Royal Navy, who prepared us all for battle, and to the living memory of submarine officers and men lost at sea—
H.31, H.49, SALMON, SEAHORSE, SHARK, SNAPPER, SPEARFISH, STARFISH, STERLET, SWORDFISH, SYRTIS, TARPON, THISTLE, UMPIRE, UNBEATEN, UNDINE, UNIQUE, UNITY, UNTAMED, VANDAL, NARWHAL, SEAL, OXLEY, THAMES, P.514, P.615, ODIN, GRAMPUS, ORPHEUS, PHOENIX, OSWALD, RAINBOW, TRIAD, REGULUS, USK, UNDAUNTED, TRITON, CACHALOT, UNION, P.32, P.33, TETRARCH, PERSEUS, TRIUMPH, TEMPEST, P.36, P.38, P.39, PANDORA, UPHOLDER, URGE, OLYMPUS, THORN, TALISMAN, UTMOST, TRAVELLER, P.222, P.311, P.48, TIGRIS, THUNDERBOLT, TURBULENT, SAHIB, SPENDID, REGENT, PARTHIAN, SARACEN, USURPER, TROOPER, SIMOON, SICKLE, STONEHENGE, STRATAGEM, PORPOISE, not forgetting Allied losses—0.13, 0.22, K.VII, K.IX, K.XVI, K.XVII, 0.16, 0.20, *(Dutch)*; DORIS SURCOUF, NARVAL, *(French)*; GLAUKOS, TRITON, PROTEUS, KATSONIS, *(Greek)*; UREDD, *(Norwegian)*; ORZEL, JASTRAZAB, *(Polish)*; SUNFISH, *(Russian)*.
MIDGET SUBMARINES, CHARIOTEERS and FROGMEN.

*

'There is no branch of His Majesty's Forces which in this war has suffered the same proportion of fatal loss as our Submarine Service. It is the most dangerous of all services.'

Part of a tribute paid by The Rt. Hon.
Winston S. Churchill, speaking in the
House of Commons in 1941.

FOREWORD

It gives me great pleasure to be asked to write the foreword to this book. It fills a gap in the history of British Submarines in the Second World War between the lengthy official histories and other shorter books which have sought only to cover a particular aspect.

The author has effectively covered a vast amount of ground in succint style and has managed to intersperse his record of events with some illuminating vignettes of submarine life. He is well qualified to write as he has, having been near the centre of the main activity for so much of the time. His experiences ranged from those of a comparatively junior officer in submarines in the Far East just before the war and in the Mediterranean at its shattering start (for submarines); then as a submarine Commanding Officer in Home Waters during the period of intensive training in the building up of the submarine arm and in the Mediterranean at the turn of events in our favour; subsequently as a Staff Officer at the Submarine Headquarters in London and finally back to the Far East towards the end of the war as a Submarine Commanding Officer again.

I would expect the views of an author such as Alastair Mars to be forthright and controversial, but one does not have to agree with them all, as indeed I do not, to admire his sweeping and masterly account of stirring times.

J C Y ROXBURGH
Vice-Admiral
Flag Officer Submarines

Fort Blockhouse
Gosport Hants
19 July 1971.

Author's Introduction

Although several excellent books have already been written on the exploits of British submarines in the Second World War we have, insofar as I know, not yet seen a published attempt to embrace the vast arena of all their operations. It may not generally be known that, at one time or another, our submarines were on patrol off places as far apart as Vladivostock and Madagascar, Java and Gibraltar; whilst, in the Atlantic, they ranged from icy Murmansk nearly to the windswept Falklands and from the sweaty heat of Guinea to the foggy Banks of Newfoundland.

When Mr. William Kimber suggested I write this book, in lieu of another I had in mind, my feelings were a mixture of humility at the honour of the work and of pride; for I had had the good fortune to be there and somehow last the pace.

In pondering how to handle this great and complex subject, in an effort to produce a balanced and concise account, I decided to restrict myself mainly to those areas in which our submarines' presence had, to my mind, the greatest effect; with only brief surveys of other essential activities, not however forgetting colourful, rumbustious and lovable characters.

As most of our operations were closely related to those of the main surface forces of the Royal Navy, the Army and the Royal Air Force, such cooperation will be brought to light; for it is only by pulling together that any nation can succeed, in peace as much as in war.

With regard to personalities, I take a liberty for which I crave indulgence. As most of my seniors in the Navy were kind enough to address me by my Christian name, I hope none will now mind my using first names or those nicknames by which they were popularly known; although a formal list will be included in the index. As the entire Navy was, and is, a band of brothers; so were the wartime submariners a smaller band in which each was known to each, both officers and men—a regiment, one might say; a regiment which in manpower seldom much exceeded 300 officers and 3,000 men.

This book is about ships of war, their achievements, victories and disasters; but no ship can live without the men who give her sinews and courage, without the chief and petty officers who provide the backbone, or without the officers who are supposed to give an intelligent lead—and frequently do. It has long been a facet of the Navy that, because of their compactness and highly centralised nervous systems, ships in battle are often spoken of by their captains' names; and this is particularly so in submarines. Nevertheless I would ask my readers constantly to remember that through the failure or mistake of a single man, a surface ship can be destroyed or a submarine sunk; that an honour to one is an honour to all and that those who escape their ship's destruction are usually limited to the hardiest and the luckiest.

It is fitting that I should pay tribute to all civilians who fought and suffered, to the Armed Forces of Commonwealth and Empire and to those of our Allies; lest it be thought that I am attempting to raise the British submariner above others which is a thing he would not ask; nor, physically speaking, would he attempt to achieve it.

I express also my admiration for Allied submariners under British operational control who gallantly surmounted human stresses we never had to bear; that is to say those of homelands devastated with no news of their loved ones, those sometimes of conflicting loyalties and broken links, all overshadowed by memories of flight, defeat and disaster; but never of despair. Their losses are listed in the dedication with our own.

And my heart goes out to the families of the men who fought, because theirs' was the hardest lot of all; always anxious, often bereaved, sometimes homeless and mainly poor, they won through with valour, perseverance and even gaiety: so to uphold that faith and morale by which all peoples must live . . . or die.

Since time immemorial, war has invariably been thrust upon the civilisations of the world and it has, in the long run, inexorably destroyed them. I feel it to be a dangerous vanity to assume that human nature improves; although people must strive to better it. After all, one might ask: 'Which was the worst, Alexander the Great, Tamerlane or Hitler?' To me, there seems little doubt; and the answer is disturbing. Hitler failed; but others might succeed by different and even more vicious means.

I hope that young people will read this book, and particularly those who have come recently to make Britain their home; because we now have a fine new generation and the events herein described, however ineptly, are a part of their maritime heritage.

My task is set. I go to it with a will and, I trust, objectivity.

Chapter 1

Before the Second World War

The idea of the submarine was not new when, in the last decades of the nineteenth century, the invention of the internal combustion engine provided propulsion and that of the Whitehead torpedo an effective weapon. It was natural that the Admiralty of the greatest fleets afloat, both naval and merchant, should regard this new and dangerous type of vessel with alarm and loathing. So, in the usual inimitable way of mankind, instead of developing submarines and then finding a means of destroying them, they at first ignored them; but later built the 'A' and 'B' class, relegating them to the duty of coastal patrol. These and the 'C's were petrol-driven boats; but the 'D's had diesel engines and, with the 'E' class, came our first proper ocean-going submarines.

During the First World War the majority of British submarines were employed on reconnaissance duties in the North Sea where we also had some attack successes, particularly against U-boats: but the main role lay in reporting enemy squadrons in order that our superior surface forces could intercept and destroy. The Germans however showed a remarkable capacity for evasion, in the knowledge that a comparatively undamaged 'fleet in being' posed a tremendous threat to this country, whilst their U-boats created a nauseating havoc in the Atlantic—a strategy they repeated in the Second World War.

The specially designed 'R' class submarines, with a submerged speed of about 13 knots, were for hunting U-boats; but proved little more successful than other types. In the First World War, our submarines sank 18 U-boats, or half the number sunk by depth charges. But public imagination was fired mainly by the early exploits of such men as Dunbar-Nasmith who won the V.C. in the Sea of Marmora where the gun was used to great effect and later of Max K. Horton D.S.O., whose great tenacity and success in the Baltic made him the perfect choice as Flag Officer Submarines for nearly three years during the last war.

Another special design constituted a few submarine monitors which carried a 12" gun for coastal bombardment; but the most interesting, to my mind, was the staff requirement for a fast submersible to operate as a unit of the fleet, usually with the battle-cruisers working from Rosyth. This led to a shipbuilding feat of considerable magnitude in the production of 14 'K' class of 2,600 tons submerged displacement, *steam-driven* on the surface at the (then) staggering speed of 23 knots; and one is reputed to have achieved 26 knots . . . Juggernaut indeed!

This description is unfortunately apt; for K.13 was lost on trials in the Gareloch and a ghastly mishap in 1918 caused two divisions of K-boats to run into a battle squadron at night off the Firth of Forth, resulting in the loss of two more and a great many men. The tragedy is somewhat casually described by submariners as 'The Battle of May Island'.

The object of the 'K's was to steam in close company with the battle-cruisers and, on nearing the enemy, dive and attack if possible; otherwise to surface after sighting them, then to shadow and report enemy position, course and speed by wireless. These ideas were not very productive because the Germans seldom put to sea. Nevertheless the principle was sound enough and, if nothing else, it elevated the submarine's position from that of a patrol boat to a ship of the fleet. And when together with great ships of the past such as *Lion* and *Tiger,* these speedy 'K' class submarines must have made a thrilling sight. Despite comparative mechanical success and good submerged behaviour, they were amongst the first to be banished by post-war economy. More important, the staff requirement for speed had lapsed and, with four exceptions, unfortunately was not again imposed until 1945. Later, a slower type of fleet submarine appeared; but in the concept of wolfpack tactics against superior surface forces of possible enemies: this subject will be elaborated in Chapter Three.

Between 1918 and 1922, British submarine strength was reduced from 138 to 55, of which 11 were in reserve. Nor were any new submarines completed until 1927; excepting the cruiser X.1 of 3,600 tons submerged displacement, armed with six 21" torpedo tubes and four 5.2" guns in twin turrets.

By virtue of her size and gun armament, X.1 was bound to be largely experimental as her name portended. Laid down in 1921, she took nearly four years to build, was not considered a success and went to the scrap-heap in 1931; or that is the official story: but, as Leslie Gardiner suggests in his intriguing work, *The British Admiralty*, many decisions have been made in that seat of power which remain unrecorded. Also, I seem to recall *X.1*'s ghost swinging around a buoy in Portsmouth harbour much later than 1931—or perhaps this was X.2—and have certainly heard that she handled beautifully when submerged, that her guns were more efficient than rumoured and the troubles of her powerful newly-designed engines exaggerated. These last were bound to have teething pains, as one would expect from diesels created to replace steam at comparable speeds and at a time when the former were in their infancy. Many of the lessons learnt became incorporated in the engines of later sizeable submarines and particularly in *Thames, Severn* and *Clyde* of 22½ knots, last successors to the pre-war 'K' class Juggernauts, until the advent of the 'nuclears', also steam-driven.

One unofficial reason given for the early demise of *X.1* was that the *success* of the biggest submarine in the world had scared the Admiralty into the thought that other navies might copy her (and the French did), thus threatening our trade routes; so it was bruited around that she had been a costly failure. But there is, I think, a broader and more pertinent reason; and that lies within the compass of the plethora of disarmament conferences and treaties which followed in the wake of the First World War; and here are things not too well remembered today.

In 1919, Europe lay back from war, aghast and exhausted by the most gruesome slaughter in the history of the West. During the summer of that year, as a wee lad, I watched Alcock and Brown take off from Newfoundland for their epoch-making Atlantic flight; then followed them across the Western Ocean to visit Britain with my parents. My impressions of London in the summer of 1919 are vivid and can be summarised in one word . . . 'zest.' A tremendous zest for life electrified the air. The sky of the future looked bright. President Woodrow Wilson was prophesying paradise, and the peoples of the West put more faith in him than in the Almighty: they also believed and really believed that the war to end wars had come and gone. It was against this background, despite reverses, that disarmament treaties were to be hopefully, but not wisely negotiated.

Two years later, Crown Prince Hirohito of Japan, Britain's great naval ally, landed at Portsmouth from a Japanese battleship for a relaxed and friendly tour—the first time an Emperor or Crown Prince had left his native land. But it was also the last time of friendship between the two great island trading countries, until recently. In 1971, Hirohito comes again, as Emperor: let us welcome him in the knowledge that his second visit presages events less ominous than his first, which may have been a cover for Japanese ambition or an appeal for the renewal of the Anglo-Japanese Naval Treaty of 1902.

In 1915, Japan, taking advantage of a Europe at war, presented China with an ultimatum known as the Twenty-one Demands which would have destroyed that country's independence, had not Britain, France and the United States interceded on China's behalf. But the writing was thus put plainly on the wall; and remained there more and more starkly until in December 1941, it fused with the violent betrayal of undeclared war.

At the Washington Conference of 1921-22, Great Britain abandoned her century-old two-power naval standard, accepted parity with the United States and a ratio of five to three with Japan, which country was already embarked on a gigantic building programme. This single stroke of an altruistic pen made Japan the supreme sea power in the Western Pacific; with the Russians hemmed in at Vladivostok, the Americans 3,000 miles eastwards in Pearl Harbour and the British almost as far to the south, at Singapore; for the British and American advanced bases at Hong Kong and Manila were barely tenable, and more than offset by the Japanese hold on Formosa.

This handsome present to a potential enemy, of which the Japanese made full use by further incursions into China, must go on record as the bloodiest blunder ever to redden the oceans; yet it was made on land, by politicians sitting around a table.

Insofar as the Royal Navy was concerned, the effects of the Washington Conference created a situation unknown for one hundred and fifty years: Britain became a power with inferior naval forces, not only in the Far East but everywhere; for a European coalition of France and Italy—with the later addition of Germany—could outnumber the available British forces.

The U-boat ravishment, between 1914 and 1918, of the seaborne supplies essential to the life of this country had shown beyond all doubt that, however horrible, the principle weapon of an inferior naval power was the submarine. History dictates that a rule of war successfully infringed is seldom restored, and certainly never in the same century.

British politicians, it seems, do not much care for history because, at the Washington Conference, they made the Royal Navy inferior in fighting strength with the right hand, simultaneously grasping the Root Resolution to their breasts with the left. This resolution ordained that submarines could attack only enemy warships and known auxiliaries: it then went on to impose such strict conditions on the interception of merchant vessels as to ban submarines from such activity and to make it difficult for even surface warships. The Root Resolution was accepted at Washington but not fully ratified.

And all this at a time when the British were building *X.1*, the largest, most powerful and fastest submarine commerce raider yet conceived! Small wonder they called her a cruiser—and a failure at that.

Successive British governments persisted in their efforts to hamstring the submarine and, in the London Naval Treaty of 1930 (Part IV.), achieved success. By 1940, they wished they hadn't!

In an environment of political anti-submarine activity, over two decades, it seems surprising that British submarines survived at all; and they might not, except that their existence became guaranteed by another form of anti-submarine activity—the practical. The Admiralty, now determined to beat the U-boat, made themselves champions of the Allied Submarine Detection Investigation Committee (A.S.D.I.C.) and developed its results far more vigorously than others, establishing a lively and demanding anti-submarine (A/S) school at Portland. The demand was for submarines upon which asdic-fitted destroyers could practice; and this became a major peace time 'staff requirement' (magic words these!).

Despite all adversity there was never a lack of volunteers for submarines, in which the inherent dangers had been well advertised by a series of disasters—too many accidents, in fact, which may have reflected the 'gay cavalier' outlook of those who joined for adventure. Whilst such an attitude is laudable at the outset; it must be subjected to a long period of intense training and concentrated attention to detail before it can be unleashed with advantage. When a man knows what he is doing with, and about, submarines, he can be as gay and high-spirited as he likes. We were blessed with many such.

Some were attracted by the extra pay, an understandable reason but one ringed with qualifications. Those who had only this as their motive were not always our greatest assets, particularly amongst officers. The best probably sprang from the category which sought more responsibility, combined with danger and extra punch.

The latent question assails me; so here is the answer. I myself joined in 1936 for the warm atmosphere of the submarine base at

Fort Blockhouse and the thought of a command in the war I could see just around the corner.

People have often asked what special qualifications are required in the captain of a submarine, as opposed to the captain of any other warship. If it is not presumptuous, I would say that exceptional power of concentration is one, immense determination another. In war, the submarine C.O. requires the moral courage to oppose an impossible demand from his own side and the ability to put his case to seniors without rancour. For, if he attempts something he knows he cannot achieve, he will certainly kill his crew and lose his ship. Above all, he must be not only self-sufficient but also self-contained. At sea, although usually surrounded by a crew of friends, he is alone, and *all* alone for very long periods.

By 1933, the Rising Sun—and power—of Japan had caused this lonely paragon to be provided with temples less antediluvian in which to practice his cult. The Admiralty had previously convinced the government that the only possible British challenge to the Japanese battlefleet anywhere north of Luzon was the submarine. Sixteen large boats of the 'O', 'P' and 'R' classes had been built, commissioned and based on the splendid new depot-ship *Medway,* mainly at Hong Kong. The great advantage of depot-ships is their mobility; thus the most powerful submarine flotilla yet assembled could, and did, range the fabulous Seven Seas from the Great Barrier Reef to Sumatra, their navigators eternally correcting thirty folios of charts upon which such exotic names as Arafura, Timor, Java, Flores, Banda, Sulu and Celebes were commonplace. More familiar yet was the China Coast from Wei Hai Wei to Hainan and most exercised of all was the South China Sea where the great battle for Singapore and the clash of empires would surely take place. Significant was the fact that, for the first time since the 'K' class, British submarines had again become major war vessels; and actually the most powerful vessels in our China Fleet, for the cruisers, aircraft-carriers and destroyers constituted only a force strong enough to necessitate very heavy convoy cover being provided by the Japanese.

On 5th January 1938, Commander G.C.P. Menzies wrote in his diary:

'*Regulus* started her 28 day patrol. We sailed from H.K.* at 0800 and were seen off in great style by 'S' † who was as charming as ever. Our first move is for 10 of us to intercept *Medway* off Manila on passage to Labuan. Our company sailed

* Hong Kong. † Captain (Submarines) Claude Barry D.S.O., R.N.

in great heart, I think largely because of 'S's good speech to us yesterday.'

On 31st January, he wrote:

'Surface patrol. After tea we attacked *Norfolk* (Commander-in-Chief, East Indies) and got in a beauty at 500 yards. Unfortunately she had us in sight for *five minutes* before we dived. Martin *sent for me* (instead of diving at once), after all his training! I could have killed him: I do not think that he will make the submarine grade.'

I am happy to say that my great friend, the late Commander J.D. Martin D.S.C., Royal Navy did indeed make the grade—in the testing cauldron of the Sicilian Channel. So, on this occasion at least, George Menzies was wrong; but I understand his feelings only too well.

At 2155, Singapore time, on 2nd February 1938, Captain Claude Barry D.S.O., commanding *Medway* and the Fourth Submarine Flotilla, sent the following signal:

'Commander-in-Chief, China, repeated to—Rear-Admiral Submarines, Commodore Malaya, *Regulus*. CONFIDENTIAL.

'*Regulus* has completed twenty-eight days war patrol exercise. She has steamed 3,940 miles on surface and 390 miles submerged, carried out 14 submerged attacks, 3 night contact exercises, been hunted by A/S destroyers and aircraft. Patrol was all in tropical waters (no air-conditioning then) with 23 days spent south of Lat: 06 degrees north. Has returned with no defects and experienced practically none. Health of crew excellent partly due to special diet adopted. It is nearly eighteen months since *Regulus* was refitted. This patrol exercise is twice as long as any yet done in peace time. I consider that great credit is due to the Commanding Officer, Commander Menzies and all in *Regulus*.'

George Menzies was known as 'The Colonel'; and, as Senior Submarine Officer of this great flotilla, he was indeed the Colonel of his Regiment. By his then unheard-of patrol did he set the edge for combat, and no Commanding Officer in that 15-strong submarine battle squadron failed to follow his lead. It was therefore with trepidation and uncertainty that I myself, after a long bout of illness and only a year's submarine experience, became the armament officer of a newly-refitted *Regulus* in August of 1938.

A month later several submarines were on exercise patrol off South East Johore; and the diary reads:

'24th September. Recalled to S'pore because of Hitler getting fresh.

25th September. *Olympus, Perseus, Pandora and Proteus* prepared for war in 12 hours.

26th September. They went off on detached service. It is sad that we thereby lose four of the nicest C.O.s

27th September. Order to fuse shell.

28th September. Ordered to prepare for war, though the warning telegram did not arrive . . . . The order to prepare arrived at 1030 and eight of us were through by 0130: 15 hours, which seems satisfactory. Our system went well and everybody dug out like mad.'

But in the Navy as a whole the mobilisation did not go so well, only adequately: the lessons were not lost. A special book was prepared. Its code names affected every department of the Navy, including civilian victualling and store yards, and its contents covered every requirement from sailmaker's needles through provisions and oil fuel to torpedoes and 16-inch shell. When, in August of 1939, the codes in this confidential book were signalled to the fleet, their effect proved magical. All the paraphernalia and accoutrements of war flowed swiftly to the ships, reflecting a colossal administrative effort by civilians and naval personnel working in harness.

In the Far East, British submarines had another year in which to swank the China seas, a thorn in the side of Japanese ambition; but, in 1940, the flotilla was ordered to abandon its familiar and friendly Neptunian seas to meet not Victory but Nemesis in the Mediterranean.

Chapter 2

Home Waters
before the Invasion of Norway

The submarine operational picture in the Far East was clearcut: to attack and destroy the Japanese battlefleet, other heavy units and large troop convoys. As submarines were the only effective means of so doing—until, and if, our own battlefleet arrived—there was no doubt as to their role, under the absolute orders of the Commander-in-Chief, then the astute and dashing Sir Percy Noble.

In the United Kingdom things were by comparison chaotic.

Home Waters is a deceptive term: roughly, for submarines, they extended northwards to the ice-edge, southwards to Gibraltar and the Azores, west to Greenland's Cape Farewell and eastwards past the Skaw of Denmark into the Kattegat—and the Baltic, if we could get there.*

In theory, we had complete naval superiority in this vast area, a handful of dangerous German U-boats excepted. In practice, we lacked some 500 asdic-fitted escorts for ocean convoys, about 30 cruisers and, above all, modern aircraft-carriers to fly effective fighters. Of the twelve battleships and three battle-cruisers in the British fleet, only two were post-1918, and these two, *Nelson* and *Rodney* were, literally, so aborted by the Washington Conference that their maximum speed touched only twenty knots, and a sizeable proportion of their designed armament vanished when their sterns were cut away. Whilst many capital ships had been given extensive modernisation refits, money was skimped, as in the glaring example of H.M.S. *Hood* which blew up whilst being properly handled† at her best fighting range against the *Bismark*. She did so because gold had been saved at the expense of her magazine protection—even after the disasters to our battle-cruisers at

*See maps, pages 41 and 43.
† According to the Fighting Instructions, although an unconventional conduct of the action might have yielded better results.

Jutland—and that is the only reason the mighty *Hood* blew up. After that tragedy, no admiral in his right mind would willingly have pitted the smaller *Repulse* or *Renown* against anything more powerful than a German pocket-battleship, and even this might have been risky.

Another weakness lay in the high-level internecine conflict between the Navy and Royal Air Force, the effect of which—whatever the rights or wrongs—was to leave Coastal Command depleted and the Fleet Air Arm with obsolete flying machines, or 'stringbags' as they were succintly called.

That the greatest sea empire the world has yet seen should so unashamedly reduce itself to an obsolescent battlefleet in the face of a blatantly arming, treaty-breaking tyrant, constitutes a profound disgrace that was to be redeemed by six years' struggle for freedom.

At the tail-end of this nightmare procession of mistakes, incompetence, sloth, cupidity and self-deception straggled, forlorn and unwanted but fortunately not unhappy, the British submarine in Home Waters. Almost an embarrassment to her exalted sisters of the surface this pathetic Cinderella was about to have her ball; but without a Fairy Godmother (unless Max Horton could later have been so described!), certainly with no charming escort: she crept softly and in rags to her dance of death; more brazenly and better clad through the fire-dance, to emerge triumphant . . . six years and more than 3,100 lives later.

The world strategic situation in July of 1939 was indeed an unhappy one for Britain and France. Attack was imminent; but . . . when? . . where? . . . how? The enemies were clearly Germany, Italy and Japan. In respect of the two last, and from the naval angle, the main question was . . . when? As early as 26th June, the Admiralty had been directed to consider the possibility of reinforcing our submarine strength in the Far East, *even at the expense of the Home flotillas.* This instruction, from the Commitee of Imperial Defence, came two years too late, as will be shown in Chapter Three.

Near the blurred fringe of this frightening global picture, Rear-Admiral B.C. Watson, D.S.O., a submarine veteran of the First World War, was in the throes of moving his headquarters from Fort Blockhouse at Gosport to Aberdour, near Rosyth; this last being supposed to become the Home Fleet's operating base: already nearby was the Area H.Q. for Coastal Command of the Royal Air Force. The idea had been mooted by Admiral Watson on 5th September 1938; but no suitable accommodation could be found at

Rosyth. This in itself is an interesting reflection on the lack of urgency in a country which, three weeks later, faced the Munich crisis. Eventually Admiral Watson himself found Corriemar House, not at Rosyth but at Aberdour which was reasonably close. Only in June of 1939 were the necessary alterations started, being completed just in time. And, when the Admiral drove 488 miles northwards with Captain George Menzies on 30th August to instal his operational staff and himself in this new H.Q., some submarines had been at sea for a week! The administrative staff remained at Gosport.

Operational control of submarines in Home Waters had never been a happy one. The Rear-Admiral Submarines, as he was then known, held only a general administrative charge, liaison duties and total responsibility for training. Operational control, and even the efficiency of individual submarines, had always been the responsibility (with one short and minor exception in World War I) of the Flag Officers commanding fleets or areas. This system, on the whole, worked reasonably well overseas; but not at all well in the United Kingdom. The main reason lay in the extremely involved and complex nature of the general home command set-up, in which the position of even the Admiralty was not always clear. To simplify, the captain of a submarine flotilla abroad had only one master, his C-in-C. In Home Waters the Admiral Submarines had several, frequently pulling in opposite directions.

However, an advance had been made when the Home Fleet War Orders were revised in 1938; because the Rear-Admiral Submarines, in war, was to command flotillas operating in the North Sea, under the immediate orders of the C-in-C Home Fleet. Thus Bertram Watson found himself with direct and full administrative, operational and fighting efficiency control over the depot-ship *Forth* with her 2nd Flotilla at Dundee, and the old *Titania* with the 6th Flotilla operating out of Blyth. He also controlled, more remotely, seven training submarines at Gosport and Portland, four refitting submarines and twelve new 'T' class building, the ill-fated *Thetis*, now renamed *Thunderbolt*, included. It should be remembered nevertheless that a rear-admiral, no matter how distinguished, was not then a great power in the overall command hierachy.

The Second Submarine Flotilla, based on Dundee, was by far the most powerful at home, comprising eight 'S' class, three 'T' class and the ageing *Oxley*.

At Blyth were based three of the new small 'U' class, two vintage 'L' class and the most elderly and tiny *H.32*. In all, on 3rd September

1939, we had only eighteen operational submarines in Home Waters, of which four were really too old for the job.

Overseas, at Gibraltar, were the large and fast *Clyde* and *Severn*, assigned to duties out of Freetown, Sierra Leone; at Aden, the large and new minelayer *Seal* was on passage to the China Station where we already had the 15-strong 4th Flotilla, two of which were refitting. At Malta lay an assortment of three large minelayers, four 'S' class, two 'O' class and the *Otway* which, with her sister *Oxley*, had a bad electro-mechanical record.

Summary of Seagoing Submarines at Declaration of War.

China	13
Indian Ocean	1
Mediterranean	10
Atlantic	2
Home	18

TOTAL OPERATIONAL 44 (of which 5 were too old or 'poorly')

Training submarines,
seagoing   7 ('H' class, mostly 1918)
           1 *(Oberon)*

GRAND TOTAL   52 (+ 18 building, trials or refitting)

When taking into consideration the speed, armament and exceptionally high efficiency of the China flotilla, it can readily be seen from the above table that our main submarine strength lay in the Far East; and that the Admiralty therefore half-expected the Japanese to open hostilities; as I myself, who was there, know only too well!* The proportion of first class submarines in the Mediterranean, which included three splendid minelayers, reflects a most watchful eye on Italy.

Germany started the war with twenty-two operational U-boats which could, initially, range the areas roughly comparable to British Submarine Home Waters as I have previously described them. Their immediate sinking of the westbound British liner *Athenia* with her harmless passengers, including neutrals, women and children, made revoltingly clear the manner in which the Germans intended to conduct the war at sea. Nor can Hitler be blamed entirely; because it had happened before, starting with the *Lusitania* in May 1915.

It would be the grossest of errors for me to give the impression that I underestimate the devastation caused by the U-boat campaign

*See Chapter Four, for opinions differed.

in World War II; because Britain only avoided this mortal blow by a hair's breadth; and faces a potentially even more dangerous situation today; and for the same reason—unpreparedness, for the *third* time in a human lifespan.

But for the first year, at least, the U-boats' task was relatively easy as British escorts, although good, were few; and the Germans' worst enemy the weather: frequently the weather was their only enemy. Neither is it difficult to attack a convoy of fifty old ships puffing along at eight knots; particularly when a 'strong' escort might comprise a couple of ancient destroyers and three trawlers. Nor, with some notable exceptions, was the German overall showing a good one. Throughout the war, Hitler's 1,175 U-boats sank just over 2,500 ships for a loss of 781 U-boats: that is to say, slightly more than two ships for each U-boat; and three for each U-boat lost. As a strategical and tactical achievement under relatively easy conditions, I don't think much of it. Nevertheless the lethal and outdrawn Battle of the Atlantic in the Second World War constitutes the closest rendezvous with death this country has known since 1066, Spanish Armada and the great Dutch Admirals of the 17th century included.

Unlike the U-boats, British submarines operating in the North Sea, particularly during the early part of the war, were so ringed by restrictions, moral, political and those inbuilt by training omissions that it took three months, to the day, before a sinking of importance was achieved. This, most appropriately, was the outwardbound *U.36* which was blown to pieces by the *Salmon's* torpedoes (Lieut. Cmdr. E.O. Bickford R.N.). A fortnight previously, on 20th November 1939, the German anti-submarine (A/S) trawler *Gauleiter Telshow* had been skilfully sunk by Lieutenant G.D.A. Gregory's *Sturgeon*, mainly because he felt her to be a pestilential nuisance. It is not easy to sink a trawler with an ordinary torpedo, even if she is stopped; but Gregory's idea was to keep these pests on the move, thus reducing the efficiency of their listening gear—and he certainly did that!

Salmon's action took place in the open waters west of the Skagerrak whereas *Sturgeon* was well in towards the Heligoland Bight and inside the huge German mined area, 60 miles across and 180 miles long, which stretched from Dutch territorial waters, north of Terschelling, nearly to the latitude of Lim Fjord on the coast of Jutland, or Dundee in Scotland.* In international law—which hardly exists today except in principle—minefields must be declared and must be effective. As it suited Germany, she declared this one on the outbreak of war, and made it reasonably

*See map, page 41

effective; but there were channels through it, which our submarines later reported.

On the forenoon of 12th December, Bickford's *Salmon* (recently recalled from the Mediterranean) sighted the German liner *Bremen* homeward bound. *Salmon* surfaced and ordered *Bremen* to stop. The order was ignored and just as Bickford was about to fire a warning shot, a Dornier aircraft forced him to dive. He decided he could not torpedo a passenger ship, even though she had been warned: and this decision was confirmed swiftly by the Admiralty telling *Ursula,* further south, that *Bremen* should not be sunk.

It could be argued however that it was the captain of the *Bremen's* duty to have obeyed *Salmon's* order, thereby saving life. Also, *Bremen* was being escorted by military aircraft. My view is that Bickford's decision constituted an act of mercy; and the world's press saw things in that light, giving this country great credit by reminding the human race of the savage sinking of the *Athenia,* which was not escorted, and received no warning.

Twenty-four hours later, Bickford was rewarded by scoring a hit on both the enemy light cruisers, *Leipzig* and *Nürnberg.* Next day, on 14th December, Lieut. Cmdr. G.C. Phillips' *Ursula,* very close to Heligoland, scored another hit on *Leipzig* and sank two of her small escorts at the same time.

As a result of these attacks, *Nürnberg* was out of action for five months and *Leipzig* for a year, thereafter being used as a training cruiser, these disappointing results demonstrating the extraordinarily efficient watertight subdivision of German warships.

Amidst wild national acclaim, Bickford and Phillips were promoted to commander and awarded D.S.O.s; and none too early either, for there was considerable depression and misgiving both within and without the Submarine Branch of the Royal Navy.

While Bertram Watson and George Menzies were motoring up the main road to Scotland, on 30th August, five submarines of the 2nd Flotilla already patrolled a line stretching west-sou'west from Obrestad near Stavanger, and outside Norwegian territorial waters, their main object—reconnaissance until declaration of war. By 31st August another six submarines, from the 6th Flotilla, had sailed for positions in the Heligoland Bight.

In this southern area, there was no action until 9th September when *Ursula* unsuccessfully attacked *U.35.* The U-boat sighted discharge splash and avoided the British torpedoes. This incident must have proved galling to Lieut. Cmdr. Phillips and his crew; for, with correct drill, there should be no splash on firing. A few minutes later, *Ursula* passed another U-boat too close for attack. Later still, a trawler tried to ram *Ursula* and she had to bottom. This was all most irritating; but there was worse to come on the Obrestad line, 250 miles to the north.

The submarines arrived marginally too late to report the August break-out of *Graf Spee* and *Deutschland,* * both pocket-battleships, for ocean raiding in the Atlantic and beyond. On 3rd September, *Spearfish* was attacked by a U-boat, saw the torpedo tracks and dived. Three days later, *Sturgeon* and *Seahorse* were unsuccessfully bombed by our own aircraft; and this resulted in new routes and bombing restrictions. Protection against attack by friendly forces is indeed a problem for submarine staffs, and will be mentioned again, more than once, as this book progresses.

Now was to occur the incident which was so sad and which upset all submariners everywhere in the world-wide disposition of the British flotillas. Navigation of the accuracy essential to all submarine operations was not easy in the North Sea where visibility on a fine day may be only five miles, and on many days less than one. Sun and stars are usually blanked by cloud or mist; and the bottom, in many parts, is of an even nature, making it difficult to obtain position by a line of soundings.

On 10th September, *Triton* sighted *Oxley* which was out of position. *Triton* challenged thrice and fired a recognition grenade and, receiving no reply, sank the *Oxley.* Thus the first British submarine torpedo to explode on target in this war, sank a sister ship. The Commanding Officer and one rating from *Oxley* were rescued and the former exonerated; mainly, I think, because both his signal lamp and grenade failed at a crucial moment. But *Oxley's* lookout drill could not have been up to scratch.

Four days later, *Sturgeon* fired a salvo at *Swordfish,* fortunately without hitting. The reason here was that *Sturgeon* had not been fully briefed.

So, by mid-September, it seems that a severe shake-up was needed; what with submarines too close together for prevailing conditions, a captain improperly briefed and 'friendly' aircraft attacks. At sea there had been two drill errors and a failure in vital recognition material.

As a very junior captain, George Menzies did not cut much ice on the submarine staff. On 24th August, then at Fort Blockhouse, he wrote in his diary: 'I am told that my job will be to mess about on R.A.(S) staff. What a fate; though the man is charming.' He was, in

* Later re-named Lützow.

fact, appointed 'additional' and later Chief Staff Officer, under the Chief of Staff.

On the Sunday upon which war broke out, he wrote a most prescient comment: 'If we rely upon economics to finish the war, I foresee six years. If we attack again in the west, then eight months?'

In the first fortnight of the war, Captain Menzies, one of the most able submariners I have ever met, makes three complaints about the staff. One can see that he was worried and, to judge from the gentle manner in which the diary is written, I would consider that he was very worried indeed—and certainly not for himself.

By the end of 1939 our submarine successes amounted to damaging two cruisers, one severely, sinking one U-boat and three small escort vessels. We had lost the *Oxley,* suffered a few not too serious (by later standards) counter attacks and *Triad* had fractured her after hydroplane shaft which was quickly repaired on a Norwegian slipway at Stavanger, to which the destroyers *Maori* and *Inglefield* had towed her. *Triad* returned to base unmolested after the Norwegian Naval Commander-in-Chief had personally reconnoitred his own coast for her. Our 'U' class submarines had suffered delaying engine defects and, on 26th December, *Triumph* hit a mine north of the big German declared area and was severely damaged. Fortunately her bows and torpedo tubes took the brunt of the mine's explosive—the fact that her torpedo warheads did not detonate is a tribute to those who designed the firing pistols—and she came safely home, after R.A.F. Hudsons of Coastal Command had driven off air attack. Miraculously no one was hurt; and one sailor slept through the whole business! But the overall picture was bleak, especially when compared to the German U-boat highlights of sinking the aircraft-carrier *Courageous,* torpedoing and damaging the battleship *Barham* north-west of Scotland and penetrating Scapa Flow to sink the battleship *Royal Oak.*

This last achievement of Prien's in *U.47* particularly shattered British submariners at home and abroad, because we all knew our own unsuccessful record, so far; but we did not know the defence set-up at Scapa, nor were we told. So it was easy to imagine that *U.47* had not only dodged blockships, but also minefields, loops with electrically controlled mines, nets and machine gun (or heavier) pill-boxes. It made a depressing thought for a long time.

This brilliantly conceived operation resulted from pre-war spying, and a correct appreciation that the British would leave things much as they had been in 1918. Its success lay in Prien's iron nerve, cool head and a superb piece of inshore navigation, made only a little easier by readily identifiable land shapes. But the fact that unnetted, unmined and undefended gaps were there at all, makes a sorry reflection upon the general state of mind of this country in the early days of the war. One could almost sum it up by: 'We'll wait and see what happens.'

Then, as if all that was not enough: in four days we lost *Undine, Seahorse* and *Starfish* to enemy attack in or near the Heligoland Bight, on 6th, 7th and 9th January respectively . . . with no success to show. *Seahorse* was detected, depth-charged; then an oil leak betrayed her and, after a twenty-four hour hammering, the German 1st Minesweeping Flotilla adjudged her sunk with all hands. *Undine* attacked two enemy trawlers, missed and was then heavily depth-charged in shallow water. With hydrophones and asdics out of action she came to periscope depth in order to see, and was again hammered until her fore-ends were flooded. She managed to surface, but had no gun with which to return enemy fire. So the ship was abandoned and sunk, the crew being rescued and well treated by the German trawlers' men. But her warning signal did not get through to base. *Starfish* started an attack, was detected by a trawler and the resultant depth-charges put both hydroplanes out of action. She was bottomed; but more heavy damage followed. After dark, she surfaced in an attempt to slip away, having made one engine workable, but came under gunfire from two trawlers. Ship was abandoned, some of the crew returning on board to make sure she sank, which she did before the enemy boarding officer could retrieve anything. The crew were rescued.

All three sinkings were announced by the German radio on the afternoon of 16th January 1940, which added that there were survivors from *Undine* and *Starfish;* but our side had only a rough idea where these submarines had been sunk, were not sure how, and believed that *Seahorse* had been mined.

That evening 'Colonel' Menzies wrote in his diary: 'It is all terribly sad (and bad from the staff point of view).'

The news came swiftly across the world at midnight to 'my *Regulus*', as the 'Colonel' used to call her, then on a freezing patrol near the ice-edge north of Vladivostok; and it shook John Money, our new skipper, Joe Martin and myself, firstly almost to tears; then to anger. Someone had blundered.

But had they? Let us examine that difficult situation from the longer and dispassionate range of time, in the light of all that is now revealed and in the knowledge that two more bitterly frustrating months were yet to come for the Home flotillas.

At Aberdour, on 18th December 1939, it was thought that Bickford and Phillips had each *sunk* a light cruiser; it being beyond belief that they should not sink (and I can state categorically that at least *Leipzig* would have sunk had she been built in a Royal Dockyard, where compartment pressure tests were seldom properly done in my knowledge of these yards—1937 to 1951). Therefore, on that day, 'all was happiness,' as the diary says; but Rear-Admiral Watson was to be relieved, so the good news had come too late for him. Apparently he had been 'seen' by the First Lord of the Admiralty (Mr Winston Churchill), the First Sea Lord (Sir Dudley Pound) and the Commander-in-Chief, Home Fleet (Sir Charles Forbes), and been given a rucking. But Menzies says, and I personally agree with him wholeheartedly, 'it may have happened a little because of his (Watson's) good and correct disinclination to press the submarines in too quickly.'

A point conveniently overlooked was the indisputable fact that the fighting efficiency of operational submarines had lain with Commanders-in-Chief (including Sir Charles Forbes) until the baby was handed to Rear-Admiral Watson a few days before the declaration of war.

Another known fact is that operational submarines at home were seldom given much opportunity to train themselves for war, or even time to think about it. At least from 1937 onwards they were used relentlessly and ruthlessly for the training of destroyers and other A/S vessels, not only working out of home ports and the A/S school at Portland, but in the Home Fleet itself. And, in view of the Atlantic Battle, none can say that this policy was wrong. The same applied to a lesser degree in the Mediterranean; but not at all in the Far East, where submarines outnumbered destroyers. So we were stuck with the ironically tragic situation that the best trained crews were in the China Fleet; but in submarines far too large for either the North Sea or Mediterranean.

The truth was that we had too few submarines for our commitments and that priorities for their fighting equipment were too low. As the submarine, even then, was known to be the longest-ranged, logistically the most mobile, the most lethal and the most economical weapon of war in existence, it is a sad paradox that the meanest (militarily speaking) country in the world should not have paid more attention to them.

Winston Churchill was angry at our submarines' failure to light the dismal cold-war scene, and particularly annoyed that we had not been able to intercept *Scharnhorst* when she sank the gallant

Rawalpindi. * But Churchill did not know much about submarines; and in that he was by no means alone. Nevertheless, we were all glad to have this great political leader and statesman back at the Admiralty; but he pressed too hard for results. He got them—the wrong way.

It is not the last time in this book that I shall criticise the greatest leader of our century, for two reasons. First, I have no doubt that his reputation will stand it: secondly, I myself have felt the lash of his willpower in similar cases; and have, on occasion, resisted it successfully. But it needed a man more powerful than the charming Bertram Watson to cope with this double-edged situation; and this man was soon to appear, in the form of Vice-Admiral Sir Max K. Horton, K.C.B., D.S.O., who shared with Sir Martin Dunbar-Nasmith V.C., the distinction of being the toughest submariner of World War I, on either side.

But the manner in which the Admiralty handled the change was disgraceful. Rear-Admiral Watson, on 22nd December 1939, received a letter from the Naval Secretary (to the First Sea Lord) which announced that he was to be promoted to Vice-Admiral, and retired (in war!). Watson was most distressed. His comment: 'The Home Fleet, nor anybody else, have been anywhere near the Bight in the whole war.'

Happily and within a week the Admiralty relented and Watson was appointed Flag Officer at Greenock where, from Admiralty House, he conducted a superb administration of Britain's greatest war-time port and convoy assembly harbour, later being promoted to Vice-Admiral and awarded the C.B.

I would have had two criticisms of the operational conduct at that time, as I have now:

First, after *Sturgeon's* sinking of the *Gauleiter Telshow* on 20th November, an order should have been made banning such attacks, except *in extremis.* Trawlers are not, and never have been, targets for non-homing torpedoes.

Secondly, there was no system by which one submarine reported 'out' of a position or area before another went in. This precaution had been practised in World War I, and should have been instituted at the start of the second war. Both these measures, it will be noticed, are defensive; and probably would not have been popular.

On 9th January 1940, George Menzies' diary reads: 'The famous Admiral Horton arrived, and we all had a jolly good shake-up, which is exactly what we need; no revolutionary changes.'

* Captain Edward Kennedy, V.C.

'The famous Admiral' was immediately faced with the loss of the three submarines already mentioned: but 'took it well.'

Having known Lieutenant D.S. Massey Dawson of *Seahorse,* I do not myself think that he would have attacked A/S vessels; and all the available evidence shows that he had the misfortune to be detected. But *Starfish* and *Undine* were, almost certainly, detected *because* they attacked.

Two factors apply here. The first was that the Germans, quite unwittingly, had laid a trap. We did not know that, in the early stages, their A/S trawlers were unarmed—no guns, no depth-charges—because the necessary equipment, although on order, had not been manufactured. This explains our submarines' reports of trawlers not fishing but acting suspiciously. The second was that, despite good peace-time intelligence reports, few at home seem to have appreciated the efficacy of German hydrophones, particularly when their A/S vessels were stopped in the water. Of course, 'acting suspiciously' without attacking is no great criterion that a vessel is actually fitted with hydrophones.

So, the evasive tactics employed in the first three months of the war were successful only because enemy A/S trawlers in the Heligoland Bight had no depth-charges

The loss of a submarine can normally be attributed to a chapter of mistakes in peace-time; a chain of circumstances in war. I hope that, in this instance, I have brought that chain to light.

Before concluding this somewhat dismal chapter, I must add that there were many unsettling changes during the first months of the war which bore on the submarine world from the outside. For instance, the Home Fleet going off from Rosyth to Scapa Flow; then returning, without the *Royal Oak*. There were demands for submarines from Commanders-in-Chief as far distant as the South Atlantic where, at one time, *Severn* hastened to reinforce Rear-Admiral Harwood's squadron, then guarding the defeated *Graf Spee* in Montevideo and 1,800 miles from *Severn*. There were calls for submarines as convoy escorts, as anti-U-boat patrol west of Ireland and for reconnaissance when the weather was too bad for flying. All such matters necessitated conferences, appreciations and other distractions from the operational job in the North Sea. Also, it meant a great deal of tedious travel for Rear-Admiral Watson and his staff officers.

The obvious place for submarine headquarters was London, close to, or in, the Admiralty, as had been proposed by Rear-Admiral C.P. Talbot, Watson's predecessor, as early as 1935—when the Admiralty had been non-committal. Vice-Admiral Sir Max K. Horton K.C.B., D.S.O. had the power to move his H.Q.; and did so, by setting it up in 'Northways', a block of flats in London's Swiss Cottage, esconcing himself there with a full administrative and operational staff in March 1940.

Chapter 3

The Influence of British Submarine
Power in the Far East

Leaving behind the as yet untroubled Mediterranean and the dangerous North Sea, in neither of which areas had our submarines so far exercised significant influence, let us fly against the sun and back in time to those distant oriental waters in which the incipient power of British submarines had been felt.

In this century, the Japanese had achieved two naval victories of worldwide importance. The first had been the resounding destruction of the Imperial Russian Fleet by Admiral Togo at the Straits of Tsushima in May of 1905, a victory of seemingly epoch-making dimensions, such as Lepanto. Their second great success had been the easy winning of a concessional contract at the Washington Conference, a contract which they thoroughly abused.

As the accepted sea kings of the Western Pacific and the China Seas, they were free to move; and did so, after several years' delay caused by the terrible earthquake of 1923. In 1931 they invaded Manchuria, setting up the puppet state of Manchukuo early in 1932. China retaliated with an unofficial trade boycott. The Japanese landed at Shanghai where only strong international pressure made them desist from fighting Chinese troops outside the international settlement; but the embargo was lifted and many other demands met.

Despite Japan's breach of the Nine Power Treaty to respect China's sovereignty, the League of Nations proved ineffective. Also and more important, there was a credible report that the Japanese had planned an attack against Singapore at divisional strength in the event of the crisis widening. Thereafter for the next five years, Japan consolidated her positions and planned a full scale invasion of China.

When, in May of 1937, Captain C.B. Barry, D.S.O., and Commander G.C.P. Menzies were voyaging to the China station in the P.&O. liner *Rajputana*, the Japanese were secretly putting the finishing touches to their plans for this invasion which culminated in the 'China Incident' of the 7th July.

Menzies had read the Odyssey during the passage and 'enjoyed it'. On arrival, he wrote: 'Now for a job of work'. That job was to put the 4th Submarine Flotilla on a war footing: Barry and Menzies set about the task with verve.

Happily their arrival more or less coincided with an extensive review of service conditions which belatedly raised the status of Chief and Petty Officers and indeed of all naval personnel to a higher and more realistic plane, however without increasing basic pay.

There ensued a series of conferences, revision of orders, a general sharpening-up of programmes and procedures; and realistic apprais-als of the logistic, operational and manpower situations. The 'Colonel's' diary reveals an enormous amount of work, from 'nuts and bolts' to Chinese boys. There was also 'much talk with many men'—from Sir Charles Little, the then C.-in-C., down to submarine C.O.s and his own navigator, 'Baldy' Hezlet. These talks frequently took place on social occasions; but the emphasis lay always on the China Fleet, its role, its ships, its men; and particularly its submarines.

Having taken over *Regulus* from Commander Garwood, George Menzies took her to sea and found her efficient. He then sat down and re-wrote the captain's standing orders to improve that efficiency. He reorganised the entire flotilla into divisions—as with destroyers—to promote both teamwork and competition, these being the essence of the mobile patrol (wolfpack) tactics then being brought to their peak of efficacy.

With Murray-Smith, Commander of *Medway,* and her Engineer Officer, the complex spare part, torpedo, accommodation and store positions were thoroughly investigated and the conclusion reached that *Medway* could support fifteen submarines in peace and eighteen in war. The necessary arrangements to meet the demands of these numbers of submarines were then put into effect.

After consultations with the C-in-C.'s staff, the senior submarine officers drew up a great 'appreciation' on the numbers and duties of submarines required for war with Japan, within the compass of the general war plan.

This last should be elucidated, if only to illustrate our own awareness of British soft spots, particularly in the light of later events. In the first place, the war plan envisaged (and because of our abandonment of the two-power standard, could only envisage) a single-handed war between Britain and Japan.

The Hongkong garrison consisted of a machine-gun battalion of the Middlesex Regiment and three battalions of foot, supported by a small number of gunners and sappers. Allowing for a fifth battalion scattered around the China coast, the garrison was of brigade strength; and there was no point whatsoever in reinforcing it. A brigade of this nature was enough to repel Chinese brigands and war lords; and that, until 1937, had been its main function.

This policy was explained to me by Lieutenant-Colonel Lance Newnham of 1st Battalion the Middlesex Regiment who later became General Staff Officer (1) at Hongkong. By this time the Japanese had reached the border and had already made at least one serious attempt to cross it, not by infiltration (the Chinese would have massacred small numbers); but by a bold move at company strength across the frontier bridge spanning the Sham Chun River. The gambit was frustrated by a cool-headed subaltern of the guard, Lieutenant H.M.F. Langley, who pointed to machine-guns, deliberately mounted to enfilade, and said: 'They cover the bridge. If you cross this line, they open fire'. The Japanese withdrew. The machine-guns were not loaded!

Colonel Newnham also explained that, even in the face of the Japanese, there was no advantage in reinforcing the garrison; because Hong Kong was untenable. All a determined enemy had to do was to destroy the water supply. With a population of some two and a half million, that would be the end. When I asked how long the colony could resist, he replied: 'the pessimists say two and the optimists six weeks; but I wouldn't give it a day over three.' He proved right; and himself met a heroic end. Colonel Lanceray Arthur Newnham MC was one of four posthumously awarded the George Cross after execution following upon prolongued and barbaric torture. Neither he nor the others betrayed many comrades involved in an intelligence and break-out organisation.

The war plan accepted the early fall of Hong Kong and tentative arrangements had been made for fleet advanced bases at Labaun in North Borneo and Cam Ranh Bay in south-east French Indo-China, 1,000 and 650 miles from Hong Kong respectively. Singapore, where dockyard and fortifications neared completion, would be the main base for the British Fleet whose arrival from the west was expected three months after the commencement of hostilities; although this period might be shortened.

The much vaunted fortifications at Singapore were designed only to repel a frontal assault by Japanese heavy ships during this three months' period; and for that purpose they may have been adequate,

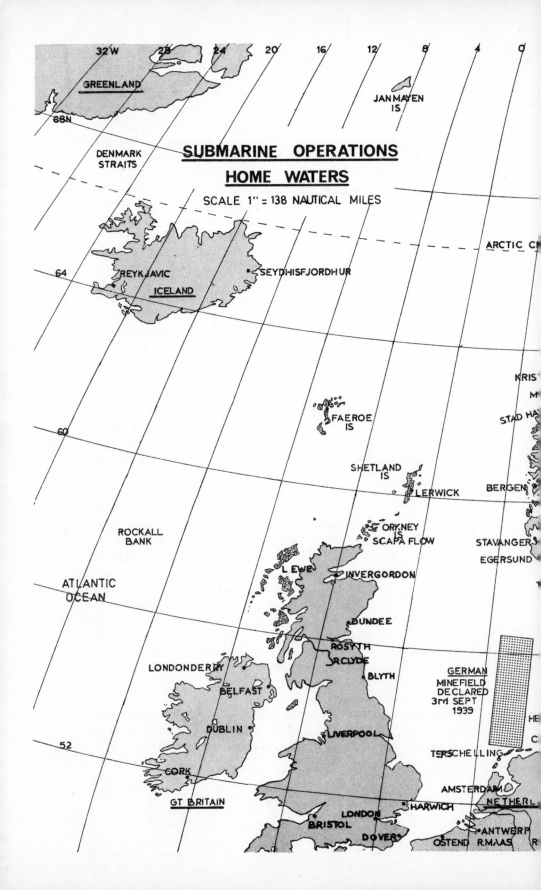

SUBMARINE OPERATIONS
HOME WATERS
SCALE 1" = 138 NAUTICAL MILES

particularly in view of the fact that enemy battleships would have had to run the gauntlet of British submarines—something I do not believe they were prepared to do.

Similarly, the landward defence of Singapore—based mainly on air squadrons which never arrived there—had only the object of holding the Malay Peninsula until the arrival of our battlefleet, with whose support naval and air forces would then have cut Japanese supply communications in the South China Sea. During that vital three months' period, our submarines would have been attacking these Japanese supply routes, again I believe, with devastating effect.

In the event, and with little air or naval support, Singapore lasted two days short of six weeks, the capitulation being tragically embarrassed but unaffected by the late arrival of some 55,000 comparatively untrained troops whose fate was to be barbaric, merciless captivity. Singapore was in fact irretrievably lost at 4 a.m. on 8th December 1941 when the Japanese landed unopposed at Singora and Patani in Southern Siam—and the War Cabinet should have known it.

It was in the context of this war plan that the 4th Submarine Flotilla 'appreciation' of 1937 was drawn up. One of the most difficult problems lay in reconnaissance. In many although not all circumstances air reconnaissance was the best; but there were, in this case, no airfields from which aircraft could operate even a modest line from Amoy to South Cape in Formosa, thence to Luzon's Cape Bojeador, a total stretch of 400 miles. Friendly American assistance might reduce the distance, but this could not be relied on. Nor could we keep aircraft-carriers long at sea for the purpose, in the face of Japanese air, submarine and capital ship power.

With his usual thoroughness Commander Menzies had a great day's flying in the *Eagle* where he was impressed with the efficiency of the pilots; but not with the performance of their aircraft.

The net result of the 'appreciation' was that we needed twenty-one submarines for attack, plus another seventeen for reconnaissance with a second depot-ship in support. This paper must have arrived at the Admiralty with emphasis, for the Japanese were then on the rampage throughout the length and breadth of China. It seems to have had no effect.

The Naval Staff had become obsessed with the thought that the submarine was a weapon of position, an idea which relegated speed to a secondary place in design. Therefore the new and formidable 'T' class were being built for only 16 knots, as opposed to *Regulus's* 18½

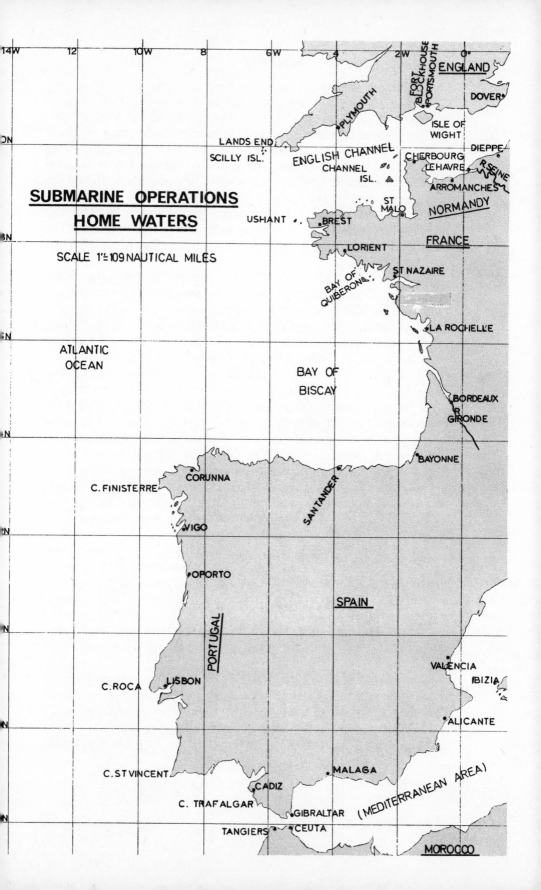

knots—a most retrograde step, enforced at a time when submarine C.O.'s were screaming for more speed in the mobile patrol exercises then conducted in all three fleets, although mainly in the Far East.

The essential requirement could, with reasonable economy, have been incorporated in an improved 'T' class of greater length, giving 20 knots with a longer range and improved habitability in tropical waters. Their deadly bow salvo of ten 21" torpedoes was already the most destructive in the world, and could have remained unaltered.

As our mobile patrol tactics were good enough to scare the Japanese, they merit some mention here, if only to demonstrate the coordination of which a division of four or five British submarines was then capable.

In war, as in every walk and aspect of life, the word 'communication' is magic. Without it, the human race is nothing and cannot exist. The submarine is no exception: her need is telepathy and without that, the next best. I think that both before and during the last war, this need was supplied to British submarines. Largely as a result of Lord Louis Mountbatten's initiative and drive in the naval signal world, our radio communication had shown a marked improvement and this applied also to submarines. The greatest boon of all lay in our ability to receive radio signals submerged, thanks to the enormous power of some shore transmitting stations. Incoming messages were routed through one of these stations which covered the principal operational areas. For instance, *Regulus* could receive Rugby with ease from 50 feet submergence when operating in the Sea of Japan. To reply, we had to surface and break radio silence, thereby risking detection and pinpointing by radio direction finders (D/F). But, in a well-organised outfit, replies were seldom either necessary or desirable.

If the C-in-C at Singapore wished to send *Regulus* a signal, it was enciphered and sent by 'fixed' shore-shore transmission or by ocean cable to Rugby, thence to be sent out on the apporopriate frequency at the next 4-hourly routine time. Sometimes only thirty minutes elapsed between despatch from Singapore and receipt off Japan, the message having encircled most of the Eurasian land mass, via Rugby. Only occasionally did the delay on priority signals exceed four hours.

There were failures, particularly in the North Sea during the early days of the war; but not many. I personally never experienced any of significance. So that kept us happily in touch with the outside world.

High frequency (H/F) submarine-to-submarine communication had also been developed to a marked degree. At periscope depth, submarines could raise a hydraulically operated mast for this purpose, talking by Morse code to consorts up to fifteen miles off, depending upon conditions—usually, the higher the aerials, the greater the range; up to the point where the 'ground wave' left the earth's surface. The 'sky wave' could be picked up thousands of miles away, but this was relatively unimportant when only tactical operations were concerned. An advantage of high frequency in those days lay in the fact that the waves were difficult to direction-find (D/F).

We also had another means of inter-submarine submerged communication. The asdic sets fitted were known as S.S/T, the letters standing for supersonic transmission. These could be used at ranges up to seven miles, depending upon water conditions. Caution was required however in the presence of an enemy; for the supersonic beam, although directional, was wide and might be intercepted.

Contrary to what most people accept as the obvious, a surfaced submarine with good lookouts (in the absence of radar) should, in clear weather, sight enemy aircraft in comfortable time to dive and remain unseen. I quote the rule, not the exception; for there were many occasions upon which both British and other submarines were 'caught' on the surface, sometimes with disastrous results.

In the knowledge of this rule, and with H/F and S.S/T as aids, Captain Barry and Commander Menzies set out to make of the 4th Flotilla the most dangerous submarine force in the world.

In the twenties and early thirties, the objects of submarines exercising at their attack functions in war had largely been confined to two goals. Firstly, a great deal of attention was devoted to the use of the gun. To practise this the submarine would approach a towed target, endeavouring to get within a range of 700 yards. She would then 'crash' surface, fire ten rounds 'rapid' and crash dive. There were frequently ten hits on the target and the whole operation seldom took more than ninety seconds. This evolution was usually highly spectacular, very exciting and therefore extremely popular. Proud indeed was the submarine captain who won his flotilla gunnery cup. Furthermore it was an exercise which proved of the greatest value in war. Complete surprise at pointblank range, particularly when her decks were sprayed with machine-gun fire, usually so shattered an enemy vessel that she had no time in which to reply before her assailant had dived again.

The second highly developed exercise concerned the main armament—torpedoes. It was adjudged the acme of success if a submarine could penetrate through a destroyer screen and obtain a single hit from close range on a battleship—using a torpedo fitted with a special collision head. The torpedo would then be recovered and the squashed head give evidence of hitting.

In their efforts to win the great satisfaction of these two accolades, submarine commanding officers were all too frequently apt to ignore both long range gunnery and the potential of torpedoes fired in salvoes, also at longer ranges. Detailed instructions for the latter were laid down in the appropriate book; but often ignored.

Although, as I have mentioned, mobile patrol exercises were conducted in Home Waters and in the Mediterranean it was only in China that they were given full rein. I wish therefore to enlarge upon the enormous amount of work and training that was put into the achievement of this object.

The close tactical cooperation of numbers of submarines may well be a matter of the greatest moment for the future and will be mentioned at the end of the book. Such tactics were practised only by the Germans during the war, and that in a somewhat half-hearted manner. The British sailor has at times an aptitude for teamwork as exemplified in the past by many leaders, notably Hawke and Nelson, more recently by such men as Harwood and Warburton-Lee. This teamwork at its rare best can give to one squadron the strength of ten.

With power loading and the ability to reload six torpedoes in about seven minutes, the submarines of the 'O', 'P' and 'R' classes possessed enormous torpedo fire power. Had fifteen such submarines been brought into close contact with a large Japanese convoy, they could have fired no less than 210 torpedoes in a matter of ten minutes. In practice this would be a tactical impossibility but it does however demonstrate the potential which could then only be equalled by three or four flotillas of modern destroyers attacking with little or no element of surprise.

In order to achieve such attacks successfully, destroyer flotillas had built up superb coordination and manoeuvrability. Taking a page from the destroyer book, Commander Menzies proceeded to manoeuvre his submarines, when on the surface, in a similar manner. I have already mentioned our submerged communications; on the surface we had three others. Firstly, by Morse code using an Aldis flashing lamp. Secondly, by radio or wireless communication. Thirdly, and most instantaneously, by flag signal. Naval flag signalling had been coded by Admiral Kempenfelt in the 18th century and brought to perfection in the First World War. It was, and probably still remains, the most efficient for surface manoeuvring.

The newly-formed divisions of the 4th Submarine Flotilla always went to sea in formation and returned to harbour in the same style, usually at 12 knots. At sea we manoeuvred constantly, thus not only improving our communication but also increasing the altertness of watchkeepers on the bridge, in the control-room, in the engine-room and in the motor-room. In submarines there is a special edge to manoeuvring in close formation. If one destroyer collides with another, it is bad and people may be killed: if two submarines collide, it is disaster. These exercises brought about a very close understanding between the captains of the submarines in the division and between the officers of the watch. One always knew who was on watch in the other boats and, more important, knew their likely reactions to any given situation. It is by such means, with the added incentive of danger, that close teamwork can be developed in peacetime.

I remember particularly some of the more hair-raising episodes when I was Menzies' navigator and signal officer in the first division which comprised *Regulus, Regent, Rainbow* and *Rover.*

One, off Hong Kong, was my first grid-iron, a favourite of the 'Colonel's'. Our division was in line ahead with the second division, also in line ahead, a mile on our port beam. Menzies ordered the grid-iron signal to be hoisted, which was done. When it was hauled down, the two divisions would turn inwards *towards each other,* each submarine in the first division turning 90° to port and each submarine in the second division turning 90° to starboard, all together. The difference between success and disaster lay in the amount of rudder used by the submarines of each division. As I remember, one division was to use 15° of rudder and the other 25°, until the courses of individual submarines were parallel, opposite but *offset.* Deliberately to place four pairs of submarines in a position where they were converging at 30 knots to pass very close, required not only iron nerve but such confidence in others as few men would accord. Only one mistake and the result could have been a shambles. Heart in mouth, I watched until all had safely passed and we resumed our original courses in line ahead, the first division now being on the port beam of the second division. And that was the object of the exercise for battleships or cruisers; namely to transpose the divisions. This unlikely and dangerous manoeuvre had been developed before the turn of the century, when fighting range was some 6,000 yards, in order that a battered division could be protected by one from the disengaged side, and had already resulted in the loss of the battleship *Victoria* after being rammed by the *Camperdown* in the Mediterranean during the nineties. In the face of that, that a senior submarine officer should have the courage to repeat it *with submarines,* I found remarkable. But it kept us on our toes . . . and how!

I recall another occasion, on leaving Manila, when the first division was taken out of harbour in formation and in the 'reverse sequence of fleet numbers'. It meant that *Rover* was at the head of the line, although not leading it. *Regulus* had to lead the line from its tail-end. As navigator, I was required to order *Rover* when to alter course around navigational hazards of which there were fortunately not many. This unusual evolution placed considerable strain on the commanding officers and navigators concerned. But strain was part of our training and that was what we were there for . . . to take it. Nevertheless, had I been captain of the *Rover* I should have been somewhat unhappy, and I expect he was. Another, and I think unique, occasion was when *Regulus* led her division into Surabaya harbour at the usual 12 knots, until almost abreast our berths on the long wharf when the division was ordered to go astern, *by signal.* This entailed using the diesel engines which sometimes failed to start astern. If that situation had arisen in any of the four boats, it would have been necessary to drain the Vulcan engine-clutches in order to go astern on the electric motors, which took all of ninety seconds! Here again was a display of iron nerve and confidence in the division's engineer officers. Our Dutch submariner hosts waiting on the jetty—whom we were to get to know so well during the war—were most suitably impressed.

It was also quite common practice that a division of submarines in close formation would all dive by signal together, fanning out as they exchanged their surface role for their true one.

All these manoeuvres may sound dangerous and even unnecessary, yet I never knew, in my time in *Regulus,* of an ugly incident, such was the cohesion and efficiency of the flotilla. In fact, I was more at hazard on the fo'c'sle of the cruiser *Orion,* as a midshipman, when we nearly rammed the *Neptune* at 22 knots in a tight turn, the latter having suddenly lost steam.

Yet I am amazed when I read the entries in George Menzies' diary. In it he lists the enormous amount of work and preparation he undertook for every objective. He portrays his fears, anxieties and modesty; with a continual underlying trend of reprimand to himself for not doing well enough. Yet to me, and I think to all of us, he was a lion at sea, a caged tiger in harbour and a lamb when relaxed.

The *Medway* was a happy-depot-ship and gave us all a splendid opportunity of knowing each other, not only the officers but the men. Wherever the *Medway* went, we played every game under the sun and in this way officers from one submarine could meet, talk with and play against the men from other submarines, thus getting to know at least many of the outstanding characters involved in sport. Social occasions also served the same object, the whole resulting in an efficient, contented but hard-working regiment, and one capable of resolving the exacting intricacies of mobile patrols.

The root of most military operations is intelligence. A secret agent may report a troop convoy assembling; or radio monitoring might deduce this by volume of enemy transmission traffic, or lack of it. 'Intelligence' will try to corroborate such reports, passing them to the C-in-C (and direct to operational commanders) with an evaluation of the contents. If the report is credible, the C-in-C will make precautionary dispositions and demand reconnaissance.

If at any time between 1937 and September 1939 the Commander-in-Chief China Fleet had faced the Japanese threat against Singapore—latent since 1932—he would have found himself with an amazingly well-balanced force. The 5th Cruiser Squadron consisting of five 8" gun county class cruisers was the finest in the world. The accuracy of their gunnery could be rivalled only by the Germans, while their rate of fire was second to none. The two aircraft-carriers *Hermes* and *Eagle* were both old and because of the limitations of their obsolete aircraft, their striking power was feeble. But the pilots, and more important the observers, had been highly trained in the difficult art of aerial warfare over the sea. However weak, this threat of torpedo bombing would have ensured that the Japanese sent to sea some of their most modern fleet carriers. Also for short periods the reconnaissance value of aircraft from *Hermes* and *Eagle* would have been most effective. In addition there was a fine and modern destroyer flotilla.

This balanced surface force would have made it essential that the Japanese put at risk not only fleet aircraft carriers but their battleships. With only nine battleships and, at that time, three fleet carriers, Japanese ambition prohibited the loss of any of these capital ships. And this is where the 4th Submarine Flotilla came in.

In the summer of 1937—when I, in *Swordfish,* was doing mobile patrol exercises of a more elementary nature in the North Sea—George Menzies' 1st Division could keep station one mile apart using S.S/T only. One can imagine the impact of such a division if brought into close contact with a squadron of Japanese capital ships.

I suspect the anti-submarine pundits will say that such close quarters is dangerous from the point of view of the submarines because the enemy destroyers, having found one, would find them all. I would refute this by saying that the first submarine to attack would lead off the escorts thus giving the others free rein. the second submarine to attack would cause havoc and disorganisation in the entire enemy force. Also, in those days, the 4th Flotilla submarines were capable of diving to 500′ where no depth-charge could be effective against them.

Mobile patrol tactics were basically very simple: communications were the be all and end all. As at full war strength our submarine divisions would have been five and not four boats; I will use a division of five as an example.

The duties of this division will be reconnaissance. The five submarines are at sea somewhere between Formosa and Singapore, in daylight with clear weather, keeping station at five cables with course and speed zig-zagging. In this situation they are vulnerable only to U-boat attack and to being sighted by enemy aircraft. But one must remember that they should sight the aircraft first and the whole division can then disappear in forty seconds. In the opaque waters of the Eastern Seas, they cannot be seen from the air even at periscope depth, except in certain unusual conditions of sunlight. At 60 feet they cannot be seen at all. The division is now approaching its operational position. So, by a simple signal, orders are given to form mobile patrol on a line of bearing 045° - 225° distance apart 15 miles, course north, speed of advance eight knots, executive signal to follow. These instructions are repeated back by each submarine to the senior officer. On his further signal 'proceed in execution of previous orders' the submarines start fanning our for their positions, the leader heading direct for the operational position which will be the first pivotal point of his mobile patrol.

As they fan out, the submarines keep in touch by H/F; and by judicious use of course and speed they should all arrive at their pre-ordained positions simultaneously. When the senior officer comes into his operational position he should have the following situation—

2 submarines to the north-east, the first 15 miles and the second 30 miles distant.

2 submarines to the south-west, at similar distances.

When the executive signal is made, all submarines alter course to the north and advance at eight knots. This slow speed gives them plenty of opportunity to zig-zag and, if necessary, to dive for a few minutes and listen on their asdic sets. As they advance northwards into the approaching darkness the division now covers a line of vision 75 miles long, this line probably being an extension of air reconnaissance. From the point of view of immunity from radio detection, the division now occupies a box measuring about 100 miles in length and 40 miles in width. Outside that box, their H/F radio signals cannot be heard except perhaps in California or Tasmania where it does not much matter. And even inside the box, they are virtually immune from being pinpointed by radio direction finder. If the conditions of the night's visibility preclude their seeing an enemy heavy unit at 7½ miles, they can overcome this by diving momentarily and listening on their asdic sets every so often; for the beat of a big ship's propellers can usually be heard outside night visibility range.

Nor are they alone, as the Captain 4th Submarine Flotilla (Captain S/M 4.) in the *Medway* at Singapore will be feeding them information about the enemy's latest movements gleaned from intelligence, air reconnaissance and perhaps from both British and neutral merchant vessels.

In the light of this information, the senior officer of the division has considerable elasticity. He can, for instance, swing his line to a bearing of east and west which, if the enemy is approaching from the north, will give the best chance of sighting. If a positive enemy report is suddenly received, and the division finds itself in a good attacking position, he will probably be ordered by Captain S/M 4. to concentrate and attack. He can then bring his outlying submarines in towards him whilst the whole division at the same time is making for a position to attack the enemy.

Although we would certainly have had aircraft to help us, I have assumed for the purposes of this demonstration, that there were few available. Let us assume also that at midnight the left-wing submarine detects propeller noise on her port beam and dives. Submerged she can hear better and identifies what can only be a very large convoy ten miles to the south-westwards. This immediately puts the whole of the 1st division out of the picture insofar as attack is concerned. The left-wing submarine surfaces and reports to the senior officer on H/F. Of course, all the other submarines in the line receive this signal. The senior officer immediately orders the right-wing submarine to break wireless silence and inform Capt. S/M 4. Thus the enemy report emanates from a source 70 miles away.

Captain S/M 4, having received the enemy report, immediately orders the 1st division to retire at 16 knots to the southward with a view to attack the next night or the day following. He also orders the 2nd division to take up a mobile patrol at five mile intervals with the dual role of reconnaissance and attack at daybreak. In reserve is the 3rd division, concentrated and always submerged by day, awaiting orders. If the reader looks at the diagrams in Appendix I, he will see a graphic outline of the possible achievements of the 2nd and 3rd divisions. Also, in Appendix I, I have produced a 'War Game' of the battle that never was. It comprises merely my own idea of what might have happened had Japan entered the war with Germany on the 3rd September, 1939, thus fighting Sir Percy Noble.

Japanese spying activities were quite open and notorious. In Hong Kong, Singapore and throughout the Malay Peninsula they made copious notes on the military defences, jungle tracks, the habits and unreliability of some planters, movements of warships, the building of airfields, the condition of aircraft and many details of our communications set-up and naval, military and airforce equipment. Although many complaints had been made by the armed forces concerning these spying activities, the latter were allowed to continue unchecked for expedient political and economic reasons. However, the Japanese did not do as the Russians do today and dog our naval exercises with the presence of their warships. Whilst they were reasonably proficient at radio interception and monitoring, it is unlikely that the Japanese knew much about our submarine H/F or S.S/T communication; but they saw enough of the 4th Flotilla to appreciate its efficiency.

From 1936 onwards, British submarines were not allowed to enter Japanese-held ports and with minor exceptions this rule was maintained. An exception I recall was when as temporary navigator of the *Otus* in the summer of 1938, I visited Tsingtao for four days, the submarine being British guardship pending the arrival of a destroyer. The Japanese heavy cruiser *Ashigara* lay at anchor very close to us and we naturally observed the courtesy of sending our officer of the guard over to her. He was politely met on the quarter-deck and not invited below. The Japanese returned the compliment by sending three officers armed with note-books, but without pencils, an omission which distressed them sadly. The armament officer of the *Otus* lent one of them a pencil and while he scribbled the others told him what to write down. They could not see our asdic set and the aerial arrays of our hydraulically operated radio mast were always dismantled before entering harbour. After five minutes scibbling, it was politely indicated to the Japanese officers that their welcome had ended.

I myself was glad to have seen the activities of the *Ashigara* in detail through binoculars. She was indeed a formidable ship with a most efficient crew, as her war record later proved. But when both ships swung to the tide and at times our torpedo tubes pointed straight towards her, it was easy to observe dismay and hatred on the faces of the men who lined her upper deck.

It was fashionable or expedient to say in those days that the Japanese were no good, that their ships would roll over, that their soldiers could only fight the Chinese and that their pilots were as blind as bats. All these silly, even traitorous, suggestions were in direct contradiction of the intelligence reports made by experts who said exactly the opposite. Like so many good peacetime intelligence reports, they were conveniently ignored.

I had always known the Germans well and suffered no illusions about them: and now the *Ashigara* had given me the measure of the Japanese—and it did not make for peace of mind.

It is an unhappy reflection that the edge was set for disaster at Singapore during those very years in which we were supposed to be preparing for war against Japan, namely between 1932 and 1939. The only two forces provided with the hardware essential for the performance of their duties were the China Fleet (its aircraft apart) and the garrison at Hong Kong, which was bound to fall anyway and therefore relatively unimportant.

In Malaya the Royal Air Force was never provided with the front-line aircraft essential to its role as the principal defender of the peninsula. Also in Malaya whenever the Army called for labour it was refused, with the result that airfields and the roads leading from the north remained virtually unfortified and constituted an open invitation to Japanese invasion. Even the sea fortifications covering the entrance to the naval base and Singapore harbour caused more damage than good for they were acclaimed by the press as making Singapore impregnable and unfortunately even prominent politicians believed it, particularly as this suited them. This left only the Navy with *Prince of Wales, Repulse* and no aircraft-carrier; a few attendant destroyers and some very old 6" gun light cruisers. I do not intend to criticise the actions of Admiral Sir Tom Phillips. But I will say this. It is a very bad principle to appoint as Commanders-in-Chief officers who have spent long periods as senior members of the staff, to the exclusion of executive command in high rank.

Had the Japanese made war in September 1939, the situation would have been much better for us. A combination of the 4th Submarine Flotilla, the balanced surface forces of the China Fleet and submarine reinforcements rushed from the Mediterranean could seriously have delayed Japanese plans and caused them grave losses at sea. And if the 4th Submarine Flotilla had, by September 1939, received the twenty-three additional submarines requested by Captain Barry on the 11th June 1937, we could have stopped an invasion of Malaya from the sea. Similarly had a total of 38 submarines been available in the Far East in 1941 the Japanese would never have mounted a seaborne invasion of Malaya. To get at Singapore they would therefore have had to enter northern Siam and advance down the Isthmus of Kra where they would probably have met defeat, as they later did in Burma.

I hope I have been able to demonstrate the considerable influence exercised by our sea power in the Far East, exercised as it was by small naval surface forces in conjunction with what might well be termed a most economical submarine battle squadron. This influence was to be maintained, mainly by the submarines themselves, well into 1940, the actual events being described in the next chapter.

Chapter 4

British Submarine Operations in the Far East

SEPTEMBER 1939-JUNE 1940

In July of 1939 the 4th Submarine Flotilla's recreational and exercise period at Wei Hai Wei was abruptly terminated. The flotilla moved to Hong Kong and then to Singapore, arriving about the middle of August. It was realised by all that there could be no second Munich Agreement and that 'Der Tag' would not be long delayed.

On 1st January 1939 Commander Menzies had deservedly been promoted to Captain but remained in *Regulus* for another three months, when he was relieved by Commander J.M. Money as Senior Submarine Officer. At the same time Captain Barry was relieved by Captain G.M.K. Keeble-White who became Captain S/M 4 and had also the command of *Medway*.

At Singapore we again prepared for war and in the early hours of the 19th or 20th August *Regulus* led her division past Seletar Creek outwardbound for Hong Kong. The division now included *Phoenix* since *Rover* was refitting.

I can particularly remember the scene at the parting because all the junior officers believed the Japanese would enter the war and therefore thought, as indeed we in *Regulus* did, that we had been sent off to do and die. On arrival at Hong Kong the division was kept at two hours' notice for sea and war; since our intended patrol positions were only 24 hours steaming, in the Bashi Channel between Formosa and Luzon.

Thus it came about that on the afternoon of the 3rd September I played tennis at the United Services Recreation Club in Kowloon, had a shower and was sitting with friends over a whisky and soda when signalman Cheale rang up from the *Regulus* to inform me that hostilities had just commenced against Germany but not Japan. Having ensured the captain had been informed, I returned to my table where a discussion developed as to the duration of the war, which to the consternation of the others I forecast at seven years.

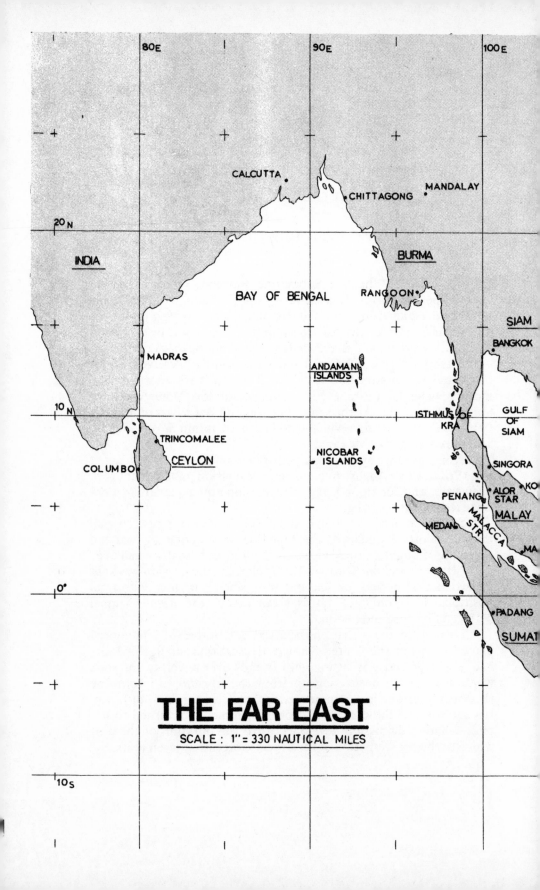

THE FAR EAST

SCALE : 1" = 330 NAUTICAL MILES

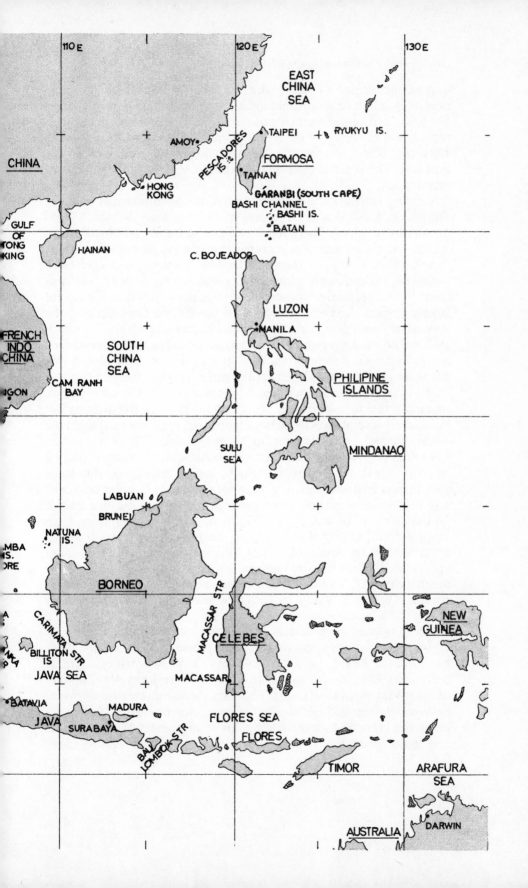

Amongst senior officers, who were better informed, the view prevailed as indeed it did in Whitehall, that the Japanese would sit on the fence consolidating their gains in China. The junior officers, who would bear the brunt of the fighting, inclined to the opinion that the Japanese, being treacherous, might make undeclared war at any moment. This in itself was not a bad thing since it kept us voluntarily on our toes.

Leaving aside for the moment operations of submarines based at Singapore, I will deal with patrols from Hong Kong in which I was personally involved. There were no German warships in Far Eastern waters but their forty or so merchant vessels imposed quite a serious threat. In the first place many of these vessels were suspected to be potential raiders, with guns and fire-control equipment crated in their holds; secondly, those not so equipped could make useful supply vessels. In the vast waters of the Pacific Ocean where the Australians and New Zealanders disposed only a handful of warships such enemy raiding could achieve untrammelled success. Our surface forces were of course already at sea searching, and blockading Japanese ports against the inward or outward movement of German ships. They also examined some Japanese vessels for contraband, much to the fury of those proud islanders. But the submarines languished several days in harbour before being sent off to patrol the Bashi Channel, our orders mainly reconnaissance. There was in fact not much else we could do because our hands were completely tied by the Naval Prize Manual which, being based on the Root Resolution, had us hamstrung. I cannot recall that *Regulus* or indeed any of the other submarines made sightings of significance on this 14-day patrol. In any event, German vessels would have been disguised and impossible to identify without the thorough search from which we were barred. I think the Commander-in-Chief appreciated this difficulty; for our next patrols were altered to the south coast of Japan where we could receive positive information from the British Embassy in Tokyo of any potential German raider sailing from Japanese ports.

The power of such raiders is illustrated by the fate of H.M.A.S. *Sydney,* the battle-experienced 6" gun cruiser which, in July 1940, had sunk the Italian cruiser *Bartolomeo Colleoni* north of Crete. In November 1941, *Sydney* met the disguised German raider *Komoran* off the West Australian Coast. The enemy's legitimate *ruse de guerre* proved only too successful. For some unknown reason, *Sydney* got much too close when investigating this strange vessel. With good drill and great precision, *Komoran* suddenly declared herself, fired torpedoes and blazed away with her powerful guns. The last seen of *Sydney* was a mass of flames vanishing over the horizon. It is assumed that she must have blown up, later on. There were no survivors. But *Kamoran* had also been severely damaged by *Sydney's* return fire, and had to scuttle herself. Many members of the German crew reached the shore, and the story came out.

By the end of October 1939, most of the ships in the 5th Cruiser Squadron had been dispersed to other duties, leaving only the submarines and the sloop *Bideford* to blockade Japanese ports. In these, there still remained several German merchant vessels of which five were fast and thought to be potential raiders. Those at Yokohama came under the close watch of the British Embassy staff in Tokyo thus necessitating only an intermittent patrol in Tokyo Bay, at times of German activity.

Also there were at least three more German ships in the Inland Sea, a more difficult proposition; for there are three outlets, the Kii and Bungo Channels in the south and one at Shimonoseki to the westwards. The generally accepted rule for territorial waters was three miles and our orders forbade operations inside this limit; excepting those of 'continuous chase', if an enemy auxiliary warship should escape into them.

The policy had now changed and our submarines were ordered to show themselves on the surface at night: we were also provided with dummy periscopes which could be dropped overboard in a position just about to be vacated. One night *Regulus* narrowly avoided being deliberately rammed by a Japanese merchant vessel and, from then on, it became obvious that our presence had incensed the Japanese into giving orders for British submarines to be rammed (Success could be cloaked with the claim that the submarine was showing no lights and that the collision had been accidental).

Submarines on the surface are highly vulnerable to a surprise gun attack (i.e. from a 'Q' ship) and they are, of course, wide open to ramming when lying stopped. These disadvantages almost entirely precluded any possibility of searching neutral vessels in the manner required by international law and laid down in the Naval Prize Manual. We did in fact have an organisation for doing this; but the chances were negligible and I cannot recall any submarine searching a vessel off the coast of Japan. Nevertheless we achieved a measure of negative success because none of the German vessels under surveillance left Japanese ports during the period of these patrols.

The Japanese exercised great secrecy in the building of new warships, a secrecy much enhanced by the closed waters of the

Inland Sea. Therefore it was with great delight that *Regulus,* in either the Bungo or Kii Channel, found herself in the middle of Japanese Fleet exercise. We were at periscope depth by day and recognised many of the ships; but one we found particularly interesting.

Whilst John Money, our captain, kept a lookout through the attack periscope, I busied myself at the high power periscope sketching details of a brand new Japanese aircraft-carrier. As I remember, this ship was so secret that we did not even know the Japanese had built her. We also gained some experience of Japanese A/S measures which we thought feeble and I do not remember any British submarine being detected by them during those patrols.

Weather conditions are extremely important at sea and with the nearest friendly but low-powered wireless stations as far away as Hong Kong and Manila we were hampered by the lack of good meteorological reports. One evening in October when the typhoon season had officially closed, *Regulus* surfaced south of the Bungo Channel into an oily, very calm but ominous swell. The barometer had dropped markedly so I reported my conclusions to the captain who asked: "What do you suggest Vasco?"*

"That we bat off, like blue smoke," I replied. "It's our second last day in any case."

Within two minutes *Regulus* was on a south-easterly course at 18 knots, reaching for sea room.

It was accepted practice in those days that a submarine did not dive to avoid very bad weather, because for a moment during the period of diving and surfacing she lacks stability. Normally this moment of time is passed through so quickly that there is no danger. But in rough weather a submarine may wallow half-submerged, half on the surface, thus extending the period of danger to the point where there is a theoretical possibility of rolling over.

During the speed run on that October night we prepared for the worst weather that any of us was likely to meet, having been left with the choice of trying to avoid the typhoon close inshore or of blasting through it with plenty of sea room. The latter was preferable because typhoons are apt to make rapid alterations of course and, had we tried to avoid, we might have faced the ugly situation of being in the typhoon's grip, on a lee shore.

By ten o'clock we had gained forty miles to seawards; but the wind had risen to force 11 and the seas were enormous. At this point 'Johno', as Money was nicknamed, said to me:

"Mars, I'm turning in. Call me when it's all over."

* After Vasco de Gama, famous Portuguese navigator.

I liked that. After all, there was little a captain could do; so why remain on the bridge and get soaked?

For four hours we battled with the monster, lashed to the periscope standards, while the wind and spume gusted to 120 knots; and the crests of colossal waves surged 80 feet above our heads. In the vortex the wind dropped and we even saw a star or two, but the seas remained mountainous, jumbled and confused. Then another four hours was spent battling our way out of the cyclone, until we were left exhausted and still in very rough weather. The damage proved amazingly slight. Our gun-mounting suffered and the enormous ship's refrigerator broke its steel straps and came adrift. Fortunately the engineer officer, Mr. Northwood, and his damage control party were able to wedge it, before any serious harm was caused.

On making a landfall in the Ryukyu Islands, we found ourselves well over 30 miles away from the estimated position, this being an indication of the strong currents running in the typhoon's periphery.

All in all, personally I quite enjoyed it. Typhoon by submarine is an unusual experience.

The depredations of the German pocket-battleship *Graf Spee* affected the movements of submarines all over the world and even the Far East was no exception. It was thought at one time, in view of the German-Soviet Pact, that *Graf Spee* might break for Vladivostok. There was a further possibility that German U-boats might make use of that port. So, after another session off Japan, *Regulus* received orders to patrol in Peter the Great Bay and investigate the Bosfor Vostochny Strait leading into Vladivostok. We spent Christmas Day 1939 well inside this strait which could almost be described as the port's outer harbour. One evening a submarine approached from seawards and we found her difficult to identify. Carrying out attack procedure, just in case she should prove to be a German U-boat, we gained a beautiful firing position, completely undetected; but because of light conditions, could not identify her ensign. Wisely John Money gave her the benefit of the doubt and *Regulus* withheld her torpedoes—which was as well because we subsequently discovered that no German U-boats had used, or ever used, Vladivostok.

At another time we became involved in a Russian submarine and anti-submarine exercise, remained undetected making copious notes and came to the eventual conclusion that the Russian equipment was two decades out of date. Then, we had nothing to fear from Russian submarines. Today, we are completely at their mercy.

Regulus had further orders to reconnoitre the ports on the Soviet side of the Gulf of Tartary and we did this, taking photographs, northwards to the ice-edge. It was here that I myself first conceived the idea of taking a submarine under the ice (by this I mean for operational rather than exploratory purposes), an idea I developed in my 1955 book *Arctic Submarine*; and later dramatised in *Atomic Submarine*.

Regulus did not suffer any mechanical failures through cold weather; although the gun became iced-up and the 2½-inch jumping-wire, running from the top of the periscope standards to the bows, collected so much ice that it resembled a 14-inch towing hawser. By January, conditions had worsened and when *Rainbow* relieved us, sheet-ice prevented her closing the coast and she had some difficulty in diving because the main vents tended to ice-up. In March 1940 *Proteus* was still having similar troubles when the operation was abandoned. Although these Siberian coast patrols did not result in the sighting of any German ships, they did provide us with some useful information about the Russians and gave valuable experiece of operating under ice conditions, much rigorous general training and provided a good area in which the efficiency of radio signals from Rugby could be thoroughly tested.

Meanwhile the eight submarines based on Singapore had not been inactive. By the time hostilities opened, patrols had been established at focal points and in the various straits around and about the Dutch East Indies, whilst observing Dutch neutrality. Their objects were to intercept, if possible, German vessels; to observe the activities of the Japanese, if any; and later to block the penetration of the Indonesian Island barrier by *Graf Spee,* then operating in the Indian Ocean.

Towards the end of October, four 'O' Class submarines were sent to set up a new 8th Submarine Flotilla operating from Colombo, as the East Indies station also lacked cruisers and, at the same time, was plagued by a surfeit of small islands in the shelter and anonymity of which German supply ships could lurk whilst awaiting orders to replenish raiders or U-boats. This new flotilla was commanded by Commander S.M. Raw, who hoped to be able to pit his submarines against *known* raiders, these being fair game. But the problem of examination and search of neutral or supposedly neutral vessels still remained. Later the 32-year-old small ex-Hamburg America liner *Spreewald* (renamed *Lucia*) arrived as depot-ship; but foetid messdecks led the crews to prefer their own submarines, even when in harbour. However her stores and workshops provided useful.

It may not generally be remembered that, in the autumn of 1939, the *Graf Spee* was usually referred to as her sister ship *Scheer* and for a considerable period the British thought there were two German pocket-battleships conducting raider activity in the southern hemisphere. And the widely separated appearances of the *Graf Spee* fortified this misconception. The areas mainly covered by *Olympus, Otus, Odin* and *Orpheus* were those of the Chagos Archipelago, the Seychelle Islands and the Maldives all, it will be noted, widely separated. When *Graf Spee* sank the *Africa Shell* in the Mozambique Channel on the 15th November, Commander H.V. King in *Olympus* was sent in pursuit; but her search proved unsuccessful and after a time in the area she put into Diego Suarez (North Madagascar) for fuel and provisions. On the 10th December she sailed to chase a raider reported by D/F bearings to be near Prince Edward Island, over 2,000 miles to the southward and about 3,300 miles from the submarine base at Colombo.

Whilst the naval stores department at Hong Kong had been able to provide splendid arctic clothing for *Regulus,* Commander King and his crew were not so fortunate: they sailed southwards with tropical kit only, supplemented by watchkeepers' trousers knocked up from the small supply of ship's canvas. The excessive humidity inside a submarine always accentuates the effects of both heat and cold; so these bold 'Olympians' felt only too keenly a 60 degree (F.) drop in temperature in less than a week. Discomfort was greatly increased by the filthy weather usually associated with the Roaring Forties. In mountainous seas with fierce wind-whipped crests of driven spume, vision became such a problem that watch for icebergs was kept by asdic.

And this was not all; for the lubricating oil, so important to the smooth running of diesel engines, which had been embarked at Diego Suarez proved of poor quality thus causing a crop of defects. Engine-room staff were worked off their feet, under appalling conditions of cold and the dangerously violent contortions of the vessel, as they wrestled to repair and nurse their machinery.

Both the Prince Edward and Crozet Islands were carefully inspected; but Commander King reported that they were unlikely places for lurking raiders because of the terrible weather and lack of both shelter and safe anchorages. A measure of the rigours of this patrol, really a cruiser's job, is evidenced by the award of an O.B.E. to Commander King—a most unusual honour but an appropriate one, although no ships were sighted.

Whilst the 8th Flotilla engaged in this Indian Ocean cruiser work, the first Anzac convoy had been assembling to take the advance part of that famous Australian and New Zealand force to join General Wavell's Army of the Nile. This convoy of twelve liners was covered by *Odin* and *Olympus*. The two submarines combed all the islands—Chagos, Addu Atoll and the Maldives—for enemy raiders; then gave submerged cover as the big ships steamed safely through the Nine Degree Channel, between the Laccadive Islands and Minicoy, on their way to Suez.

By March 1940, the Mediterranean situation had become more threatening; so preparations now went ahead to send *Medway* and all the 4th and 8th Flotilla submarines to that area. The depot-ship arrived at Alexandria in May, accompanied by half the old 4th Flotilla, the remainder following at short intervals. With this move, the 4th Submarine Flotilla (and the new 8th) became incorporated in the 1st Flotilla, traditionally the Mediterranean designation. But before relating their fate, it is now necessary to turn to momentous events in Home Waters.

Chapter 5

The Norwegian Campaign

Under the aegis of Rear Admiral Watson, in November 1939, there had been a reorganisation of the submarine flotillas and this embraced several of the new 'T' class submarines as they became ready for operations. In the subsequent five months there ensued a great deal of chop and change brought about by a demand for submarines from various commands; and these fluctuations must have been most unsettling for the officers and men, if not confusing.

However, by early April 1940, the base situation was beginning to crystallize and was now as follows:

H.M.S. Forth and 2nd Flotilla (Captain G.C.P. Menzies) at Rosyth.
> Ten new 'T' class of which two were undergoing repairs.
> Two minelayers.
> Polish submarine *Orzel* which had had an amazing escape from the Baltic.

H.M.S. Titania and 6th Flotilla (Commander J.S. Bethell) at Blyth.
> Three 'S' class.
> One 'U' class.
> One minelayer.
> *Clyde* and *Severn.*

H.M.S. Cyclops and 3rd Flotilla (Captain P. Ruck-Keene) at Harwich.
> Seven 'S' class of which two were undergoing repairs.

French 10th Submarine Flotilla at Harwich.
> Four submarines, operating mainly off the Dutch coast.

Despite all our efforts, we achieved no successes in the North Sea between mid-December 1939 and the 21st March 1940, when *Ursula* sank the *Heddernheim* in the Skagerrak, a 6,000-ton vessel taking iron ore to Germany. Two days later *Truant* chased the *Edmund*

Hugo Stines into Norwegian territorial waters where the German ship scuttled herself.

The British Government was desperately aware of the importance of the iron ore trade to Germany; but this kept almost entirely inside territorial waters and the chances of interception within the framework of existing international law were remote. Even after the German occupation of Norway, traffic kept to the confined waters between the fjords and outlying islands, known as the Leads, where enemy ships proved very difficult to attack because of protecting minefields, aircraft and A/S vessels.

On 1st April 1940 Captain Menzies attended a conference at Northways on the Norwegian situation. With government approval, the Royal Navy planned extensive minelaying operations off the Norwegian coast on the 4th April (later postponed until 8th April) and it was feared this might precipitate a German attack on Norway, whether or not the enemy already intended to invade that country. It was therefore decided to sail all available submarines to patrol off the Norwegian coast, in the Kattegat and north of the German declared mined area, whilst *Unity* was put in the Heligoland Bight.

The campaign was opened by *Orzel* intercepting and sinking the German troopship *Rio de Janeiro,* about 6,000 tons, off Kristiansand(S) early on the 8th April. *Orzel's* signal gave the alarm that a German invasion of Norway was actually proceeding. Ignoring for the moment two British and two French submarines on patrol in the south-western waters of the North Sea, we had engaged in the Norwegian operation ten submarines with six more on the way.

The German plan was a daring one. They aimed to land small but effective forces in the key ports of Narvik, Trondheim, Bergen, Stavanger, Egersund, Kristiansand(S) and Oslo all more or less simultaneously. They also crammed their warships with soldiers, embarking as many as 800 in the heavy cruisers and as few as five in E-boats. In addition, they intended heavily to mine the Skagerrak.

In the interests of simplicity, let us follow the German squadrons one by one:

Ten destroyers with over 2,000 troops on board sailed from the Weser late on the night of the 6th April escorted by *Scharnhorst* and *Gneisenau.* Passing between the British submarines patrolling north of the German minefield and those off the coast of Norway, they proceeded northward and undetected to the Lofoten Islands where the destroyers were sent to Narvik for the assault, *Scharnhorst* and *Gneisenau* peeling off into the Norwegian Sea with the object of drawing away British warships. This led to a brief action with the

British battle-cruiser *Renown* (out-armoured, out-gunned and out-sped) in which both enemy ships were damaged and retired at speed to the north. The weather at the time was execrable with a full gale blowing and frequent snowstorms. On their southward journey *Scharnhorst* and *Gneisenau* were able to make Wilhelmshaven by approximately the reverse of their outward route.

Also on the night of the 6th, *Hipper,* four destroyers and 1,700 troops left the Elbe for Trondheim and although this force also evaded our submarines, its journey did not remain unopposed. On the forenoon of the 9th April the destroyer *Glowworm* had been detached from *Renown's* screen to look for a man overboard and ran into the German force. Although the German guns made great execution in *Glowworm,* the British destroyer with superb audacity managed to ram the *Hipper* before sinking, and seriously damaged this enemy heavy cruiser. Nevertheless the German occupation of Trondheim was accomplished, and *Hipper* limped back to Wilhelmshaven unmolested.

On the evening of the 7th, the cruisers *Königsburg, Köln* and *Bremse* with an E-boat flotilla sailed from Wilhemshaven for Bergen, which the two last mentioned cruisers left on the evening of 9th April, arriving at Wilhemshaven on the 12th without incident—successful assault landing apart. But *Königsburg* was sunk at Bergen by a splendid Fleet Air Arm attack in Skuas from Orkney.

Also on the 7th, the 2,400 ton German gunnery-ship *Brummer* accompanied by two torpedo boats sailed from Cuxhaven for Stavanger; again this force successfully evaded our submarines and carried out its mission. Although not in chronological order, we can now dispose of *Brummer;* for she was sunk by *Sterlet* in the vicinity of the Skaw on the 15th April. Unfortunately *Sterlet* did not report this attack, nor did she return from her patrol; and the most probable cause of her loss is counter-attack by German A/S vessels.

On the 8th April a force comprising *Karlsruhe, Tsingtau, Greif* two more destroyers and E-boats sailed from the Weser for Kristiansand (South), Egersund being looked after by minelayers from Cuxhaven. *Karlsruhe* was also to meet her end from a British submarine's torpedoes.

On the evening of the 9th April, Lieutenant-Commander C.H. Hutchinson's *Truant* sighted this German light cruiser after her departure from Kristiansand(S). The submarine's initial attacking position was a good one but *Karlsruhe* zigged away thus putting *Truant* well abaft her beam and in a position from which a hit would be difficult to achieve. But 'Hutch' pressed in as far as he was able and unleashed, so correctly, his tremendous bow salvo of ten torpedoes, admirably spaced. The tracks were sighted from *Karlsruhe* which immediately took avoiding action; but the salvo was so well spread that this failed and the cruiser received a hit near the stern. Damage was such that neither engines nor steering could be used and it soon became evident that the *Karlsruhe* was sinking slowly. The escorting destroyers' counter-attack proved severe, causing considerable machinery damage in *Truant* and starting some leaks. The water fortunately being deep, *Truant* was taken to over 300 feet where she remained for nearly three hours. An attempt to regain periscope depth was thwarted by a new team of enemy A/S vessels which had arrived on the scene. In the meantime the enemy destroyers were busy embarking *Karlsruhe's* crew; for it had now become apparent that the cruiser could not be saved. About ten o'clock that night the destroyer *Greif* finished off the *Karlsruhe* with torpedoes.

'Hutch' and his crew had managed to keep *Truant* under control; although breathing had become difficult because of a high pressure in the boat caused by internal air leaks. Also electric battery power was nearly exhausted and the air had become very stale, the submarine having been dived since dawn. The next attempt to come up was successful and *Truant* surfaced silently, to find no enemy vessels in sight. She returned safely to base after avoiding several aircraft attacks. For this patrol Lieutenant-Commander Hutchinson was awarded the D.S.O. (Perhaps I should say here that when the commanding officer of a submarine receives an award it is usual for him to recommend officers and men to share the honour. Unfortunately it is never possible to recommend them all).

Now was to occur an event which so vividly demonstrates the fortunes and misfortunes of war that I propose to describe it in some detail. It concerns the only German force not so far mentioned, which sailed from Swinemünde (in the Baltic) on the 7th April with Oslo as its objective. This force with troops embarked comprised the pocket-battleship *Lützow*, the heavy cruiser *Blücher*, the light cruiser *Emden* and three torpedo boats. Proceeding through the Great Belt, the German ships were later sighted by *Triton* which attacked from a very unfavourable position, having mistaken one of the ships for *Gneisenau*. The torpedoes missed because the enemy force increased speed only a few seconds after firing. The Germans also evaded *Sunfish* which was too far away for attack; but able to make an accurate enemy report, this being received by the C-in-C Home Fleet in only half an hour.

Unfortunately our submarines in the approaches to Oslo had been moved to cover Larvik which had a direct railway line to the capital, it being thought that the Germans would prefer to land at an undefended, rather than a heavily defended port. The Germans had however decided to accept that risk in order to gain surprise; and in the event their heavy cruiser *Blücher* sank, a victim of Norwegian guns.

Apart from the main striking forces which I have outlined, the Germans were also sailing convoys under the general protection of their navy but sometimes unescorted; although *Triton* (Lieutenant Commander E.F. Pizey) was to be accorded no favours. On the evening of the 10th April, the *Triton* attacked a large convoy with an angled salvo of six torpedoes and sank three ships of about 5,000, 4,000 and a small vessel of 300 tons. This convoy was escorted and a severe depth-charging ensued, nearly eighty charges being dropped but fortunately not too accurately, and *Triton* got away, partly because her attackers had now latched themselves on to *Spearfish* which occupied the next billet, off the Skaw. These attacks at the end of a long day submerged, could prove dangerous if the enemy vessels persisted, in the knowledge that the air in the submarine would be becoming foul and that the battery would be low. The German A/S vessels probably unloaded the remainder of their depth-charges on *Spearfish* because they dropped over sixty in the next hour. *Spearfish* was hunted for another three hours but managed gradually to creep away and eventually to surface. In the darkness, two hours later, the somewhat shattered lookouts on *Spearfish's* bridge sighted a large bow-wave which was believed to be that of a destroyer. *Spearfish* turned away but, soon realising that she was in contact with a heavy ship, altered course to attack. In this way a quite unsolicited depth-charging had put the British submarine in sight of a prize target; for the enemy vessel was none other than the pocket-battleship *Lützow* returning from Oslo.

To complete the chain of events it is necessary to view matters through German eyes. Remarkably, for those early days of radar, the *Lützow* had detected an object at eight miles and, shortly afterwards, altered course to avoid it. This alteration caused a large stern-wave (sighted by *Spearfish)* and also interfered with *Lützow's* radar which, as I have mentioned, was not very advanced. A few minutes later *Lützow* altered back to her original course, this move putting *Spearfish* in an excellent position.

Lieutenant J.H. Forbes, in *Spearfish*, fired six torpedoes by eye and quickly made off. One or more of these torpedoes hit the pocket-battleship near her stern, blowing off both her propellers and rendering her steering gear useless. *Lützow* like *Karlsruhe* was sinking slowly. As she gradually settled, her damage control parties fought effectively to stem the flood water. But it was not until the following forenoon that help arrived, in the form of a destroyer escort and a Danish tug which towed the crippled pocket-battleship to Kiel where it took the dockyard a full year to restore her operational capacity.

During the first week of the Norwegian campaign, the patrol positions of our submarines were frequently shifted to follow up intelligence reports received, mainly from Norwegian sources. Unfortunately much of this information proved highly unreliable and led to many a wild goose chase. The enemy had complete command of the air in the Skagerrak and Kattegat which, combined with intense A/S activity, made it particularly difficult for our submarines to charge their batteries on the surface at night, a situation not helped by very short periods of darkness.

It has been seen that the seven German naval assault forces reached their destination without being damaged by our submarines whose dispositions, considering the scant information available, were reasonably good; although in the light of after knowledge these obviously could have been improved. This is a criticism, not of the submarine operating staff, but of our intelligence organisations in northern Germany and the Scandinavian countries which were either inefficient or too thinly spread. A further disadvantage we suffered lay, as ever, in political inhibitions. As enemy aircraft wellnigh prohibited surfacing in the long hours of daylight, suspicious vessels could be examined only through the periscope. For this reason it was, almost without exception, not possible to establish the identity of large numbers of merchant ships in the area. Thus many German troopships approached the Norwegian coast unmolested.

The War Cabinet belatedly decided, on the 9th April, that all German ships in the Heligoland Bight, the Skagerrak and the Kattegat should be sunk at sight; but by that time most of Norway's key ports had been lost to the enemy.

I can remember, later in the war at Trincomalee, Jackie Slaughter telling me about his dramatic receipt of this signal, when commanding *Sunfish* in the Kattegat. He had a 7,000 ton German vessel in sight and, very wisely, was carrying out a dummy attack, since he was not allowed to sink her. The vital signal was deciphered, read out to him at the periscope, just in time to enable torpedoes to be fired.

In this way *Sunfish* sank the German ship *Amasis.* The following day
Lieutenant-Commander Slaughter made two unsuccessful attacks
but was rewarded during the long evening twilight when he sank the
Antares of 2,500 tons. *Sunfish* was hunted but got away without
being depth-charged. Jackie Slaughter rounded off a splendid patrol
by sinking a 3,000-ton merchant ship and the 6,000-ton *Florida*
before returning safely to base.

Off Oslo Fjord on 11th April *Triad* sank the transport *Ionia,*
about 3,000 tons, whilst *Sealion* despatched a 2,500 ton ship just
south of Anholt Island in the Kattegat.

Also on the 11th April the War Cabinet extended the 'free for all'
zone up the Norwegian coast as far as Bergen to a distance of ten
miles off.

Perhaps I have not made it clear that Vice-Admiral Horton was in
direct operational control of all submarines, his signals to them being
repeated to the various flotilla captains. On 12th April he made
various dipositions to intercept an enemy heavy force reported
southbound off the Naze (southernmost tip of Norway); but these
efforts failed, the German force reaching safety in harbours south of
Heligoland. Nevertheless on that day Bill King in *Snapper,* having
missed by torpedoes, surfaced and sank a tanker by gunfire, thereby
depriving the Luftwaffe of valuable aviation spirit. Two days later
Snapper, moved north by FOS/M (Flag Officer Submarines),
virtually destroyed two small vessels off the Skaw. About this time
Narwhal laid her fifty mines north of Laeso Island in the Kattegat
and, on withdrawal, attacked a convoy unsuccessfully, being later
foiled by A/S vessels in her attempts to close another. *Narwhal's*
mines are thought to have destroyed four small ships.

Tarpon (Lieutenant-Commander H.J. Caldwell) failed to return
from her patrol in the Heligoland Bight, having either hit a mine or
met destruction at the hands of A/S vessels. As captains of the latter
were not always certain of having sunk a British submarine,
sometimes they made no claim. It could easily follow that the
submarine, although seriously damaged, managed to creep away
from her tormentors. She might then sink to the bottom and be
unable to surface; or, in deep water, she might crush. Again, the
effects of the damage could easily lead to a submarine accident,
directly but not immediately brought about by enemy attack. On
the British staff side, in both Home Waters and the Mediterranean,
there was a marked tendency to assume that, in the absence of any
information, submarines which did not return had been mined. Such
assumptions were apt to have a bad effect, in that commanding

officers were sometimes misled regarding the efficiency of enemy A/S vessels.

Lieutenant-Commander P.Q. Roberts, who later lent his initials to the much ravaged North Russian P.Q. convoys, had recently arrived off Egersund in *Porpoise* where he attacked and sank a German U-boat. On the other side of the coin, *Thistle* (Lieutenant-Commander W.F. Haselfoot) was most unfortunate in the U-boat she attacked but missed. The captain of *U.4* put this event to full advantage. He lurked in the area, awaiting revenge. Nor did he have to wait long for, in the early hours of the following morning (10th April), *U.4.* surprised *Thistle* on the surface and sank her.

The first phase of the Norwegian campaign may be said to have been brought to a close Lieutenant-Commander J.W. Studholm's *Seawolf* sinking the 6,000 ton German ship *Hamm* by night attack off the Skaw on 18th April; although *Triad* sank an unknown vessel of about 4,500 tons in the Skagerrak on the 20th. Thus, in twelve days we lost *Thistle*, *Sterlet* and *Tarpon*. A summary of enemy losses at the hands of our submarines reads—

Sunk by torpedo. 11 merchant or transport vessels totalling approximately 50,000 tons, including one 8,000 ton tanker (*Posidonia*).

Sunk by gunfire. One small tanker about 300 tons carrying aviation spirit.

Sunk by Narwhal's mines. In the Kattegat, four small mine-sweepers and, in the Heligoland Bight, the A/S vessel *Emden*, from a previous minelay.

German warships sunk by torpedo. Cruiser *Karlsruhe*, large escort vessel *Brummer*, mine-sweepers *Behrens* and *C.Jansen*, U-boat *U.1* and the small escort vessel *R.6*, this last having been sunk by *Triton* during her convoy attack on the 10th April.

German warships severely damaged. Pocket-battleship *Lützow*.

Shipping severely damaged. Two vessels totalling 7,500 tons, by *Snapper*.

In a work so brief it is not possible to embrace every operation; so I crave forgiveness for omissions. Nevertheless and in view of the very short period involved, the score looks good to me. It certainly worried the Germans who thenceforward put every effort into their air and sea anti-submarine measures which, combined with even fewer hours of darkness, placed great pressure on our subsequent operations. The Germans had thoroughly mined the Skagerrak and continued to increase the numbers of minefields with all available means.

Strategically our submarines had been more successful than we knew at the time; for Admiral Raeder barred the western Norwegian ports to supply ships which were thus confined to Oslo and Larvik. Also a plan to send great numbers of troops to Trondheim in the liners *Europa* and *Bremen* was cancelled.

Because of the intensification of enemy anti-submarine measures, Vice-Admiral Horton asked for a British destroyer sweep in the Skagerrak but, although orders were given, the Commander-in-Chief Home Fleet persuaded the Admiralty to cancel this operation by saying that he was extremely short of destroyers and could not afford to lose them. The French gallantly attempted to rescue our submarines from their predicament by a sweep with three of their large and fast destroyers which, entering the Western Skagerrak, sank some small vessels. These French ships, despite close air cover, experienced a very heavy Luftwaffe attack on their return journey but managed to escape unscathed. So perhaps Sir Charles Forbes' attitude was the correct one; although I personally think more could have been done in this direction during the earlier days of the war.

Our submarine operations in the Kattegat, Skagerrak and Heligoland Bight now began rapidly to wane because of the enemy pressures already mentioned. *Tetrarch* (Lieutenant-Commander R.G. Mills) after unsuccessfully attacking a large merchant ship, went through one of the longest periods of submergement known during the whole war. She was hunted relentlessly by three escorting destroyers, frequently getting out of conttol, and sometimes going down to 400 feet—a hundred feet below the designed depth. Ronnie Mills, thinking he had managed to evade the enemy, surfaced in the middle of all this; but was forced down within a few minutes. Eventually and after the harrowing experience of being submerged forty-three hours the *Tetrarch* was able to surface, and returned safely.

Truant again left Rosyth on the 24th April to carry out a special operation, but was damaged by an explosion near Sogne Fjord, probably a mine. Nevertheless she returned safely.

Commander G.M. Sladen, in *Trident,* entered Selbjorne fjord, remaining in the enclosed waters for two days. On 2nd May he fired torpedoes at a 5,000 ton German supply ship but the torpedoes ran under, for the vessel was in ballast. Greatly daring, in an area dominated by the Luftwaffe, Sladen surfaced and blazed away with his 4" gun until the enemy ship put herself aground on Skorpa Island. The German vessel, *Clare, H. Steins* received a parting shot of a torpedo in her forehold. *Trident* left the scene hastily. Although forced to dive by aircraft, and hunted by A/S vessels, she arrived at Rosyth two days later.

Towards the end of April, the *Unity* was sunk in collision with a Norwegian vessel off Blyth, fortunately with the loss of only four men.

The French 10th Flotilla, now reinforced to eight submarines, had the rather dull but nonetheless important duty of patrolling the south-western North Sea roughly between Texel and the east coast of England. This area, vital in reconnaissance, could not always be covered by the Royal Air Force, thus necessitating submarines. In May the French submarine *Doris* was torpedoed and sunk by *U.9.*

In the twelve days previously mentioned, we had been able to maintain an average of fifteen submarines in the three operational areas. They sank nineteen enemy vessels and severely damaged three, including *Lützow.* These successes were achieved mainly in comparatively shallow water, always under the complete domination of the Luftwaffe, always in cripplingly long hours of daylight, always against the unchallenged surface mastery of the German navy; and in the face of ever increasing enemy mining and A/S activity.

In the foreword I mentioned that I would limit myself to those operations in which our submarines had the most effect. I feel this effectiveness is demonstrated by the fact that the Germans were forced to change their policy regarding the sailing of vessels along the south-western Norwegian coast. Also, although we did not delay the enemy advance into Scandinavia, we did cause him much wastage; and economy of force is one of the underlying principles of war.

No one can write about the Norwegian campaign without mentioning the gallant exploits of our destroyers at Narvik. It will be remembered that ten German fleet destroyers had entered Narvik carrying the assault force. At 4 a.m. on 10th April, the British Second Destroyer Flotilla (Captain B.A.W. Warburton-Lee) consisting of *Hardy, Hotspur, Havoc, Hunter* and *Hostile,* after a terrible passage up Vest Fjord in a blizzard, forced into Narvik harbour and immediately sank two heavier German destroyers and damaged three. Unfortunately Warburton-Lee was himself ambushed by the remaining German destroyers which suddenly appeared from a nearby fjord; he was posthumously awarded the Victoria Cross. The British ships were then caught in crossfire. *Hunter* was sunk, *Hardy* driven ashore and the gallant captain killed, whilst *Hotspur* was severely damaged; but she escaped, accompanied by *Havoc* and *Hostile.* So ended the first battle of Narvik.

With great daring the Admiralty ordered the 15" gun battleship *Warspite* to Narvik, accompanied by nine fresh destroyers. This force sank the eight remaining German fleet destroyers and, to everybody's delight, the *Warspite's* aircraft bombed and sank a U-boat. After the second battle of Narvik, German troops ashore were exposed to attack but we could not follow up, having no men to land.

To meet such an eventuality we had four cruisers at sea with troops embarked; but the Admiralty had previously ordered them to join the main body of the Home Fleet whose primary role was the interception of *Scharnhorst* and *Gneisenau*. Another precipitate Admiralty interference had been to exert such pressure that the aircraft-carrier *Furious* hurriedly left the Clyde without having time to fly on her fighters. In truth, the Admiralty, including the First Lord, should not have ordered individual ships about; but confined themselves to giving the C-in-C Home Fleet all available information. Nevertheless British troops were already on their way to Norway, notably in a convoy which left the Clyde on the 11th April.

By the end of April we had only four submarines operating in the Kattegat and eastern part of the Skagerrak, two of these being the minelayers *Narwhal* and *Seal*. *Narwhal* again laid mines near the island of Laeso, subsequently torpedoing and sinking a 6,000 ton ship whilst another of 8,500 tons was damaged.

It had never seriously been considered that any British submarine could fall into enemy hands; so not much thought had been given to arrangements for destroying a boat in danger of capture. *Seal*, commanded by Rupert Lonsdale (who had for a time been my own captain in *Swordfish*), laid a minefield south-west of Göteborg—outside territorial waters. But she had previously been sighted by aircraft and molested by A/S trawlers. This led, in the afternoon of 4th May, to a hunt by German E-boats and *Seal*, in avoiding their attentions, passed through an unknown minefield. At this point she may have picked up a mooring-wire thus trailing the attached mine in a dangerous position. Some three hours later, still attended by E-boats, *Seal* suffered a heavy explosion aft which caused flooding; and the submarine bottomed by the stern in 130 feet of water with a marked angle bow-up. The German E-boats do not seem to have noticed the explosion and later made off. In the submarine, frantic efforts were made to reduce the flooding and deal with machinery damage but the crew rapidly became exhausted, suffering from a combination of carbon-dioxide poisoning and the lack of oxygen; and it was not until 1 a.m. the following morning that she was finally brought to the surface. *Seal* proved uncontrollable; so an attempt was made to steer her stern-first into Swedish territorial waters, an effort frustrated by the early dawn. About 3 a.m. the submarine was attacked by German aircraft, only being able to reply with ineffective Lewis guns, both of which soon jammed. In this attack the 1st Lieutenant had been badly injured. The submarine was slowly sinking so, when a German seaplane landed nearby and demanded that the captain should give himself up, Lieutenant-Commander Lonsdale reluctantly did so. This left the submarine with an exhausted crew and bewildered officers. These felt they could not sink their ship with the crew, which included wounded, still on board. In fact, it might have been difficult to do so as all telemotor (hydraulic) pressure had been lost. So when a German trawler arrived at the scene, the British officers and men allowed themselves to be taken on board, believing that the submarine would sink. However, she did not sink and the German trawler was able to tow her into a Danish port, now under their control. The Germans announced this capture with great glee; but all their efforts to use the *Seal* as an operational submarine failed. It is standard naval procedure to institute a court-martial after the loss of any ship. I am glad to say that at this particular post-war trial, Lieutenant-Commander Lonsdale and his acting second-in-command were honourably acquitted.

We had now lost seven submarines in Home Waters, with many near escapes, and the continual strain imposed by the conditions previously described had started to tell on commanding officers, particularly the older ones. It will be remembered that Captain Menzies commanded the 2nd Submarine Flotilla at Rosyth, composed of 'T' class, minelayers and the Polish *Orzel.* On the 21st April 1940 he wrote in his diary—

'I had the very difficult task of telling the boys that they could afford to stay at periscope depth until the hunters were upon them and that they should not retire because they hear H.E.* What they dislike are the bangs. In the afternoon I had a good walk and then had a supper with Sladen *(Trident)* 'Hutch' *(Truant)* and Van der Byl *(Taku).* They, with Pizey *(Triton)* are a great team and I think that Hitler will know when they return to the fray.'

In the last half of April and the beginning of May no less than four experienced submarine C.O.'s from the 2nd Flotilla asked to be relieved. Two of these requests shook the 'Colonel'; but in the

* Hydrophone effect, propeller noises heard through the asdic set which, when not transmitting, acts as a sensitive hydrophone.

circumstances there is only one thing to do—relieve them. Fortunately at that time the first lieutenants of submarines were still extremely highly trained and, after a six weeks' submarine commanding officers' qualifying course, these were quite capable of taking over the smaller submarines. It was usual to have at least one spare commanding officer ready in each flotilla for emergencies. Later such reserves were not always possible; but we managed.

Simultaneously a similar trend developed in the other two operational flotillas and the older captains started drifting away, some to command destroyers with distinction and others to submarine staff work, equipment supervision and the development of new underwater projects. This drift continued and applied to nearly all concerned, those that were highly decorated included. Such resignation of command was accepted as sensible and, in fact, required high moral courage.

Early in May the French 10th Submarine Flotilla was transferred to Rosyth and the 3rd Flotilla, operating out of Harwich, was reinforced by four old 'H' class and two 'L' class submarines. The French depot-ship *Jules Verne* and the British *Cyclops* were sent north (the 3rd Flotilla operating from a temporary base on shore), this move being to minimise the risk of air attack on the valuable depot-ships.

The months of May and June 1940 witnessed the German invasion of Holland, Belgium, Luxembourg and France while, in the north, our short-lived expeditionary force into Norway was being landed and evacuated. During this evacuation the aircraft-carrier *Glorious* was sunk by *Gneisenau* and *Scharnhorst* (both of which had recovered from their action with *Renown*) whilst one of the British escorts, *Acasta,* scored a torpedo hit on *Scharnhorst* just before she herself sank.

As the Fleet Air Arm had sunk the German light cruiser *Königsburg* in Bergen harbour on the 10th April, the depredations suffered by the German Navy had now become serious, thus offering far fewer valuable targets to our submarines than heretofore. This may have been just as well, for there followed a period of virtual interregnum. The Commander-in-Chief Home Fleet was now saying most definitely what submarines he wanted and where. Admiral Horton continued to deal mainly with the Admiralty. The French submarines, with the exception of *Rubis* which is specially mentioned immediately below, returned to France and Dutch submarines started to come over, but were not operational until July, with the exception of *0.13.*

The French minelayer *Rubis* remained to fight under the British, firstly under the command of Capitaine de Corvette Cabanier and later Rousselot, achieving remarkable success throughout the war. Her score aggregated one 4,500 ton vessel sunk by torpedoes and no less than twenty-two vessels, totalling about 30,000 tons, mined. It can be seen from these figures that *Rubis* sank a large proportion of small vessels which included many sizeable minor warships such as escort vessels, minesweepers and A/S craft. Her operations illustrate the effectiveness of small minefields laid at focal points, usually in or near the enemy's swept channels,* which, in *Rubis'* case, ranged from La Rochelle to the Lofoten Islands. Recently I had the great pleasure of again meeting Admiral H. Rousselot, D.S.O., D.S.C., who is still a serving officer in the French Navy.

Of this enormous bag it is interesting to note that twenty of these vessels *sank,* only two surviving mine damage, the first being a U-boat and the second a small merchant vessel.

Generally speaking, during May and June 1940, the 2nd Flotilla with its larger and more powerful boats, operated along the coast of Norway westwards and northwards of the Naze.

David Ingram in *Clyde* had an interesting encounter with the German raider *Thor*. Believing the enemy to be a transport, Ingram gunned her and gave chase on the surface. But the *Thor* could almost match *Clyde's* twenty-one knots and escaped into a rain squall, later to take refuge in Trondheim; whence she emerged a few days later. This port was being used by *Gneisenau, Scharnhorst* and *Hipper* as a temporary base; but *Scharnhorst* had to return to Germany for repairs to the torpedo damage caused by the brave *Acasta,* leaving *Gneisenau* with *Hipper* and some destroyers at Trondheim.

On her next patrol *Clyde* was again in the area and this time scored a significant success. Late on the 20th June, in very rough weather, *Clyde* sighted this German force at sea and David Ingram achieved a most difficult attack without being detected—an extraordinary accomplishment in prevailing conditions. The battle-cruiser *Gneisenau* was hit by a torpedo and put out of action for six months. The destroyer counter-attack, although otherwise comparatively ineffective, damaged *Clyde's* main aerials and weakened transmission. Nevertheless the enemy report was picked up and relayed by nearby *Porpoise*. Lieutenant-Commander Ingram gained the D.S.C., for this skilful attack. It can be seen that awards were already being scaled down, which was a little unfair on Ingram and all who followed.

---

* 'Swept' or 'Searched' Channels—shipping lanes, usually off harbours, regularly swept of mines.

During this period the situation was fluid, at any rate whilst our troops were still ashore in Norway. This led to some incidents between friendly forces and we also suffered a large number of misses with torpedoes; but *Truant* (Hugh Haggard) sank the *Preussen* of 8,000 tons in the extreme north towards the end of May. In June *Tetrarch* (Ronnie Mills) sank a valuable tanker off Egersund, the *Samland* of 8,000 tons. In the same area Bill King (one of today's famous lone yachtsmen), in *Snapper* despatched the *Cygnus* of about 1,400 tons.

Our minelaying submarines continued their activities, *Porpoise* being ineffectively attacked by aircraft. But we lost the fine Polish *Orzel* (Commander J. Grudzinski), probably from German air attack in the western Skagerrak, towards the end of May.

It will be remembered that by now the Germans had taken Denmark, most of Norway, all of Flanders and half of France; for the French surrendered on 25th June. Many of the submarines from the 3rd and 6th Flotilla, reinforced by training submarines, were required for reconnaissance duties and anti-invasion patrol in the southern waters of the North Sea and in the Channel. This necessary but unrewarding diversion was intermittently to continue whilst the threat of invasion lasted.

The reader will undoubtedly have noticed that there has so far been no mention of any mobile patrol tactics in actual operations. There are several reasons for this which I will elucidate. First, although captains and first lieutenants were proficient in such tactics, their juniors (who would have to do most of the work) had not been so trained, and there was no time in which to train them. Secondly, German forces invading Norway had only a short hop of open sea to cross, this making it difficult for a patrol line to prove effective in the short time available. Lastly, and of overriding importance, was our appallingly bad intelligence concerning German movements, combined with an almost negative aerial reconnaissance. Earlier in the book I have mentioned intelligence as being the root of most operations and have also pointed out that Coastal Command of the Royal Air Force suffered at the expense of an obsession with bombers, an obsession which was to be encouraged by the Prime Minister, taking precedence also over the Army's requirements for more sophisticated weapons and equipment.

By the end of June we had for three weeks been at war with Italy, so it is now necessary to leave the ravages of Northern Europe and devote our attention to the Mediterranean.

Chapter 6

Mediterranean Operations

JUNE 1940 - MAY 1941

In the Mediterranean† our surface forces were inferior, in numbers and fire-power, to the Italian Fleet. In the central area our air power was virtually non-existent, whilst to the west, Gibraltar had almost complete immunity through distance, in the east air-power was a little better balanced. Therefore Admiral Sir James Somerville had been based at Gibralter with Force 'H', formed around a nucleus of capital ships; this force playing a dual role in both the western Mediterranean and Atlantic. The main Mediterranean fleet, in accordance with the war plan, had been based at Alexandria, and Malta denuded of most naval forces, including submarines. Whilst the decision to leave Malta is difficult to criticise in the light of German air efficiency, it does reflect an over-estimation of Italian bombing prowess.

The main object of all our Mediterranean naval forces had been laid down as the disruption of enemy seaborne communications to North Africa, and this applied particularly to submarines. Now the pre-war parsimony in shelving the Malta submarine shelter plan was to be keenly felt; and felt with considerable bitterness as the war progressed.

By the end of May 1940 we had amassed at Alexandria *Medway, Olympus, Odin, Orpheus, Otus, Phoenix, Proteus, Pandora, Parthian* and the minelayers *Grampus* and *Rorqual;* but *Otus* and *Olympus* had mechanical troubles necessitating their refit at Malta.* On passage from the Far East to join the 1st Submarine Flotilla were *Regulus, Regent, Rainbow* and *Perseus,* to be followed later by *Rover.*

I myself had been appointed 1st Lieutenant of *Perseus* in May and, when we arrived at Alexandria about the 8th August, we met a

---

* There were no facilities for refit at Alexandria.
† Please see map, page 89

paralysing situation. Although we did not then know the actual causes and attributed too much to mines, the stark fact remained that *Grampus, Odin, Orpheus, Phoenix* and *Oswald* had all been lost with not a single success to show; although it was later learnt mines had sunk a 4,000 ton Italian vessel, these having been laid by *Rorqual* which survived the war.

We now know that *Grampus* (Lieutenant-Commander C.A. Rowe), after laying mines off Augusta, was sunk by the Italian torpedo boats *Circe* and *Cleo* with depth-charges, off Syracuse in mid-June. *Odin*, under the command of Lieutenant-Commander K. MacI. Woods (also one of my skippers in *Swordfish*) fell to the Italian destroyer *Strale* in the Gulf of Taranto. Also in mid-June *Orpheus* may have been sunk by the Italian destroyer *Tribune* off Tobruk; but in her case, mining cannot be ruled out. We lost these three submarines, all on their first patrols, in three days.

In mid-July Lieutenant-Commander G.H. Nowell, in *Phoenix*, after having attacked and missed the Italian submarine chaser *Albatross*, was sunk by her depth-charges. On 30th July *Oswald* (Lieutenant-Commander D.A. Fraser) radioed a report of enemy cruisers and other vessels in the Strait of Messina, and this report would certainly have been the cause of her detection by D/F. On the night of 1st August *Oswald*, still patrolling in the vicinity, was caught unawares, rammed and sunk by the Italian destroyer *Vivaldi* which rescued Fraser and most of the crew.

Distressing losses of this magnitude cannot be allowed to pass without comment. As we have seen, these large and conspicuous submarines were designed mainly for operations in open waters. They took, under the best conditions, about forty seconds to dive, usually a little longer. This time compared unfavourably with twenty seconds for the 'U' class of small submarines; and thirty seconds for the 'T' class. The night silhouette of an 'O' class submarine was greater than that of an enemy torpedo boat, although less than a destroyer's, and therein lay a grave disadvantage. I have already mentioned what large asdic targets these submarines made and how easily visible from the air. But there was more to it than just the shortcomings of material, especially when one considers that the submarines sprang from the 4th Flotilla which I have eulogized. First, when Captains Barry and Menzies left the 4th Submarine Flotilla, early in 1939, the high pressure mobile patrol exercises tended to lapse. There was an inclination amongst submarine C.O.'s to aspire to being given a large patrol area, plenty of information and told to get on with the job, without interfering orders from others.

Also, with the exception of *Grampus,* the commanding officers of the five submarines lost, although experienced, had not long been in their commands: whereas those that had were able to achieve marked success even under these disadvantageous conditions. Another factor lay no doubt in the physical state of junior officers and men for, in the vast majority of cases, they were long overdue for home leave, having spent more than two years continually exercising and training under tropical conditions, without proper air-conditioning. They were, in fact, tired; and tiredness slows down reaction. Furthermore, many of the submarines themselves had spent as much as ten years almost continuously in tropical waters which corrode metals much more readily than the colder seas. These submarines, therefore, again with the exception of *Grampus,* were nearing their age limit. The loss of this last particularly affected me, for she had been my first submarine as a sub-lieutenant, brand new in 1937; and I knew many of those killed who had first commissioned her at Chatham.

The Submarine Branch being so small, a loss became very much the personal affair of all submariners. Both officers and men not only knew their own contemporaries in the sunken submarine; but had at least an acquaintanceship with many others, both senior and junior. For instance, I do not suppose there is a single submarine captain already mentioned in this book whom I did not know, or had at least met. Naturally, by late 1940 and after four years in this small band, I was friendly with many of the junior officers, several of the captains, and well acquainted with a large number of chief and petty officers and junior ratings. So the loss of even a small submarine in distant waters always made a very sad personal occasion, such as grief for a brother and, later, a son.

Sadness did not, however, prevent a critical summing-up of the circumstances if we knew them, which was infrequently. There was, for instance, severe criticism concerning the surrender of *Seal;* but the post-war court-martial gave honourable acquittal. In her case, the main complaint remains; that she should not have been sent into the Kattegat at that time.

In the early and tragic months of Mediterranean operations, as in the opening months of the war in the North Sea, there existed amongst commanding officers what I call 'early stage amorphism'. They found themselves faced with dangerous situations of which they had little knowledge—and none could be provided for them, as there had been no submarine operations since 1918. The unknown frequently leads to indecision. Some officers, being more imaginative than others, could visualise events which might befall, analyse their own reactions to those circumstances, and physically exercise their submarines and crews in suitable manoeuvres and tactics, thus both forewarning and fore-arming themselves for the future.

Personally I had been lucky in this respect; for Captain Menzies constantly exhorted his officers, when on watch with little to do in peacetime, to exercise their minds not with girls but with situations that might arise in war and with the necessary counter-measures. In this connection I recall particularly on one occasion in the Formosa Strait at night, seeing white streaks approaching from port. I altered course to comb the tracks and dived—so touchy was the situation with the Japanese that I really believed that they might be torpedoes. But we were only surrounded by a shoal of dolphins; nevertheless the 'Colonel' was delighted; particularly by the good reaction of a surprised crew!

But in the balmier days of the late twenties and early thirties, many submarine captains were not so exacting; with the result that some who became commanding officers in the early stages of the war had not enjoyed similar good fortune.

Other contributing factors to this amorphism were, as already mentioned, the obligations of international law, in some cases the ill-appreciation of the principles of salvo firing and orders which did not too clearly define proper targets for torpedo attack. In the light of after knowledge, unprovoked attacks upon trawlers, torpedo-boats and destroyers—unless large sitting ducks—were dangerous. Additionally, in a general lack of war experience, some captains tended wildly to underestimate the enemy's capabilities; whilst others were over cautious. Also, a matter of the greatest concern to Sir Max Horton was the fact that details of war experience in Home Waters had been insufficiently promulgated to other flotillas. The blame was sometimes attributed to bad or lost mails, but I do not feel that this excuse holds water.

When the Japanese entered the war, early stage amorphism again made itself apparent to a small extent amongst the Dutch submariners and almost universally amongst American submarines in Far Eastern Waters, as was to be expected.

It will be remembered that in the year of this chapter's review the background in Northern Europe was that of evacuations from Norway and Dunkirk, the collapse of France and Soviet occupation of Lithuania, Latvia and Estonia. Later came the preparations on both sides for the invasion of England, the glorious Battle of Britain, Japanese entry into Indo-China, the sea war in the Atlantic, including the gallant *Jervis Bay** being sunk by *Scheer*. All this was to be followed by the severe bombing of London, more rigorous rationing, the loss of *Hood* followed by the sinking of *Bismark,* and the ever growing realisation in the United States that Britain intended to hold on, and that therefore their increasing aid would not be wasted.

In the Mediterranean and Middle East theatres of war on land, we witnessed German troops entering Rumania early in October and Greece rejecting a vicious Italian ultimatum later in that month. Greece was invaded early in November, repelled Italian attacks and, on the 22nd, the Greeks captured Koritza in Albania. After earlier strategic withdrawals, in December, General Wavell's small Army of the Nile captured Sidi Barrani and began the destruction of Italian forces in Africa, which led to the capture of Bengazi on the 7th February and Mogadishu, capital of Italian Somaliland, on 26th.

However imperative the political considerations of diverting a proportion of General Wavell's army to help defend the gallant Greeks, this decision led to military disaster. The campaign started early in 1941 and lasted until the British forces were withdrawn from Crete at the end of May. On land, our distraction to Greece gave Rommel the opportunity to become established in North Africa: at sea, the operations, particularly the evacuation from Crete, vitiated the striking power of the Mediterranean fleet thus even further increasing the relative importance of the submarines.

This chapter is therefore divided into two parts, the first part covers the period, until about December 1940, when Malta was used only for refitting and as an advanced fuelling base. The second part covers the period after Malta had been reconstituted as a base and continues until the evacuation of Crete, at the end of May 1941.

Even in the absence of the much desired shelters, the withdrawal of our submarines from Malta proved to have an unsound basis. This applied also to light surface forces; but the decision had been reached mainly on the Army and Royal Air Force view that, in the face of Italian air superiority, Malta was untenable. Nor, at the time, was it for our staffs to know that the Regia Aeronautica would prove relatively impotent. So, unfortunately, were also to be our own submarine efforts, or most of them, based on Alexandria.

We in *Perseus,* having had our little weep and trying mentally to adjust ourselves to the somewhat terrifying conditions, proceeded to a position south-east of Italy's toe, from which we hoped to intercept Italian convoys making for Benghazi. Once again, through

* Captain Fogarty Fagan V.C.

lack of proper intelligence, the British staffs did not appreciate that the Italian route at that time lay west of Sicily, thence direct to Tripoli, then coastwise to Benghazi. After a few unproductive days, we moved through the Strait of Otranto into the Adriatic, in the southern waters of which an unsuccessful attack was made against a 3,500 ton Italian supply ship which was escorted by destroyers. *Perseus* was then ineffectively hunted, no depth-charges being dropped. In his evasion tactics Peter Bartlett, our skipper, endeavoured successfully to sit in a density layer with all machinery stopped. The boat sorely needed a refit and this set me, as first lieutenant, quite a problem, for our stern-glands were leaking badly. But the destroyers were prowling close overhead and we expected the depth-charges to come bombing down at any moment, so it was important that we should remain still and silent in the enveloping shroud of the higher density water. As the stern fell to greater depths, naturally the leak increased in intensity and when I went aft, I found the lonely watchkeeper at the tail—up to his neck in water in the after machinery compartment! With the stern of the submarine (as I recall) at 480 feet, I felt something must be done; elst it drop below crushing depth. Apart from that, the angle on the submarine, some 35°, could soon make her unmanageable. Grabbing an intercom telephone, I urgently requested the control-room to pump from aft. This was done and we gradually levelled off, our enemies fortunately remaining deaf.

Astronomical observations had been scarce so, when leaving the Adriatic, *Perseus* was considerably to the eastwards of her estimated position. When on watch, about 0120 in the morning, and with low visibility, I suddenly smelt marshland to port; and rang the Captain's alarm bell, whilst slowing down. No sooner had he reached the bridge than Sazan Island came up on our *starboard* side. We were heading straight into Valona Bay and the beach at its southern extremity! Making a tight turn to starboard, *Perseus* headed northwards, skirting the island. Fortunately for us, the Italians seem not yet to have laid their Valona minefield; and if they had, we passed through it unscathed. I have mentioned this patrol because it is typical of those which at the time were unproductive, a barreness greatly increased by the distance of our operational areas from the Alexandria base. On that patrol, *Perseus* was twenty-three days at sea of which thirteen were on passage. It was nevertheless a memorable patrol for myself because I was suffering from severe amoebic dysentery (first contracted about a year previously in China), could retain no food and had to exist mainly on stomach powder and brandy—a concession granted by the captain; presumably in the hope that he would not have to keep too many watches for me, and in fact I think he kept only one, which I spent in the heads. Of such mundane material are made some of the minor headaches of a submarine commanding officer at sea.

I myself went to hospital on return to Alexandria and did not rejoin *Perseus* for, when after six weeks' cure I was again fit, a signal came appointing me to the submarine commanding officers' qualifying course, starting January 1941 at Fort Blockhouse.

In October *Rainbow* (Lieutenant-Commander J.E. Moore), encountered the Italian U-boat *Toti* south of Calabria and was sunk in a gun and torpedo duel. In the same month *Triad* (Lieutenant-Commander G.S. Salt), fresh from Home Waters, was sent from Malta to patrol the Libyan coast en route for Alexandria, but did not arrive. It is thought she was mined. Saddest of all to me was the loss of 'my *Regulus*', now under the command of Lieutenant-Commander F.B. Currie, to a mine in the Strait of Otranto.

The loss of these three last mentioned submarines was presumably attributable to mines; as in the case of so many others, they just did not return and the enemy made no claim. Although reinforcements were arriving, we had lost nine submarines in the first six months of the war against Italy. That represented about half those sent out on any patrol, lost in operational areas which were, and continued to be, close to enemy shores. Equally depressing were the scant results achieved: only six supply ships and one tanker, totalling about 29,000 tons, were then known to have been sunk. Information had not yet been received that *Rorqual's* minelays had destroyed two ships of about 4,000 tons each. Although *Osiris* had sunk a torpedo boat in the Adriatic and 'Bim' Rimmington, in *Parthian*, had blown the Italian U-boat *Diamante* to smithereens off Tobruk, these more martial successes did little to compensate for the loss of splendid and highly trained crews, a bereavement which deeply affected all submariners and which seriously accentuated the manning problem.

Whilst I feel it must be admitted that tactical thought had to some extent petrified in the submarines out of China, our losses were undoubtedly magnified by crew exhaustion, no home leave and indeed very little locally; and by the serious disadvantages in the submarines themselves which have already been mentioned.

Yet, for an extra budget of three million pounds in 1937 and 1938, we could have had twenty extra 'T' class which would have enabled all the 'O's and 'P's to be relegated to convoy escort and training duties.

With the merging of the old year into the new, this dim picture was to brighten until later it glowed. During the first half of 1941 we lost only three submarines in the Mediterranean area, including the French *Narval*. Let us look now to our achievements.

I have already mentioned very briefly the military operational scene surrounding the Mediterranean. Both the landing and evacuation of British forces in Greece and Crete, made heavy calls on the Mediterranean fleet. At the same time everything possible was being done from both the west and the east to build up Malta as a tenable base. Although Italian air raids on the island had caused considerable damage, most essentials remained intact, but the Germans regarded Malta with malevolence, for they realised it threatened their communications with North Africa and Rommel's newly established army. After April, the Luftwaffe achieved complete air superiority over the central and eastern Mediterranean, with the exception of a small area in Egypt and the Nile Valley—but even here they were able to mine the Suez Canal.

In his attempts to establish British sea power in the central Mediterranean, Admiral Sir Andrew Cunningham had, as early as the 9th July 1940, encountered the Italian fleet off Calabria and repulsed them. There followed, on the collapse of France, Sir James Somerville's unpleasant task of neutralising the French western fleet at Oran; whilst their eastern squadron, at Alexandria, agreed by negotiation to a passive role. It was within the compass of this fluctuating scene that our submarines had to operate.

On 11th November the brilliant Fleet Air Arm attack on Taranto harbour in moonlight had written off the Italian battleship *Cavour* and seriously damaged the battleships *Littorio* and *Duilio;* both of which took some months to repair.

During the period under review the situation in the Adriatic and the Aegean became extremely confused and whilst some of our larger submarines operated there, only two sinkings were achieved: the 6,000 ton Italian supply ship *Cesco* by *Rover* in February and the 5,000 ton *Carnia* by the Greek submarine *Triton* towards the end of March.

Our remaining older and larger submarines continued to be based on *Medway* at Alexandria; although they often visited Malta for replenishments as part of a circuitous passage and patrol routine. At Malta where the submarine force was now rapidly growing under Commander G.W.G. Simpson, the base lacked facilities and most of the repair work had to be done by the dockyard which gave excellent cooperation. In theory, Commander Simpson remained under the

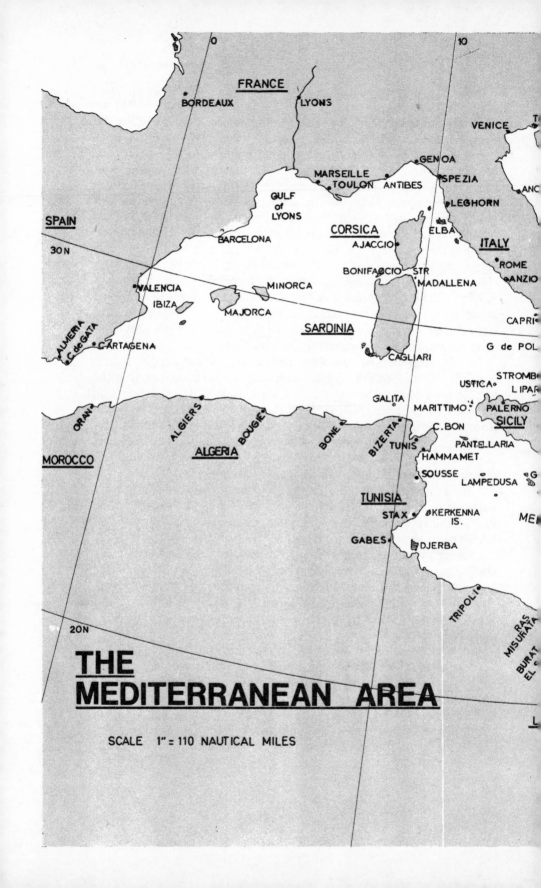

THE
MEDITERRANEAN AREA

SCALE   1" = 110 NAUTICAL MILES

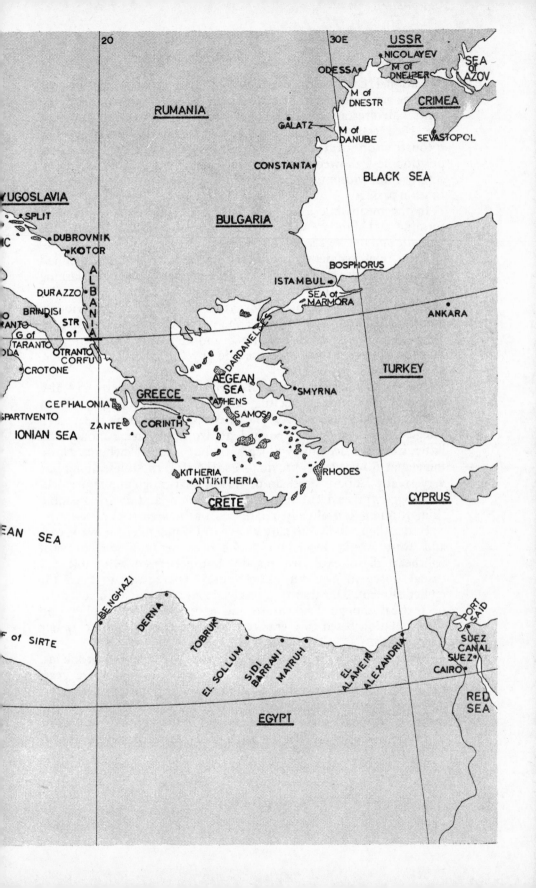

operational control of Captain S/M.1. at Alexandria; but the practice gradually developed whereby he operated submarines in the central Mediterranean, this being recognised by the establishment of the 10th (Malta) Submarine Flotilla in September 1941. The reconstitution of the Malta base with its excellent strategical position now allowed our submarines really to get across the enemy supply lines without having to spend the major proportion of their time on passage.

In the meanwhile a new 8th Submarine Flotilla was gradually forming at Gibraltar, with the dual role of activities in both the Atlantic and the western Mediterranean.

Early reinforcements from home waters (in 1940) had included that old warhorse Hugh Haggard in *Truant,* the debonair and dashing Ronnie Mills in *Tetrarch,* and sadly George Salt in *Triad,* who together with Watkins in *Triton* were lost in December as previously mentioned. Later were to come the purposeful Wilfred Woods in *Triumph* and that turbulent friend and implacable foe, Anthony Miers in *Torbay,* having been preceded by *Upright, Usk, Upholder, Utmost, Ursula* and *Unique.*

The wardroom mess of the submarine base at Lazeretto in Malta was soon to become the melting-pot of submarine thought, as fresh but battle-experienced blood and talent poured in from the west to mingle with their diehard equivalents from the east. Amongst the latter were the seemingly phlegmatic but astute Dewhurst whose minelayer *Rorqual* was proving so successful, the unassuming but very steady Hubert Marsham of *Rover,* that tough and imperturbable rugger forward Tubby Linton in *Pandora,* and the irrepressible 'Bim' Rimmington, already mentioned, of *Parthian.*

Under the friendly but shrewd eye of Commander Simpson, east and west would meet, no doubt over many a gin, to yarn lightheartedly of explosive episodes; but, perhaps unbelievable to a casual observer, without exaggeration. There was no need for embellishment. This tradition survived and so, in an exchange mart of tactical thought, adventure and experience, both policy and determination fused to a granite which the enemy could chip but never smash.

Nevertheless the start was slow because Malta had its problems. There was, for instance, a lack of torpedoes and spare gear, necessitating the overloading of submarines arriving from Gibraltar and that meant a restriction on operations until unloaded. Old destroyer torpedoes had to be converted for submarine use and this at a time when the Luftwaffe started to raid Malta, partly because of the presence of the damaged aircraft-carrier *Illustrious* after convoy operations through the Mediterranean.

Pandora, which Linton had taken over in China, had, in September, sunk a small ship off the coast of Cyrenaica but was now to meet further success on the way home to refit. In early January, when south of Sardinia, Linton sank the *Palma* of 2,700 tons and the important motor transport vessel *Valdivagna* of 5,500 tons. On the same day *Parthian* sank a 4,000 ton ship off Cape Spartivento (Calabria), before paying a visit to the Greeks in Piraeus and continuing back to Alexandria. Later in the month Dewhurst caused a terrific stir by gunning a large tug which was towing a floating battery near Dubrovnik. He sank the tug and decimated the battery, which did not sink, but gave the Italians something to talk about. Ronnie Mills' last shot from *Tetrarch* damaged a 2,500 ton ship off Benghazi before he returned to Malta, to be relieved by Lieutenant-Commander R.M.T. Peacock.

Of course, Greek submarines had entered the fray and after working with considerable success in the Adriatic, sinking the *Sardegna* of 11,500 tons and three or more troopships, they later fell back on Alexandria, coming under British operational control.

Truant had a very early success in September, sinking the 8,500 ton *Providenza* off Naples. Then, in November, Haggard surveyed inside the enemy swept channel off Tripoli, thus being able to bring back useful information. In February he sank a vessel of some 2,200 tons; but in a subsequent unsuccessful attack *Truant* was damaged by bombing. She then hit another vessel of 3,000 tons and again suffered damage to her battery before returning to Malta in mid-February. In December, Haggard had sunk, off Calabria, a vessel of 1,500 tons and achieved a splendid and important success by despatching the tanker *Bonzo* of 8,000 tons in the same area. (Oil fuel, petrol and aviation spirit, or lack of them, proved a constant anxiety to both Italians and Germans in the prosecution of the Mediterranean war. Throughout all our submarines' operations, tankers usually received our best attention, having priority over even vessels loaded with tanks, motor transport and troops, which came next). Haggard stalked another small tanker in the Gulf of Sirte and actually entered the little harbour of Burat el Sun to torpedo her by night. Unfortunately the tanker had unloaded, so the torpedoes ran under. *Truant* turned and left the harbour to a hail of vituperation from a character on the enemy vessel's upper deck!

On her last patrol in the Gulf of Sirte, *Truant*, whose captain had as varied a career as his famous ancestor had imagination, gunned and sank a 300-ton barque and, the following day, acted as navigational beacon for battleships bombarding Tripoli. Her parting shot was at the *Prometeo*, an Italian naval auxilliary of about 1,000 tons. Although the torpedoes missed, panic ensued in the enemy ship which immediately beached and scuttled herself! For all their tenacity during twenty patrols, of which about half were in the Mediterranean, *Truant's* captain and crew received a just award of honours for gallantry and a special prize in the form of a refit in the U.S.A.

The newly arrived 'U' class submarines suffered, as had their sisters in the North Sea, certain inherent engine defects which, combined with a highish proportion of misses, got them off to a slow start. During January Lieutenant A.F. Collett, in *Unique*, attacked a convoy off the Tunisian coast but forgot that the enemy would be obliged to make a navigational alteration of course and so missed. (This is only too easy to do when one's mind is occupied with a thousand other things).

The coast of Tunisia from Cape Bon* runs past the Gulf of Hammamet, the Kuriat and Kerkennah Islands to the Gulf of Gabes, thence south-eastward towards Tripoli, and is within easy reach of Malta. The enemy convoy route, which was now known, skirted this coast. Therefore we concentrated as many of the smaller 'U' class submarines in these shallow waters as possible. Here *Upholder*, commanded by the immortal Wanklyn, hit the large German ship *Duisberg* of 8.000 tons at night, putting her out of action for four months. Unfortunately Wanklyn lacked the speed to follow up and destroy his quarry. *Upright* under the command of Lieutenant E.D. Norman had an unproductive patrol in the area; so did *Usk*, Lieutenant-Commander P.R. Ward.

Although the waters of Tripoli were quite unsuited to large submarines, especially when calm, Browne in *Regent* sank the *Silvia Tripcovich* of about 2,400 tons, but suffered a damaging counter attack from which he escaped with difficulty after many an aquatic contortion.

It should be mentioned that the 'sink at sight' areas in the Mediterranean were, after the initial delay, extended much more rapidly than they had been in Home Waters. The policy pattern on this subject now became more one of expediency than of considerations in international law. However, the enemy, particularly when the Germans began to press heavily upon the Italians, usually gave us a good political excuse.

* See map page 89.

By February 1941 a veritable little flotilla of 'U' class submarines had assembled at Malta. Five were sent to attack the enemy convoy lanes down the east coast of Tunisia, but suffered from a bad crop of misses until Lieutenant E.D. Norman in *Upright* off Sfax, made an attack at night on two enemy cruisers and sank the *Armando Diaz*. Additionally a few supply vessels were damaged, but this could not have been of any serious concern to the enemy.

The redoubtable Dick Cayley, in *Utmost*, did a special operation of considerable importance and complete secrecy, which must have been highly successful, for Cayley was soon to be awarded the D.S.O.

In this case, as in many of the earlier special operations, even Commander Simpson at Malta did not know the real objectives. Secrecy in clandestine landings is important; but Captains S/M and C.O.'s of submarines necessarily had to have a great deal of secret information which might be denied to even rear-admirals commanding cruiser squadrons. Also, in my view, it is imperative that the submarine's captain should know the mission's object because it is only in this way that he can evaluate risks. But this operation must have been unique: it was most unusual for a submarine C.O. to be so highly decorated in such circumstances.

During March, Lieutenant A.F. Collett, in *Unique*, sank the *Fenicia* of 2,500 tons off the Tunisian coast, a welome success in a dull period thoughout which, however, our submarines produced valuable reconnaissance. It should also be mentioned here that our intelligence now began to improve and continued to do so, certainly insofar as the Italians were concerned.

Dick Cayley, after a long period of chasing targets without finding them, and spending very short periods in harbour, sank the 6,000 ton troopship *Kapo Vita* in the Gulf of Hammamet, later sinking the German *Herakleo* of 2,000 tons off Kerkennah.

Hubert Marsham in *Rover*, had previously sunk the 6,000 ton tanker *Cesco* off the Calabrian coast whilst *Triumph* (Commander W.J.W. Woods) destroyed two small vessels anchored off Melito at the toe of Italy.

Most of our attacks were contested by enemy surface and air forces; but unsuccessfully. The Italians were slow to achieve complete efficiency in anti-submarine work; nevertheless it was a mistake to underrate them. They were alert and gradually developed their techniques and tactics until, towards the end of 1941, they became dangerous—no doubt partly as a result of heavy German pressure.

We must now return to the general scene leading up to the victory at Cape Matapan. General Sir Archibald Wavell had strongly advised against the diversion of large forces to Greece but, having registered his complaint, executed the difficult task to the best of his ability.

In March 1941, whilst almost the entire resources of the British Mediterranean fleet were engaged to protect the conveyance of some 60,000 men to Greek territory, the Germans were able with comparative ease firmly to establish Rommel's Africa Corps in Tripolitania, whence the enemy were ready to strike by the end of the month.

As an indication of the importance of reliable intelligence, it can be said that British radio monitoring established the likelihood of an Italian fleet move against our convoys, bound mainly for the Piraeus. This enabled Admiral Cunningham to make the dispositions which led to the Battle of Matapan off southern Greece. The British fleet comprised a light force of four cruisers and nine destroyers, supported by the battleships *Warspite, Barham* and *Valiant* with the newly arrived (via the Cape) fleet-carrier *Formidable* whose torpedo bombers damaged the Italian battleship *Vittorio Veneto* in the running action by daylight. *Formidable's* aircraft again attacked at sunset, hit the heavy cruiser *Pola* and forced her to stop. About this time the Italian Admiral Iachino broke off the action and retreated, but sent back the heavy cruisers *Zara* and *Fiume* to assist *Pola,* unaware that Admiral Cunningham's battleships were in the vicinity. This seems a strange lapse, because Admiral Iachino knew we had an aircraft-carrier at sea and should therefore have assumed the proximity of British battleships. In the ensuing night action our battle squadron destroyed all three Italian cruisers at almost point-blank range. The scene of this success lay some 450 miles from Taranto and 600 miles from Alexandria, thus illustrating the capabilities of a fleet-carrier not only in attack but in reconnaissance and the denial to the enemy of similar reconnaissance. Much of the available strength of the Italian navy had taken part, so British moral and indeed fighting ascendency was clearly established and remained so until the end.

During April and May, with the exception of four destroyers attached to Malta, the main resources of the Mediterranean fleet were devoted to the evacuations of Greece and Crete. The navy brought over 50,000 men out of Greece and 18,000 from Crete, a total nearly 25,000 less than the number landed. These withdrawals in the face of overwhelming Luftwaffe attack cost us every cruiser and destroyer in the eastern Mediterranean—sunk or damaged with heavy casualties. At the same time the Chiefs of Staff in London were urging Admiral Cunningham to operate north of Crete with the object of preventing the island's invasion while the Prime Minister, presumably thinking of Zeebrugge, wanted Tripoli harbour blocked by the battleship *Barham.* Fortunately Admiral Cunningham resisted such fantasies; but the fleet did, with *Truant* as beacon, bombard Tripoli, unfortunately without much military effect.

By the end of April, Rommel, having encircled the staunch defenders of Tobruk, was hammering at the gates of Egypt and stood a good chance of breaking through the defenders' depleted ranks.

These most unfortunate events brought Malta to full prominence as the only base from which any effective attack could be made on the Afrika Corps' supply lines. The island had been reinforced, although inadequately, from the west under the protection of Admiral Somerville's Force 'H' and by Hurricanes flown in from his aircraft-carrier. But these small numbers of fighters were insufficient to prevent heavy bombing and mining by the Luftwaffe, until May, when Hitler drew off the main heat for his gamble against Soviet Russia.

So, under difficulty, Malta had her surface striking force, her handful of submarines and a few aircraft.

After several unsuccessful attacks, some of which led to counter-action, and a sustained and gallant effort to guide the Malta destroyers on to a convoy, Lieutenant-Commander Wanklyn, in *Upholder,* sank the 5,500 ton supply ship *Antonietta Lauro* off Lampedusa. He then went on to destroy a damaged German motor transport ship which had been gunned by our destroyers. The *Arta* of 2,500 tons was boarded and set on fire. A week later Wanklyn attacked a convoy escorted by destroyers, sinking the 2,500 ton *Arcturus* and damaging the 8,000 ton *Leverkusen* which he was later able to sink after evading the escorts' counter-attack. This fine patrol set Wanklyn on his way, from which there was no turning back.

Both Germans and Italians kept up their minelaying activities and *Usk* (Lieutenant G.P. Darling) probably fell victim to a new mine barrage in the Sicilian Channel, also early in May.

In April, tough rugger-playing 'Hairy' Browne was sent to Kotor, in *Regent,* with orders to evacuate the British Minister to Yugoslavia and his staff. Were it not for the casualties suffered this episode merits the comic opera touch. Entering the Gulf of Kotor *Regent* steamed around in broad daylight on the surface not knowing that Yugoslavia had surrendered the port to the Italians; nor could the British Mission be found. Therefore Lieutenant Lambert, through the good offices of what might be termed a Yugoslav liaison officer, was sent ashore as an envoy whilst an Italian officer boarded *Regent* as a hostage. Lambert was actually being interviewed by an Italian admiral when the Luftwaffe swept out of the sky and bombed *Regent,* wounding Lieutenant-Commander Browne amongst others, although some wild machine-gun fire from the shore may have been responsible for the casualties. Browne made for the open sea and dived, Lambert later being exchanged for his Italian counterpart.

There is a story amongst submariners, which I cannot substantiate although it seems to fit, that *Regent* dived with the upper conning tower hatch open. The leading stoker on the diving panel, according to the story, having opened all the main vents, chanced to look up the conning tower where, to his amazement he saw a patch of blue sky. Turning with superb aplomb to the signalman he is reputed to have said:

"Got yer umbrella chum? It's going to be a rainy day."

About this time the United States navy, having presumably seen the writing on the wall, sent one of their best submariners, Commander J. Fife, U.S.N., to gain battle experience with our submarines in the Mediterranean where he became suitably impressed with the urgency and speed of our diving and the fact that the order to dive was given instantly by the officer of the watch without reference to the captain. Much later in the war several British submarines were to come under the command of Rear Admiral J. Fife, U.S.N.

Towards the end of May our submarines' success picture improved considerably, although with one loss. As a result of recent and heavy mining by the Italians off Tripoli, it is assumed that *Undaunted,* commanded by Lieutenant J.L. Livesay, was lost in that area about the middle of May, thus making the second of the recently arrived 'U' class submarines to be sunk on her first patrol from Malta, the other being *Usk*—already mentioned. The twin heroes of the Central Mediterranean arena over the coming year were to be Wanklyn as Castor with Tomkinson in *Urge* as Pollux. 'Wanks' and 'Tommo' were to be admired by all in a way that set them at the top, a position probably shared only by Tubby Linton when he later returned to the Mediterranean in command of *Turbulent.*

On 20th May, east of Tunisia, *Urge* heard occasional depth-charges and rightly concluded that a convoy approached. (The Italian practice of lobbing depth-charges into the sea at random, presumably designed to frighten submarines away, frequently had the opposite effect, as in this case). Shortly afterwards, two cruisers and some destroyers passed, too far off for attack. A little later a convoy and five destroyers came within range and 'Tommo' pressed in a good attack, hitting the 5,000 ton *Zeffiro* which sank and the *Perseo* of about equal size. The latter suffered damage but got away, as did the two cruisers which were attacked on the next day; but do not appear to have been damaged.

A little later *Upholder,* in the Strait of Messina, attacked a tanker and scored a hit; but unfortunately the Italians were able to tow this ship into Messina. *Upholder* now underwent a very long hunt by A/S craft during which she moved her position considerably. Then, with her asdic set unserviceable and only two torpedoes left, *Upholder* came in sight of three large southbound liners with a heavy destroyer escort. To ensure success Wanklyn obviously had to press this attack home and, with no asdic set, even at the risk of being rammed. Despite his disadvantages, he managed to pierce the destroyer screen effectively and score two hits on the *Conte Rosso* of 18,000 tons. The resultant damage proved sufficient to sink the liner with heavy loss amongst Italian soldiers on their way to the front line in Africa. Subsequently Lieutenant-Commander M.D. Wanklyn was awarded the Victoria Cross—ample compensation to his crew for their participation in this hair-raising attack and the subsequent heavy, but ineffective, depth-charging.

Chapter 7

The Scene at Home

JULY 1940-FEBRUARY 1942

An important side effect of our submarine activities during the Norwegian campaign was that the Germans withdrew several U-boats from the Atlantic battle as one of their counter-measures against us. This withdrawal was reflected in our merchant shipping losses which lightened considerably for a period, unfortunately all too short.

Another effect had been to advertise, too greatly perhaps, the prowess and capabilities of our submarines which resulted in diversification and dispersal of effort. During the twenty months under review in this chapter our submarines put in a good deal of time on anti-invasion measures around the south-western part of the North Sea and in the Channel; but, as no invasion took place, they could not achieve sinkings on these patrols. However, *L.27* (Lieutenant H.N. Edmunds) sank a 7,000 ton ship off Cherbourg in October 1940. This success hardly compensated the submariners for their enormous effort in these areas.

Ocean escorts were provided for many convoys intermittently over the whole period and in March 1941 Captain Menzies took the *Forth* to Halifax where a reduced 2nd flotilla pursued this somewhat unrewarding occupation; and the gallant captain complained repeatedly about the high naval direction of the war—I think with reason.

A reconnaissance patrol was done in the Azores area and occasionally submarines were sent to the eastern North Sea. Increasing attention was paid to the Bay of Biscay, firstly against tankers and secondly to contain German warships using particularly Brest as an advanced base. Operations also continued along the whole length of the Norwegian coast, attempting the near impossible task of attack on enemy ships within the protection of the Leads and extensive minefields.

The truth of the matter was that enemy targets at sea were scarce and this is reflected in the disappointing results given below.

During the entire twenty months' period, British submarines, aided by *Rubis,* sank only about 90,000 tons of enemy shipping, with another 10,000 tons or so damaged, some three dozen enemy vessels being dealt with. Additionally, three U-boats and three A/S vessels were sunk and, in February 1942, the German heavy cruiser *Prinz Eugen* severely damaged. Ten British, one Dutch and one French submarine were lost; the last being *Surcouf* (4,000 tons and copied from X.1.) which was rammed and sunk by an American ship when approaching the Panama Canal for passage to the Pacific. Included in the British figure is *Umpire* which was lost in collision when with an east coast convoy, a disaster graphically described in 'One of our Submarines' by Commander Edward Young, D.S.O., D.S.C., R.N.V. (S) R.

In a book of this length it is not possible to mention the exploits of all submarines individually; but I have gone into considerable detail in the earlier stages because it was in this period that we were finding our way so painfully. It now becomes necessary to generalise. Nevertheless there are some episodes which must be mentioned.

About the middle of August 1940, David Luce* in *Cachalot,* having laid a minefield, torpedoed and sank *U.51* off Bordeaux; thus implementing one of the objects of our Biscay patrols. A further object was the interception of ships, and later 'Milch Kow' U-boats, supplying German surface and undersea raiders in the distant oceans. In this last, the redoubtable and ubiquitous Hugh Haggard, whilst on passage to the Mediterranean in *Truant,* intercepted a Bordeaux-bound ship which turned out to be the Norwegian *Tropic Sea* with a prize crew on board, the vessel having been captured by the German raider *Orion. Truant* rescued the Norwegian captain and his wife, also the captain and survivors of the British ship *Haxby* which had been sunk by *Orion.* This rescue, reminiscent of Captain Philip Vian's *Altmark* epic, must have been highly satisfactory to Haggard and his crew; although *Truant* could have been endangered by the scuttling explosion which blew out half the side of *Tropic Sea.*

The Italians had commenced to operate submarines from Biscay ports, to better advantage than most of their Mediterranean efforts. In December 1940, also off Bordeaux, *Thunderbolt* (ex *Thetis*) sank the large Italian submarine *Tarantini.* A comment appropriate here

* The late Admiral Sir David Luce G.C.B., O.B.E., D.S.O. and bar, who so selflessly resigned from the post of First Sea Lord when the government tried to scrap our aircraft-carriers.

concerns a bad habit practised by both German and Italian U-boats which was to proceed on the surface by daylight in areas where British and allied submarines might be encountered. This practice led to many an enemy U-boat being sunk at our hands.

I have mentioned that our submarines frequently escorted ocean convoys, usually an unrewarding task; but here is an instance of success. Lieutenant-Commander A.N.G. Campbell, in *Severn,* had orders to escort a Gibraltar convoy in the Atlantic. The Admiralty, by now proficient in the detection of U-boat concentrations, diverted this convoy from just such a wolfpack. Campbell was then ordered to patrol in the vicinity of the enemy concentration, well to the westward of the Strait of Gibraltar. About a week later, in very rough weather, *Severn* sighted and fired at a U-boat in darkness. The torpedoes missed; but the enemy remained unaware of his danger. Campbell's second salvo blew up the Italian U-boat *Bianchi,* early in August 1941.

Six weeks later *Severn's* sister ship, *Clyde* was to have an exciting brush with three U-boats off the Cape Verde Islands, where a German refuelling base was thought to be. Whilst attacking the first U-boat by night, *Clyde* was menaced by a second, and turned to ram her new opponent. This one dived just in time and David Ingram swung *Clyde* round to fire a salvo at her original target. Unfortunately *U.111* at last woke up and dived on sighting the tracks. *Clyde* also dived to safety and to reload. About three in the morning yet a third U-boat was sighted surfacing (*Clyde* by this time having reloaded and being herself on the surface). *Clyde* again tried to ram her opponent but was herself struck right aft, suffering only superficial damage.

The large *Clyde* was at a considerable disadvantage against these U-boats and probably would not have survived without the skill and verve of her captain, David Ingram. Although it does not seem to have been realised at the time, *Clyde* had surprised *U.111* in a rendezvous with both *U.67* and *U.68* for the purpose of supplying torpedoes and picking up a sick man. Despite the odds of 3-1, *Clyde* in fact gained the advantage, for *U.67* had to be withdrawn from patrol through collision damage.

Now we must jump forward six months, to the end of February 1942, for a brief look at what was perhaps the most important attack in the whole twenty-month period under review. This brief action provides another illustration of the uncertainties, errors and general vicissitudes which comprise what is usually known as the 'fog of war'. In this month the Admiralty had reason to believe that German warships would move northward to Norwegian ports with the object of attacking our P.Q. convoys. They had therefore arranged Coastal Command reconnaissance in the North Sea and ordered Admiral Horton to dispose his submarines for the interception of enemy heavy units entering Trondheim. This port lies far inland, up the fiords, and has two main entrances; Fro Havet to the north and Ytre Fjord whose entrance is commanded by the Grip lighthouse in the south. Admiral Horton correctly appreciated that the Germans would use this southern entrance and ordered the French submarine *Minerve* and '*P.37*', later *Unbending*, (I prefer to use names when available) to leave Fro Havet and concentrate on the northern channel leading into the Grip lighthouse. About noon on the 21st February, aerial reconnaissance reported one enemy pocket-battleship accompanied by a cruiser and three destroyers steering northwards past the west coast of Jutland at speed. Admiral Horton correctly deduced their intended path and was able to place *Tuna* (Lieutenant M.B. St. John) and *Trident* (Commander G.M. Sladen) thirteen and nineteen miles westwards of the Grip lighthouse respectively.

The German force had frequently been reported by our aerial reconnaissance and even attacked at one point. Our submarines which had previously been shifted around to meet likely contingencies, reached the positions given above, this being the final disposition, made in the knowledge that the enemy force had left Bergen (having arrived there through the Leads) during the evening of 22nd February and was therefore expected off Ytre Fjord about dawn on the 23rd. Admiral Horton's forecast proved so accurate that *Trident* had been placed within a mile-and-a-half of the actual route taken by the enemy and *Tuna* within one mile. These two submarines were about six miles apart; so, even allowing for their movements whilst patrolling, it became inevitable that both submarines should sight the enemy, navigational errors excepted. It will be noticed that the intelligence received by the Admiralty, or deduced by them in a number of ways, started off the whole procedure. This was followed by reconnaissance of which nobody could complain. In fact, as a result of excellent intelligence, reconnaissance and staff work, a perfect ambush had been set.

'The best laid schemes o' mice an' men gang aft agley'. Navigation in the area, despite experience, was not easy; for strong winds set up unpredictable currents and both *Tuna* and *Unbending* had already grounded during their patrols. Snowstorms were frequent, the hours of daylight few and the weather usually rough. Also our submarines had been forbidden to surface by day for taking sights, because of enemy aircraft. The positions of *Unbending,* commanded by Lieutenant Harry Winter (who had been 'number one' to me, in *Regulus*) and of Lieutenant P.M. Sonneville's *Minerve* were precautionary, putting them out of the picture.

Shortly before dawn *Trident*, on the surface, sighted the enemy force and turned in to attack. There was very little time in which to plot his enemys' speed and Sladen underestimated; but got their course right. Being very close ahead of an enemy destroyer, he then decided to dive whilst in the process of firing his seven-torpedo salvo and warned the crew accordingly. *Trident* started to dive after firing her third torpedo and immediately an explosion was heard, followed by a second explosion over a minute later. The latter came from a torpedo hit on *Prinz Eugen* which jammed her rudder and caused an engine failure with much other very serious damage. The first explosion seems to have been caused by two of *Trident's* torpedoes colliding. The pocket-battleship *Scheer,* unscathed, altered course to port; then back to starboard and, taking her destroyers with her, should have fallen straight into the welcoming arms of *Tuna.*

Trident did not fire any more torpedoes because, through a misunderstanding when the submarine dived, a sailor had moved a switch on the firing panel to 'stop fire'. *Trident* was not counter-attacked and surfaced half an hour later to make her enemy report.

Tuna, hearing the explosions, chased towards them but, seeing nothing and hearing no more, resumed her patrol; not knowing that she had made a navigational error which put her actual position five miles south of the estimated one. The enemy, firmly convinced for some hours that *Prinz Eugen* had hit a mine and that another mine had exploded not far from *Scheer,* were not unduly concerned about the lame duck limping towards harbour at 3 knots. *Scheer* was now beyond our grasp and entered Ytre Fjord without further incident.

Tuna received *Trident's* enemy report and altered course to intercept the damaged cruiser, diving when it became light. About an hour later she heard propeller noises and then sighted a vessel some four miles off. Observations through the periscope were most difficult and Lieutenant St. John thought that he had sighted *Scheer* doing over 20 knots. However, by this time, *Scheer* was about 20 miles to the eastward, in the safety of the fjord. *Tuna* had sighted *Prinz Eugen* weaving about all over the place in what might have become her death agony, the impression of speed being given by her damaged stern causing a big wake. The visibility closed in and

Lieutenant St. John had no further opportunity of sighting this splendid target, the Germans still being unaware that British submarines were after them. War is largely a tale of missed opportunity and on that note the episode must rest.

This brings to an end a very brief description of those few actions used to illustrate the activities of our submarines in the vast expanse of Home Waters in the period July 1940 to the end of February 1942, excepting British operations from North Russian ports which I will mention later in the chapter.

I should perhaps remind the reader that anything subsequently said in this chapter with regard to our own losses or the sinking of enemy vessels will not be additional to the details given earlier, that is to say—10 British, 1 French and the Dutch submarine *0.22* lost (the last off Norway); about 100,000 tons of enemy shipping sunk or damaged, 3 anti-submarine vessels destroyed, 3 U-boats sunk and the *Prinz Eugen* so heavily damaged that it took a year to repair her.

In the calendar year 1942, the British alone were yet to lose 18 submarines, 15 of them in the Mediterranean. These 1942 losses were greatly mitigated by success and compared favourably with the total of 25 British submarines lost in 1940, a partial annihilation illuminated only by the star of the Norwegian campaign. The crux of the matter, survival or defeat, depended largely upon two factors. Firstly, that the building programme should keep pace with the rate of loss, which it finally just managed to do. Secondly, and far more importantly was the replacement of all crews lost, by the vigorous training of fresh ones, from commanding officers downwards.

As I myself arrived home at the nadir, December 1940, I will endeavour to implant in the reader's mind what I myself saw and experienced as an embryo commanding officer in the threshing of this training mill which, in an amazingly short time, produced enough expertise and determination to meet the challenge. Let us start then with the scene at Fort Blockhouse in January of 1941.

Portsmouth had just been heavily bombed so, after a candle-lit night in the Queens Hotel at Southsea, I arranged for my wife to stay at the Red Lion in Fareham and crossed the harbour to report. In my qualifying course or appropriately enough 'perisher' as it was known, I found Hugh Mackenzie, Harry Winter, Michael St. John and Tommy Catlow. Even here, was a wide disparity in age and seniority, the first two being older and considerably more experienced than us three youngsters. The reason was that contemporaries of Mackenzie and Winter, who should have been on this course, had already been killed.

Rear-Admiral Reggie Darke had retired before the war, but returned to become Captain S/M.5 at Blockhouse, from where he controlled (under Flag Officer Submarines) new construction, much of the early training, and submarines operating in the Channel. After the formalities, we 'perishers' were handed over to Lieutenant-Commander Pat Steel to be taught the principles and practice of torpedo attack. Some months previously Wanklyn, Tompkinson and Pat Steel had been mainly responsible for introducing new methods of submarine attack which were practical in war.

The principle is quite simple, based on a relative triangle. It is similar to firing with a shot gun at game on the wing. One has to 'lay off' ahead in order to score a hit, But the shot gun is simpler, because you can see your quarry and your sights at the same time, whereas in a submarine you are looking in one direction through a periscope whilst firing your torpedoes in another. To take a simple case, if the target is doing 30 knots, your torpedoes' speed is 30 knots and the angle of approach of the torpedoes to target is 90° and the latter is crossing your bows from right to left, you must lay off an angle of 45° on the periscope. This means that the centre torpedo of your salvo must be fired when the target is 45° on your starboard bow. Thus you could be looking northeast through the periscope, at the same time firing a torpedo steering north. Should all your calculations be correct that torpedo will hit; or this is the theory. If the enemy's speed is less and your torpedo faster—a more normal set of circumstances—the angle of lay-off will be smaller. But it is very easy to get 'lost'. This situation is accentuated by your own alterations of course, the target's zig-zags and in that you may obtain only two periscope glimpses before having to fire; sometimes only one.

Unlike the rifle, the shotgun is not a weapon of precision, and the torpedo is even less of a precise runner. It usually suffers from slight variations of course, depth and speed. For this reason, although firing and hitting with a single torpedo may be a superb economy, it makes bad practice. Therefore salvoes are fired; and there now appears a disadvantage from which British submarines suffered, as opposed to the American ones. The latter could angle their torpedoes to an accuracy of 1° whilst in the torpedo tubes. This meant that an American attack officer could look in one direction and fire his torpedoes from tubes pointing in a second direction whereupon the torpedoes would turn and pick up the correct course for meeting the target. The equipment however was expensive; therefore we did not have it. We were nevertheless able to angle our torpedoes 90° either way, but only 90° and did achieve an occasional success by this method. Soon angling was banned to us, because of gyro failures in the torpedoes themselves. The American captain had the advantage of an attack officer, comparable to the gunnery officer in a cruiser or battleship, which left him free to concentrate on the overall situation. Although we thought this luxurious and were content with what we had, it was a sensible arrangement and one which has now come into its own.

All depot-ships had a submarine 'attack teacher' where the more experienced would teach the juniors, but our course was something rather special. The teacher itself consisted of a revolving cylinder, known as the 'box', in which the trainee stood at a short periscope. On the floor above the 'box' was the plotting room. Here the upper lens of the periscope pierced what was known as the 'attack table' upon which model targets could be placed in varying positions at different ranges. The pupil would sight his target, rap out orders for closing her, at the same time putting himself on a good attacking course and say "down periscope". The box would then revolve madly, making one quite giddy, after a beautiful Wren, up top, had put a hat over the periscope's upper lens. The initial lessons were kept simple, but later a team composed of Pat Steel his (literally) plotting Wrens, aided and abetted by one's fellow perishers, would think up every fiendish device to thwart the attack. So, on next looking, it was quite usual to see a destroyer with an enormous bow-wave coming straight towards at a distance of a few hundred yards. Then one had to go deep, and woe betide the perisher who left this too late; for although being rammed (signified by a hammering on top of the box) produced hoots of merriment from one's colleagues, it was rightly considered a black mark and a disgrace. A wartime innovation had been the introduction of Wrens to this game, thereby making it more popular and I am glad to see that these girls' successors are still there.

Most of our time, day in day out, was spent on the teacher where every attack was carefully analysed after the event. So, one was learning all the time; not only by one's own attacks but by observing the mistakes and sometimes the expertise of others. But this box was very easy to get lost in, also a disgrace after the initial stages.

There were two methods of spreading a salvo, which should be mentioned here in order to clear up any misconceptions. The first and normal way lay in the 'firing interval'. This resulting in a time spread rather than an angle spread; thus the torpedoes ran along the same actual track in the water but, as the target was moving across their line of advance, the longer the firing interval the greater the spread along the length of the target. Sometimes, and particularly if one was uncertain of estimations concerning enemy course and speed, the torpedoes would be spread over as much as three target's lengths. In this way torpedoes would be fired ahead of the target, at the target and astern of the target. Therefore, if the speed was higher than estimated, the first torpedoes in the salvo should hit and, if lower, the last torpedoes. If however the speed and course were both correct, the central torpedoes in the salvo would hit. There were other refinements as to the concentration or dispersal of the salvo.

Secondly, by firing with the submarine under rudder, one could accentuate both the concentration and dispersal of a salvo. If torpedoes were fired with the submarine swinging towards the direction of the target's advance, this naturally concentrated the torpedo pattern, the reverse also being the case. 'Firing on the swing' could be useful at night in a snap surface attack with no time to work out firing intervals or track angle—this last being the angle at which a torpedo approaches the target; thus a 90° track is where the torpedo comes in from the enemy vessel's beam.

There was no need to teach us anything more in the fields of personnel or material, all of us having been in submarines for at least four years, Winter and Mackenzie* considerably longer. It is appropriate here to mention Hugh or 'Rufus' for he was naturally the Red Mackenzie whilst Lieutenant A.J. Mackenzie was already conducting Mediterranean operations in *Ursula,* being known as the 'Black' Mackenzie, unfortunately later to be killed when his new 'S' class submarine, *P.222,* was heavily depth-charged and sunk by the Italian torpedo boat *Fortunale* in December 1942, off Capri.

Having all been first lieutenants of submarines, we had naturally enjoyed the confidence of our captains and were therefore kept in the local operational picture, thus gaining a certain amount of staff knowledge. But, as we were about to become commanding officers of major war vessels acting independently for long periods, our staff knowledge was improved by lectures, particularly in the fields of operational planning and communications.

A criticism I have of the course, and indeed of some flotilla captains, is that we were not given sufficient instruction in evasive tactics to counter heavy depth-charging The course itself was too short for me to form an impression on the subject; but later, at Malta, I had a most definite feeling that some deliberately did not dwell on such unpleasant details. Nor were submarine captains keen

* Vice-Admiral Sir Hugh Mackenzie K.C.B., D.S.O. and bar, D.S.C.

to relate harrowing experiences. Perhaps this is understandable, but it tended to leave one unprepared for the worst, and I later gained a marked impression that there was a tacit agreement not to mention such horrors in case, as I thought, the new boys might be put off, and become timid. The result was that new submarine skippers (who had not been heavily depth-charged when first lieutenants) met not only a determined enemy in the first such encounter but met also the unknown. Of the two, the latter was by far the worse.

After a fortnight's gyrations in our mechanical box, the five of us sped northwards with Pat Steel for attack exercises at sea—whilst the commanding officers of the 7th (training) Flotilla kept their fingers crossed; for it was in their boats that we hoped to practise our new art without 'any hammering on the box'.

Clustered around *H.M.S. Cyclops,* a veteran-depot ship from the First World War, were a few old crocks, part of the motley bunch of elderly submarines in which all training had to be carried out. Although not the oldest by any means easily the largest was the prototype submarine *Oberon* which, with her half-sister *Otway,* were known as the electro-mechanical monstrosities. These, with the ill-fated *Oxley,* were the forerunners of sixteen submarines of the 'O', 'P' and 'R' class whose main peacetime operational theatre had been the Far East. Commanding *Oberon* at that time was the delightful and fortunately imperturbable Bertie Pizey, a veteran of the Norwegian campaign who had already been awarded the D.S.O. For him, for Pat Steel and us perishers there ensued a two-week period in the Clyde exercise areas during which we were put through our paces. In each attack there had to be a three-way liaison between Bertie Pizey, Pat Steel and whichever perisher's turn it was. This type of teamwork can be established only by mutual respect combined with actual friendship. While Pizey had to ensure that we did not impale his submarine on the bows of a destroyer, Pat Steel, in order to train us properly, had to encourage our attacks to be realistic whilst the perisher himself, who might easily be the cause of a disaster, had the least responsiblity of all. In practice Bertie Pizey would 'give his ship' to the first attacker, Pat Steel would supervise and, after the attack, the perisher would hand over to the next trainee in turn. In this way, we were not only attacking but were in complete control of the submarine during that period, our orders being carried out by the unfortunate first lieutenant who had to suffer them. The feelings of the crew can be imagined; but they took the risks and the extremely hard work involved with cheerfulness and commendable restraint.

The practice was that the perisher doing the attack would have the periscope of his choice, whilst Steel or Pizey would use the other periscope to ensure safety. If one of these two should stretch out his hand to press the klaxon for a 'crash' dive from periscope depth to 'deep'—at least 60 feet—woe betide the perisher concerned. This was for real, and getting rammed was not on. In the winter months, we might achieve ten submerged attacks during daylight; to the utter exhaustion of the crew, the electric batteries and most of the compressed air in the submarine. Often we remained in the area to carry out night surface attacks throughout the hours of darkness. Then we might anchor, in some place such as Inchmarnock Water, for a short nap followed by breakfast: then it was on again. Our targets, which must not be forgotten, were usually A/S vessels such as yachts and small destroyers attached to submarine flotillas for escort duties, frequently commanded by older submarine office⁻ now above the age limit—about 35, although not a statutory limit.

On my course, Hugh Mackenzie proved the most successful attacker and the best potential commanding officer; for we were being closely watched for other necessary attributes such as judgment, determination, power of command, reaction to crisis and general grip of any situation.

This seems a good place to mention the personal relationships between all submariners. Firstly the captain was (and I'm sure he still remains) next only to God, controlling a mass of intricate machinery operated by men, those men being an extension of the captain's brain . . . in fact his fingers. In order that these fingers could react speedily and effectively, there had to be complete understanding down the line of communication to the most junior man; and not only understanding but intelligent understanding. This meant that the captain's wish must be implemented as soon as indicated, whether by gesture, order instrument or word of mouth—and frequently it was anticipated. These instantaneous reactions required a discipline so rigid that there are few parallels; and even if the watchkeeper on the after pump was dressed in filthy overalls and occasionally smoked an illicit cigarette in the confines of his distant dungeon, such minor irregularities hardly came into the picture. But conversely, there was almost universal friendship and respect between all members of the crew whatever their ranks—a friendship which became conspicuous in the chief and petty officers messes and on the messdecks of the depot-ship, where her first lieutenant often had a difficult job trying to persuade his own men that the submariners were not privileged.

In the wardroom this amicability was perhaps even more marked. Here, C.O.'s and first lieutenants, with very few exceptions, did not stand on their dignity or throw their weight around. Even in the middle of a party when guests were being entertained, a quiet word from a C.O. to his duty officer would ensure his submarine being brought to immediate readiness—perhaps for patrol or perhaps her officer of the day would quietly take the boat off to an anchorage because she was bumping through bad weather. It was (and still is) through the social occasions of mess life that junior officers could realise their skipper was not always the exacting and blood-thirsty tyrant which he seemed to be at sea. Captains also could chat and even rough-house with their juniors in complete relaxation; so acquainting themselves with finer points that might easily be missed under the stress and strain associated with a submarine at sea in war.

Depot-ships and particularly submarine shore bases were a great venue for skylarking . . . a sailors' licence that so often led to amusing and ridiculous letting-off of steam which frequently confounded the more austere senior officers in whose areas we were based. This is not a book of reminiscences, so I have no space in which to elaborate some fantastic peccadilloes. But we were very well looked after, in all ways, by the officers and men of our depot-ships and bases: most of whom would be the first to claim that they had, by their efforts and patience, become honorary submariners. If scenes, in the wardroom particularly, became too riotous, the commanders of depot-ships had a choice. They could squash it or join it. For the most part they joined it and, by their very presence, brought the situation under control unobtrusively.

Now that our exacting, enjoyable qualifying course was over, our little group of five split up, some going to other flotillas as spare commanding officers, in which capacity I remained in *Cyclops* whilst, I think, Hugh Mackenzie and Michael St. John received immediate training submarine commands.

In the first sixteen months of the war, up to December 1940, the British had lost 26 submarines or half the original seagoing number of fifty plus, a rate of sinking which at times overtook the accelerated building programme; although in general the building programme was just adequate to replace submarines lost. The crew situation however had become little short of desperate. Including only a handful captured, we had lost some 1,300 officers and men, which figure with the addition of natural wastage, amounted to half our original strength. We had not only been decimated but decimated five times over. The year 1941 was to prove a merciful relief, with only ten British submarines sunk; but the greatest destruction of all was as yet long ahead; for, in the seventeen months from January 1942 to May 1943, we lost no less than 28 submarines.

Fortunately Sir Max Horton and other senior officers, foreseeing the future, had made urgent arrangements; the most important being the establishment of the 7th Submarine Flotilla with the depot-ship *Cyclops,* at Rothesay in the Clyde estuary. After basic training at Blockhouse, all new personnel were now being channelled into the 7th Submarine Flotilla for an arduous period which varied according to operational requirements. A brief description of the intensity or white heat at which we were trained will come a little later, at the point where I took permanent command of a training submarine.

Before the war all, or nearly all, ratings joining submarines were volunteers; which meant that their papers were sent to Fort Blockhouse for scrutiny before an acceptance was made. Thus the submariners could pick and choose from a large selection of petty officers and junior ratings. For instance, no man without at least one good conduct badge was accepted and the idea of taking ordinary seamen into submarines was ridiculed. Furthermore, all the chief petty officers and men accepted for submarines had not only completed a long period of general service training, but also of specialist training (i.e. seamen torpedomen, seamen gunners) whilst the engine-room department stokers would have their good conduct badge and at least three years' training in the Navy, probably considerably more. Therefore these men were firstly good sailors and secondly, had their professional qualification. All that had to be done at Blockhouse was to train them in submarine work and submarine equipment. This might take between three and six months, whereupon the men were sent to sea. Then, after a year or so, it could be judged whether they were going to turn out good submariners or not. In war this tempo could be increased, reducing the whole process to a period of about six months; but always providing the men had been trained in the Navy to begin with.

By 1941, the enormously enlarged surface fleets were themselves extremely short of trained men. The barracks in all the manning ports had become inundated with requests from all types of ships. Every conceivable warship needed trained engine-room ratings whilst destroyers were howling for seamen torpedomen; merchant vessels for seamen gunners; ocean escorts for A/S ratings; battleships for gunners' mates; cruisers for telegraphists, and aircraft-carriers for every highly specialised man their captains could lay their hands on. It is therefore hardly surprising that the submarines found it difficult to obtain ratings already well trained in general service.

But necessity is not only the mother of invention: it is also a sword which cuts knots, in this case the knot of preconceived ideas, carefully formulated in the balmy days of peace. Sir Max Horton, with his usual foresight and intimate knowledge of the personnel situation in 1918, decided that men could be drafted direct to Fort Blockhouse after a few weeks' initial training in barracks. There followed a period of instruction at Blockhouse after which they were pitch-forked into the training flotilla.

If volunteers were lacking, men were pressed. A difficult case was that of torpedo gunners' mates. These chief petty officers were mainly to be found in destroyers where, at least in harbour, they had comfortable quarters and a nice well-equipped workshop in which to service their outfit of torpedoes. In addition they probably had two quadruple but simple upper deck torpedo tube mountings and, of course, all the depth-charges and throwers to look after; but for this work they had a reasonable amount of room and quite a few men. In a 'T' class submarine, the torpedo gunner's mate had no workshop (excepting the torpedo stowage compartment which was also used as a messdeck; and generally bunged full of stores, hammocks, suitcases and any prisoners or survivors that might be taken), seventeen torpedoes to look after and eleven complicated torpedo tubes. Furthermore after an uneventful patrol, all eleven tubes would have to be unloaded in order that water-shot or air-shot tests could be carried out; all seventeen torpedoes had to be routined and the tubes reloaded again. Compared with a destroyer, living conditions were abominable and not compensated, in the minds of many, by the extra submarine pay. We therefore had few torpedo gunners' mates volunteering to leave their destroyers for the discomfort of a submarine; so they were pressed. In fact anybody needed, including officers, were pressed into submarines when required. Such 'tyranny' probably horrifies the civilian of today, but it worked very well: only a tiny minority could not settle down and pull their full weight.

The shortage of junior officers was not so easily remedied; but Admiral Horton sought and obtained Admiralty approval for the impressment of *all* the regular R.N. officer intake. So in this way we obtained the services of many young sub-lieutenants who had to subjugate their ambitions to become gunnery or torpedo officers, and even flag lieutenants, to the urgent demands of war. These young officers proved quite invaluable for, already having been midshipmen in war, they needed only to be trained in the peculiar submarine aspects of our life. Many served with great distinction, gaining early command, which still left enough time for them later to specialise in their desired branch.

Whilst on the subject of manning, I feel it pertinent here to dip into the future and explain an experiment which failed. It was probably in 1943 that both the Admiralty and Flag Officer Submarines felt submarine captains were becoming too young. It was not meant by this that they were not proficient at their duties; but rather that their age was too tender for the weight of responsibility involved. Therefore it was decided that experienced destroyer first lieutenants would be given a six months' period of specialised submarine training, followed by the submarine commanding officers' qualifying course. They were then to be sent to sea as captains of submarines. This, to me at least, is of considerable interest; because similar schemes were adopted by the Germans, thus contributing, in my view, to their disastrous rate of loss during the later stages of war.

The British scheme was soon dropped, it having become abundantly apparent that you could not place an officer with only six months submarine experience—however accomplished a seaman in other respects—over a first lieutenant who knew submarines and their capabilities inside out. The situation arose that the first lieutenant was advising the captain: this of course is fatal.

We now come to commanding officers themselves. One of Admiral Horton's earliest reforms was erroneously considered to be a purge of submarine captains over 35. This rumour may, with good reason, have been deliberately spread for the consumption of junior officers, chief and petty officers and men, who might otherwise have thought that some of the older C.O.'s were opting out too easily. But in truth it was only a rumour. The facts I think are clear from my comment, based on Captain Menzies' diary, that many of the older captains were relinquishing their commands voluntarily. I would suggest that it is probably more difficult to display this sort of moral courage, than to go to sea and face the enemy. But there can be no doubt whatsoever that, if the captain of a submarine decides he must go, then go he must. In this connection, the only thing approaching a purge might have been a reminder to a few commanding officers that perhaps they were getting on a bit, for the strenuous work involved, and that it might be a good idea to make way for a younger man. In addition, it became customary to relieve a commanding officer who had missed many attack opportunities; but this usually arose from inaccurate torpedo firing.

I had not long been spare C.O. in *Cyclops* when the great day came that I was to take a submarine to sea for exercises, all on my own. One evening I was sent for by Captain S/M 7, 'Sluggie' Edwards of great patience and renown. He eyed me dubiously and said:

"Mars, Bertie Pizey has had to go to Northways. I want you to take *Oberon* tomorrow. Think you can manage her?"

I hadn't expected to be allowed to start on this monster but replied firmly: "Yes, sir; I'm used to large submarines."

Just to show him, next morning and after having done my homework, I took *Oberon* out through the Kyles of Bute, a short cut to the exercise area in Inchmarnock Water; but also a tide-swept and extremely narrow channel for such a large submarine. 'Watty' Phillimore, *Oberon's* first lieutenant, being a clever lad, was senior to me; and this illustrates an anomaly which sometimes occurred. Phillimore had had less time in submarines than myself and had not therefore yet been selected for his command course. This odd situation sometimes arose; but never, as far as I know, led to any grief.

Oberon behaved well that day and, in common with most large submarines, handled beautifully when submerged. So on Bertie Pizey's return I was able to hand him his boat intact.

My next duty was that of temporary staff officer (operations); for the boats of the training flotilla had been ordered to the Bay of Biscay, and our proper staff officer whisked off to Blockhouse. Here, Rear-Admiral Darke had assumed direct operational control of the 6th, 7th and 9th Flotillas. The 3rd Flotilla was to operate itself. The larger submarines proceeded direct to their billets while Falmouth was used as an advance base for the smaller boats.

For the previous two months *Scharnhorst* and *Gneisenau* had been on the rampage in the Atlantic; although not too successfully because our convoys were being escorted by battleships as well as submarines and A/S craft.

Hipper was also out and so were the U-boats. *Scheer* which had been raiding in the South Atlantic, managed to return to Germany safely; likewise *Hipper* towards the end of March. But the Admiralty thought all four might enter Brest and had ordered the 'Iron Ring' of submarines. Bad weather had precluded all aerial reconnaissance.

Somehow we managed to rake up 22 submarines for this duty, these being spread on a wide arc between the latitudes of Bordeaux and Brest; but well out in the Atlantic, at an average radius of 200 miles from the latter port. The submarines concerned were— *Tuna, Taku, Torbay, L.26. L.27, Undaunted, Sturgeon, Sunfish, Sealion,*

Sokol (Polish), *H.31, H.32, H.33, H.44, H.50, Cachalot, Union, Unbeaten, Tigris* and the Dutch *0.9, 0.10* and *0.24.*

The whole operation was completely abortive, because *Gneisenau* and *Scharnhorst* had already returned safely to Brest before most of our submarines had even sailed. Owing to the neglect of Coastal Command in peacetime, a neglect fortified by the night bombing effort on Germany, British air reconnaissance over the sea left a great deal to be desired. Nor had it in any way improved a year later when the *Scharnhorst* and *Gneisenau* were able to escape up channel undetected until too late by R.A.F. Coastal Command and almost unmolested by R.A.F. Bomber Command, both of which had been forewarned by the Admiralty.

The equinoctial gales were fierce that year and our submarines suffered accordingly, particularly the tiny 400-ton 'H' class—nearly a quarter of a century old—and the small Dutch training submarines *0.9* and *0.10* The two last caused a mild furore by running out of distilled water and lubricating oil respectively; but the Dutch were not alone. *H.50* ran out of fuel and, like *0.9* and *0.10,* had to return to harbour. *H.32* also returned to harbour with damaged hydroplanes whilst *H.31* also damaged hers but managed to stick it out. Admiral Horton had not favoured this 'Iron Ring' and it seems to have been foisted upon him by the Admiralty. Gradually he was allowed to reduce the strength until, by the middle of April, all our submarines had returned to their previous duties. But the evolution was not a complete loss because, for once, the training submarines had been allowed experience in a proper submarine function under the most adverse conditions and, although the whole affair was highly uncomfortable and perhaps unnecessarily dangerous for these old boats, it did have an element of value for the submarine crews concerned. With proper reconnaissance, the four British submarines already on patrol in the Bay of Biscay might well have intercepted the German battle-cruisers returning to Brest. But bad weather apart, we were denied the good reconnaissance which could have been obtained had we been allowed to use airfields in the Irish Republic. This refusal of cooperation on the part of the Irish cost us many a ship, one way or another.

In May of 1941, I was appointed to command the training submarine *H.44* which then lay at Londonderry.

Although the depot-ship *Cyclops* mothered her brood of training submarines, most were employed exercising, not from Rothesay but from widespread harbours. The 7th Flotilla then was split around Scottish and Irish ports upon or near which our anti-submarine ocean escorts were based, to wit Belfast, Larne, Londonderry, Campbeltown, Ardrishaig, Oban, Tobermory, Scapa Flow and Hollyhead, this last being handy to Liverpool where the Commander-in-Chief Western Approaches had his headquarters.

Therefore the majority of training submarines, usually very old and very small, could not for most of the time use the living facilities of their depot-ship. For war purposes, a submarine's crew was divided into three watches, red, white and blue. By this arrangement, one-third crew were always on duty both at sea and in harbour. For maximum relaxation and comfort (both important to morale and physical condition) the best arrangement was one whereby two-thirds of the crew lived in the depot-ship or suitable shore accommodation, leaving one watch for duty. But even as late as May 1941, very little shore accommodation had been provided.

At that time, it was common to see scores of boiler-cleaning destroyers, corvettes, trawlers and other escort vessels berthed four abreast in the River Foyle at Londonderry. These represented only a proportion of Atlantic escorts, enjoying a four-day boiler clean and rest period. Escort groups were continually arriving and leaving; so it was for the benefit of these groups that we usually kept three submarines exercising from Londonderry.

Therefore, after having relieved Willy Knox* as captain of *H.44*, it came as no surprise to me that my crew were living in appalling conditions. 'H' class submarines were of American First World War design and many still in service had been built in the U.S.A. Good little boats for their time, they displaced about 400 tons and had a total complement edging 30. Right for'ard, was a tiny space around the four torpedo tubes; then came a watertight bulkhead and the torpedo compartment. This measured some 22 feet in length and perhaps 9 feet across at the widest point. It contained four torpedo racks and, under these conditions, a mass of hammocks, suitcases, kit-bags and a collapsable mess table. About fifteen men were expected to live in this confined space, both at sea and in harbour. Going aft, through another watertight door, one came to little square messes for the chief and petty officers and engine room artificers: then came a minuscule wardroom. Abaft this, was the control-room, another watertight door, then the engine-room and motor-room combined. Throughout the boat, headroom was at a premium; whilst under the living spaces were 'battery tanks', the large cells being covered by floorboards which had frequently to be lifted, in order to replenish each individual cell with distilled water.

* Lieutenant W.N.R. Knox, lost when commanding *Regent* in the Mediterranean, 1943.

One or two men would usually sleep on the control-room floor and another in the engine room. The majority managed as best they could—even in torpedo racks if these happened to be empty—in fact a torpedo rack was considered quite luxurious.

No lodging allowance was given for sleeping ashore, and it was usually only the commanding officers who could afford to live in a hotel. In fact, in an 'H' boat, the captain *had* to live in a hotel because there were only two bunks in the wardroom. We did not spend much time in harbour and most of that was usually only to undertake repairs, but not enough had been done to alleviate foul-aired, congested conditions which were certainly unhealthy and contained the seeds of danger.

The submarine berths were alongside the Transatlantic shed, just below the bridge where the tidal flow was so strong that one could only come alongside at the high and low-water stands; and the 20 foot rise and fall of tide caused the greatest inconvenience.

I had never fancied myself as an administrator but felt something must be done. So, having gained the support of Captain Philip Ruck-Keene who was then Commodore, Londonderry, and himself a submariner, I put up a plan to commandeer the Transatlantic shed and to have pontoons placed alongside the jetty for the greater convenience of the submarines berthed there. Not surprisingly to me, the scheme ran into opposition on the score of expense; but finally we had our way. So, by mid-summer, the crews had messing facilities and hammock billets in this rambling warehouse which was not ideal, but at least provided fresh air, being exceedingly draughty. In its day the Transatlantic shed must have seen some bizarre birds of passage, but none who so urgently needed the shelter of its corrugated iron and rotting timbers. As *H.44* was typical of most training boats, I will enlarge upon her condition and her crew.

In the tide-swept and shoal-ridden River Foyle, a reliable anchor was a necessity. *H.44* boasted only one which invariably failed to drop when required to drop and was equally as perverse in the opposite direction. When weighing, the electric capstan fuses always blew and, on one occasion off Moville, I had to slip and buoy the anchor. Unfortunately the buoy sank, thereby causing me much piffling correspondence, because the loss of an anchor is considered a serious crime in the Navy. Fortunately it was later recovered and the quill-driving ceased. Although our electrics usually worked, all insulations were low and the boat a hotbed of 'earths.' This necessitated constant and infuriating work for the electricians. We also suffered one particularly distressing defect, a leak from the sea into one of the battery tanks. This leak was never found, probably because it had rusted up; but for quite a period, whenever we dived, a frantic and useless water-divining effort ensued.

Nevertheless we made do with yards of electric tape, bits of old rope and many a Heath Robinson expedient thought up by the Chief E.R.A., who fortunately was experienced.

In the crew, the coxswain had considerable experience, as had one or two other petty officers; but most of the remainder were as green as little green apples. My 'No. 1', Lieutenant Trickey, R.N.R., proved willing, hard-working and of adequate experience; but, with more gallantry than wisdom, he had failed to report that his eyesight was not up to the high standard required—as I found out one day when a destroyer nearly whipped the periscope out of his hands. Our only other officer, straight from training class, was the worthy and excellent John Haig Haddow, a lanky and determined young Scot who later became my first lieutenant in *Unbroken*.

This set-up was typical so, in common with other C.O.'s of training submarines, I, at the age of twenty-seven and without command experience, set out to train not only these men, but the equally raw crews of the A/S vessels with which we exercised.

Perhaps the most intense hive of activity lay at Tobermory where Commodore Stephenson reigned in holy terror, supreme over the early training of corvettes and trawlers. A typical week's running out of Tobermory would go something like this—

At 6 a.m., we would leave harbour and chug out to the exercise area between Tiree, the Skerriemoor Lighthouse, Colonsay and Iona. About two hours later, a corvette or two would turn up: *H.44* would then dive to 60 feet for a simple anti-submarine exercise lasting about three hours. This was usually to a pre-arranged plan in which the submarine's course and speed were restricted, so that the instructing officer in the corvette could re-direct his pupils onto the submarine if necessary. Also the submarine usually towed 'buffs' to indicate her position, but of course the learner asdic operator could not see these. In summer we would continue this activity until about eight o'clock in the evening, perhaps returning to Tobermory around ten o'clock.

Then, on the Tuesday, we might continue with similar exercises until the evening, when perhaps a destroyer would turn up. With her, we might do a less restricted practice, thus giving ourselves experience in evasive tactics. Then, if we were very lucky, we might be allowed to attack the destroyer. Later the destroyer might anchor in the Sound of Iona or some other sheltered spot; when we would go alongside for a few hours. This was considered a great treat, bath day, one might say. Our non-duty watches would probably be entertained to a meal whilst the destroyer's men were acquainted with the novelty of a conducted tour in a very old submarine. Then, as the short hours of darkness approached, we would be off again for a night encounter exercise; although in twilight conditions these were not very realistic. Nevertheless they had to be done in order that drill and procedures could be perfected.

However, the luxury of these meetings with destroyers were more the exception than the rule; and we spent most of our time doing the more tedious exercises first mentioned. As our anchor always seemed to work better in a slight seaway, we would frequently anchor off for the night; because, with our slow speed, it was sometimes hardly worthwhile returning to Tobermory.

By Sunday we would probably be back in harbour dealing with our many defects, hopeful of a nice run ashore in the evening; but our hopes were usually dashed. Commodore Stephenson was a man of energy and enterprise who rightly considered that peace and quiet were not compatible with war training. Therefore many schemes, often explosive, were divised to keep his corvettes alert. At no time was any ship in the harbour immune from being surprised and boarded by gangs of enterprising pirates, festooned with arms and accoutred with such objectionable pyrotechnics as thunderflashes, flares and even gas capsules. And woe betide the corvette captain who had his ship boarded, captured, set on fire and his sailors blinded by tear-gas.

Submarines were not immune from these attentions and we were sometimes subjected to a clandestine visit in order to confiscate the log book. The theft, if undetected, could land a C.O. in trouble. Having no boats of their own, submarines relied on others; but the sight of the local inn, only 200 yards away, frequently remained just a tantalising vision—all boats being engaged in mock battle!

In a fortnight at Tobermory, I think I only got ashore once; and that ten minutes before the pub shut. In that period, *H.44* must have spent something like 200 hours at sea. The pattern was much the same for the whole flotilla in all places from which we exercised; but little harm was done and, after a few months in the training flotilla, both officers and men became fit for operational patrols.

Miles away, at Northways, Admiral Sir Max Horton worked day and night, the dynamo and architect of training, home operations and vital new construction and equipment. His name had become a byword in the upper command hierarchy; and he was not a man to be crossed. As an example of this, I will try to describe from memory a proforma document issued under the Admiral's signature which illustrates his attention to detail. Learning that commanding officers of operational submarines (perhaps back from a three-week patrol) often had to stand for many hours in the corridors of trains, he produced a written authority to ease their problems. Addressed to all Naval, Military, Royal Air Force and Civil authorities concerned, the pith went something like this—

'The bearer and undersigned is a submarine commanding officer travelling on duty. You are required to afford him every facility of which he may stand in need. The submarine commanding officer concerned has orders to hand you this document as authority. Further, he has orders to complete and detach the bottom half of the form, stating which facilities have been requested, which granted and, if not granted, the reasons.'

The précis immediately above is not of course word for word; but it does illustrate the Admiral's intent. It is a pity that such biting language should have been necessary: but necessary it was.

When the training submarines were with *Cyclops* at Rothesay, they were exercised in their proper functions. In the Clyde areas, we worked by day and night with converted yachts and small destroyers attached to submarines; and, in these cases, the practices were for our sole benefit.

To recapitulate briefly upon the training situation, we come face to face with the difficulty of turning a cowhand into a submariner before he has yet become a sailor on the one hand; whilst, on the other, R.N. sub-lieutenants and senior ratings are being pressed into submarines. There is the training flotilla with multifarious tasks and only a gaggle of old crocks to undertake them.

The Americans used to call their early submarines 'pig boats' and that certainly applied to the 'H' class. 'Electric Sieve' became my name for *H.44* and the handful of old American submarines we acquired about this time enjoyed such descriptions as 'Reluctant Dragon' and 'State Express', a goer carrying the number P.555.

For much of the time the irrepressible Lieutenant-Commander Harvey commanded that electro-mechanical monstrosity *Otway*. His was a case of a true submariner who preferred to remain in this unlikely boat, rather than advance himself by gaining command of ever-increasing numbers of destroyers and escort vessels, and thereby promotion. *Cyclops,* in addition to Captain Edwards who was Captain S/M 7 for a long period, was blessed with a retired officer, Commander Spragge and that most understanding of doctors, Surgeon-Lieutenant-Commander Derrick Logan, amongst many others.

Much later in the war some of the smaller 'U' class were detailed for training duties; but, in the main, the brunt of submarine training had to be taken by worn and sometimes dangerous craft, *L.26* probably being the best of a bad lot. As regards personnel, it became perforce a case of 'blind lead blind'; but by perseverence and the efforts of the elder submariners, who acted as senior submarine officers at the various ports, success was achieved not only for ourselves but for hundreds of ocean escorts. In addition there were a number of calls for operational duties, to wit anti-invasion patrols and notably the 'Iron Ring' previously mentioned. The pattern set above continued with minor variations until the end of hostilities.

To return briefly to the operational scene at home. Towards the end of May 1941, *Hood* was sunk by *Bismarck* which very nearly escaped into Brest, only being prevented by the Fleet Air Arm's torpedo attack from the aircraft-carrier *Ark Royal* which, less than a week before, had been flying Hurricanes to succour Malta. When on 22nd June 1941 Hitler attacked Russia we were quick to offer help by sending Rear-Admiral Vian (to Murmansk) who soon reported the general state of unpreparedness of the Russian Fleet in Arctic Waters including that of their submarines.

The Russians asked us to intercept German troop movements by sea along the Norwegian coast and for this our submarines needed a base closer than Lerwick in the Shetlands. Accordingly a small party of British naval officers was sent to Polyarnoe,* being joined by a submariner, Commander G.P.S. Davies who came up from Moscow where he had been on our ambassador's staff. Commander H.F. Bone in *Tigris* and Commander G.M. Sladen's *Trident* were chosen for these North Russian patrols and arrived at Polyarnoe early in August. The Russians were most impressed with our submarines' efficiency and enthusiastic about their successes—eight ships sunk and two damaged, mostly in very confined waters and in broad daylight, as this was the height of the Arctic summer. These sinkings have already been included at the totals given earlier in this chapter.

Our relations with the Russians at this time were quite cordial but later deteriorated—our allies expected too much and were boorishly ungrateful for what they received.

In November 1941 *Tigris* and *Trident* were replaced by Lieutenant George Colvin's *Sealion* and Lieutenant R.P. Raikes in *Seawolf,* both of which had some success; but as the winter closed in,

* Near Mermansk

conditions became intolerable. Anyhow, by January 1942, the new German super-battleship *Tirpitz,* sister to *Bismarck,* had arrived at Trondheim; so our submarines had to devote their attention to containing her. The submariners were not sorry to leave their bleak and, by now unfriendly Russian base. The weather was atrocious, the food appalling, recreational facilities non-existent and the sun did not rise above the horizon; also the Russians had become jealous.

The Norwegian coast apart, our patrols continued in the Bay of Biscay although, by the end of 1941, we were woefully short of operational submarines in Home Waters: a shortage caused by losses temporarily exceeding new construction, by the increasing require-ments of the training flotilla, the necessity to reinforce the Mediterranean and mounting mechanical troubles in allied sub-marines, many of which were old. At the same time the C.-in-C. Far East was, so rightly, clamouring for submarine reinforcements, having only a few Dutch submarines on firm promise.

By December, all the signs were that *Scharnhorst, Gneisenau* and *Prinz Eugen* could soon be ready to break out of Brest. Therefore another 'Iron Ring' was instituted with eight boats from the training flotilla and the Dutch submarine *0.10;* but this also was abortive because the enemy made no move. Frank Gibbs in *H.31* did not return from this patrol, having possibly hit a floating mine. During the period, heavy R.A.F. raids on Brest claimed success against the German ships, but these claims were exaggerated.

A weaker 'Iron Ring' was maintained, but the object was to intercept the German force if it broke into the Atlantic in order to attack our convoys. Therefore our submarines were disposed on the most likely enemy route which ran southwestwards from Brest.

The Admiralty were under no illusions as to the possible movements of these German ships and had informed all authorities early in February that the most likely move was up-channel at high speed. The ships of the Home Fleet were preoccupied with *Tirpitz;* also it was adjudged unwise to risk them in the restricted and dangerous waters of the Channel,. The Admiralty then made arrangements for the enemy ships to be attacked in the Channel by torpedo bombers of Coastal Command, by Bomber Command and by destroyers and M.T.B's in the Straits of Dover; but this all depended on early Coastal Command recconaissance off the coast of Brittany, and that failed.

The enemy force was not positively identified until 10.45 in the forenoon of 13th February when it was already sou'west of Boulogne. Coastal Command's torpedo bombers were disorganised and their attack abortive. Bomber Command had planned a heavy attack; but this also failed partly because of low cloud. Our M.T.B.'s from Dover could not penetrate the enemy's heavy destroyer screen and our own destroyers' torpedoes were avoided by the German heavy ships. Lieutenant-Commander Esmonde's gallant attack, for which he was awarded the Victoria Cross, with half a dozen old Swordfish torpedo-carrying aircraft had little hope because the R.A.F. fighters meant to escort these lumbering old stringbags failed to materialise. All the Swordfish were shot down by enemy fighters and anti-aircraft fire. Fortunately the Admiralty had previously taken the wise precaution of mining along the French and Dutch coasts. Both *Gneisenau* and *Scharnhorst* hit mines without serious damage until the latter hit a second mine off Terschelling; but by that time was outside our reach.

The only submarine close to Brest was George Colvin's *Sealion*; but she was guarding the sou'western approaches, off the Chaussée de Sein. The enemy force hugged Ushant and passed twenty miles to the north of her.

Whilst there is no doubt that the Germans planned this operation with exactitude and audacity, they should not have been able to get away with it. Naturally the country was shocked and an enquiry ordered. Its results only confirmed a view long held by the Navy which was—and I hope still is—that all operations at sea, whether air, surface or sub-surface should be controlled by one authority; and that authority obviously must be the naval one.

Nevertheless one question remains in my mind. *Sealion* could have been ordered to patrol the end of the swept channel off Ushant, but was not. The reason is not clear to me; but it may have been that the Flag Officer Submarines had been told to confine his dispositions to attack an Atlantic sortie, the Admiralty being satisfied that the Royal Air Force and our own small ships could combat any Channel dash.

This episode brings to a close the period under review; so we must now devote our attention to the Mediterranean where the situation was soon to deteriorate, if only temporarily.

Chapter 8

The Ascendancy of
Malta-Based Submarines

JULY 1941 - MARCH 1942

In our quick transit from the winter waters of the English Channel to the height of Mediterranean summer, we travel back in time for seven months. By June in any year in the Mediterranean, asdic conditions deteriorate and thereby the submarine has a distinct advantage which she loses between the autumn and spring. With the high rate of summer evaporation in the Mediterranean basin and the consequent inflow of water from the Black Sea and Atlantic, there is an admixture of varying densities which tend to conglomerate into layers under which, or in which, a submarine can hide and become relatively immune from asdic beams. Conversely, the calm and improved clarity of the water makes a periscope's sighting more likely and increases the chances of being seen from the air, particularly when the sun is not at the zenith.

The reader will recall Lieutenant-Commander Wanklyn's splendid attack on the *Conti Rosso* towards the end of May, 1941. From then on, the British submarines' star in the Mediterranean was to rise markedly, an ascendancy helped by the enemy's use of Benghazi as a supply port; this making for attack areas within reasonable range of the submarines based at Alexandria. But the German invasion of the Aegean Islands proved to our disadvantage, for it was now more difficult to get surface ships through to Malta from the eastern basin, consequently 'Magic Carpet' submarine supply runs to the island base had to be made from both Alexandria and Gibraltar. But Captain S/M 8. was relieved of his Atlantic patrol work, thus enabling both Dutch and British submarines to operate in the western basin of the Mediterranean. I come to their exploits first, later moving on to the central and eastern areas.

Captain G.A.W. Voelcker, who was known as 'Vox' to his friends and whose name must have had Dutch connotations even though he came from the Channel Islands, made the ideal commander for this Anglo-Dutch flotilla based on Gibraltar. Whilst it is invidious to make comparisons, I feel it should be said that the Dutch were our staunchest submarine allies and showed remarkable skill and tenacity through all adversity. In saying this, let me make it clear that I do not intend in any way to minimise the gallantry of those few French, Polish, Norwegian and Greek submariners who fought alongside us.

That experienced veteran David Ingram still commanded *Clyde* which he took to Sardinian waters at the end of May 1941, there sinking the 3,000 ton ship *San Marco;* but missed another. Having a big area, he ranged across to Capri, where two attempted attacks on enemy destroyers were foiled; but failure was compensated by the successful destruction of a 2,000 ton vessel further south, this time with the gun. A close inspection of Palermo revealed a cruiser in harbour, but achieved no other result. On her way back to base at Gibraltar, *Clyde* fell in with a 1,000 ton Italian schooner and gunned her to destruction, taking prisoners. Perhaps it should be mentioned here that the Italians had converted many schooners to A/S uses, therefore these vessels were fair game. But as I have previously mentioned, the 'Sink at Sight' areas were conveniently extended as required, only neutral waters and some safe lanes being left for the use of those not engaged in hostilities, and the latter included prisoner of war comfort ships and other mercy vessels.

Severn, still commanded by Andrew Campbell, having missed one ship and a U-boat (which resulted in being hunted by an A/S schooner), torpedoed and sank a 1,300 ton ship in the Tyrrhenian Sea, taking survivors. Before returning to Gibraltar in early July *Severn* despatched the 3,000 ton *Ugo Bassi* off Sardinia.

Lieutenant-Commander O. de Booy in the Dutch submarine *0.24* made some sightings of distant convoys in the Gulf of Genoa before getting his teeth into a fine target, the Italian tanker *Fianona* of almost 7,000 tons. Unfortunately one of the torpedoes broke surface after firing and the target was able to avoid the salvo. But de Booy surfaced and, gunning his enemy, scored several hits before finally despatching her with a last torpedo. On the same day a 500-ton schooner was sunk with demolition charges, this economy being something of a compensation for the earlier wasted torpedo salvo.

A glance at the map* shows what a magnificent area these Gibraltar-based submarines had; all around the Sardinian coast, the

* Page 89

Gulf of Genoa with its large and important harbour, then the entire
length of the west coast of Italy to its toe, and the north coast of
Sicily; thus encompassing the comparatively open spaces of the
Tyrrhenian Sea into which one could beat a retreat if too hotly
chased. Of course, as always, staff planning had to ensure no
unexpected meetings with friendly submarines, which could so
easily lead to calamity. Naturally there was complete cooperation
between the staffs at Gibraltar and Malta; for submarines from the
latter also patrolled in the southern part of the Tyrrhenian Sea.

Now came the turn of Lieutenant-Commander G.B.M. van Erkel
in *0.23* who found a heavily-laden 5,000-ton tanker south of
Leghorn and made the unusual score of three hits from a salvo of
four torpedoes. After this *0.23* had a nasty time; for she had herself
developed an oil leak which kept enemy destroyers persistently on
her tail. However, their attentions were not sufficiently accurate—
most surprising in the circumstances—to destroy the Dutch
submarine which van Erkel took to the Gulf of Lions where the
offending tank was emptied of oil and washed out. This is an
illustration of the great advantage a large area can provide, because
after her cleansing, *0.23* could again have attacked. However, the
remainder of her patrol proved uneventful and she returned to
Gibraltar early in July.

In the meanwhile the new submarine *Thrasher*, Lieutenant-
Commander Joe Cowell, was so urgently required at Alexandria that
she had no patrol in the western Mediterranean. Carrying stores to
Malta, *Thrasher* proceeded to her new base in the east.

Apart from the damage done, our patrols in the western basin had
the effect of drawing off the enemy's anti-submarine forces from the
more hotly contested areas of the centre and east. Although patrols
from Gibraltar continued throughout most of the year, they were
apt to be reduced by the requirement to run submerged supplies into
Malta, the *Clyde* later being converted for this purpose. A similar
diminution of offensive patrols was suffered for the same reason by
the 1st Flotilla at Alexandria and it was in fact from here that the
majority of Malta's submarine supplies were run in. Before turning
to the activities of submarines operating from Malta, let us take a
brief glimpse at the large eastern Mediterranean basin.

Early in June, Lieutenant-Commander E.F.C. Nicolay, in *Taku*,
was sent to the Benghazi area where he landed a reconnaissance
party and indulged in a gun action with small surface vessels until
Taku's gun jammed. Later Nicolay was rewarded by sinking two
vessels of about 1,500 tons each before returning to Alexandria. This

area remained quiet during *Regent's* patrol which followed; but *Triumph,* on her way and when off Mersa Matruh, sighted a U-boat coming towards. Commander Woods,† finding himself in an impossible position for torpedo attack, surfaced and with great promptitude engaged the enemy by gunfire thus damaging and stopping the Italian U-boat *Salpa.* Woods then despatched her with a torpedo before continuing to his area where he sank a small coaster but had trouble with her escort, a trawler named *De Lutti* which was nevertheless severely damaged, later sinking. So close was *Triumph* to the beach that a shore battery joined in this action, scoring a hit on the submarine which caused damage to the forward tubes. Despite this, Commander Woods maintained his position for nearly a week before proceeding to Malta for repairs.

There was considerable tanker traffic at that time which emanated from Rumanian ports and passed through the Dardanelles en route to Italy; therefore the northern parts of the Aegean were given considerable attention. Lieutenant-Commander Miers* in his *Torbay* achieved an unusual success by torpedoing a tanker from right astern near Cape Helles; then hit her with another torpedo after she had hurriedly anchored. But tankers, particularly when laden, are extremely difficult to sink because their cargo of oil, being lighter than water, gives them additional buoyancy. Miers had some trouble with this one which was aggravated by Turkish patrols and an attempt to tow his quarry away. But with that determination for which he is renowned, Anthony Miers persevered, finally sinking this troublesome vessel by gunfire. Later *Torbay* sank another tanker of similar tonnage and capped her patrol with a caique and a schooner, having already sunk two small petrol-carrying caiques on her way to the area.

Cachalot (Lieutenant-Commander Hugo Newton) arrived at Malta in mid-July, having carried aviation spirit and stores from Alexandria. After a short stay she set out on her return voyage, this time carrying passengers and spare parts. Off Benghazi she sighted what she believed to be a destroyer escorting a tanker; because this combination was expected in the area. Newton, in bad visibility, shadowed and chased the supposed tanker for quite a while, eventually deciding to slow her down by gunfire. It was still dark and foggy with the result that the flashes half-blinded Newton and his lookouts. The next thing they sighted was a destroyer coming for them at high speed, blazing away with her guns. Because of a jam

† Now Admiral Sir Wilfred Woods, G.B.E., K.C.B., D.S.O., and bar.

* Now Rear-Admiral Sir Anthony Miers, V.C., K.B.E., C.B., D.S.O., and bar.

when the submarines gun's crew were trying to get down their hatch, as ordered, the destroyer was within 300 yards before *Cachalot* could start to dive. Certain now of being rammed, Newton gave the order to abandon ship in order to save his crew and passengers. The destroyer, *Generale Achille Papa* was a little one, more like a torpedo boat. Her captain went full speed astern, not wanting to smash his vessel to pieces on the stout hull of a fully surfaced and much larger submarine. Nevertheless the resultant collision so damaged *Cachalot* that she became incapable of diving. Hugo Newton then tried to trick his opponent and get away on the surface; but his bluff was called and the *Cachalot* had to be scuttled. Of the 92 souls on board all but one were rescued. This was a case perhaps of too much aggressive spirit. *Cachalot's* shadowing and chase technique must however have been good, because the little *Papa,* which had been sent into the area to search for a British submarine, knew nothing of her presence until the *Cachalot's* shells came whistling overhead! Such are the fortunes of war.

Lieutenant-Commander Miers sank many caiques and small vessels by gunfire during his Aegean patrols, some of which were loaded with petrol, some with German troops and others with stores; for the Germans used these vessels extensively to supplement their aerial supplies to Crete and the Aegean Islands. In early July, off the delightful island of Mikonos which is now so well known to tourists, *Torbay* sank the Italian U-boat *Jantina* which plunged to the bottom only one minute after being struck by one of a salvo of six torpedoes.

Many other successes were achieved in 1941 by submarines of the 1st Flotilla, including the evacuation of isolated groups of British soldiers from Crete, the landing of saboteurs and experts in guerrilla warfare and intelligence. Patrols were maintained off the North African coast westwards to the Gulf of Sirte, sometimes with success. But the shallow and difficult waters were mined more and more, thus making a close approach to the coastal harbours very dangerous. To complicate matters further, supply convoys using these ports had, because of the gentle configuration of the land, several directions from which they could approach and leave. Because we seldom had more than ten submarines in the entire eastern basin, some of which were usually engaged on 'Magic Carpet' supply runs to Malta, our forces were too thinly spread to achieve spectacular results. Before leaving the eastern Mediterranean, I feel we should take another look at the exploits of the *Rorqual* which was destined to be the sole survivor of the six large minelayers thrown into the conflict by the British. Under Lieutenant-Commander L.W. Napier, *Rorqual* was one of four submarines which carried a large quantity of mail, some stores, many passengers and almost 500 tons of petrol to Malta during the month of August alone. She then laid mines off Zante (which later sank a small ship), following this up by sinking a 3,000 ton vessel with torpedoes. In this attack *Rorqual* was rammed and suffered periscope damage, although she returned safely to Alexandria early in September. This might be described as a useful and highly rewarding round trip.

After having been relieved by *Porpoise,* in October, *Rorqual* proceeded to the Gulf of Athens where her minelay accounted for the Italian torpedo boats *Altair* and *Aldebaran,* two fine feathers in her already highly decorated head-dress. Out of Malta, she laid her final minefield in Sardinian waters before passing through the Strait of Gibraltar, and temporarily out of the picture, for a refit in the United Kingdom, having successfully completed an inspiring seventeen months' Mediterranean operations under the most hazardous conditions. Many members of her crew were now returning home for the first time in more than three years, some having gone out to China in her as far back as 1938.

Remembering the constant movements between the three submarine bases, especially fresh submarines coming in from the west and, less noticeable, half their number trickling homewards for a refit, let us go to Malta, where great events are taking place. Fortunately we have the influence to travel to Malta by what was rapidly becoming recognised as the safest way—by submarine. So let us assume that we've had a quiet passage with some amiable character like Teddy Woodward in his *Unbeaten,* and are now in the so-called submarine base at the old lazaret in Malta.

This is situated on Manoel Island between the Sliema and Marsa Muscetto creeks; both of these being immediately northwest of the Grand Harbour and divided from it by the great Lascaris bastion which housed the staff of the Vice-Admiral Malta. From here one can look down upon the whole vista of the Grand Harbour which is so minimised that one feels able to stretch out and touch the topmasts of the battleships at their buoys. But in June 1941 there were no battleships. And although the full violence of enemy air attack has not yet fallen on Malta, there is, even now, considerable bomb damage; and an air raid may take place at any minute. Lazaretto was the local and accepted name for the submarine base and, as quarantine arrangements had been conducted elsewhere for many years, the place usually served as a storehouse. The smaller submarines were berthed at buoys only a few yards off the shore and

Captain George Menzies inspecting the crew of one of his submarines on board the depot-ship *Forth*, in October 1940.

Lazaretto, Malta, 1941. *Upholder*: left to right Lt. F. Ruck-Keene; Lt.-Cmdr. M.D. Wanklyn vc dso; Lt. J. R. Drummond dsc; Sub-Lt. J. A. Norman rnvr.

could be reached by pontoons or floating catwalks. The buildings were, and I presume still are, of solid sandstone blocks and, in places, reach out to the sea wall on the upper floors; being supported underneath by pillars of solid stone. These strong and almost fireproof structures were to stand us in good stead; but, in June 1941, excavations were being made into the soft sandstone, towards Fort Manoel which dominates the small island. Although few submarines would be in harbour, one could walk into the crypt-like makeshift wardroom and consult the pictorial score boards, which must have been started about this time.

On this board would be the names of *Unique, Utmost, Union, Ursula, Urge,* and *Upholder,* the last two being the most prominent. Yet to be added were *Unbeaten, Upright, Ultimatum, Umbra, Una* and *Uproar.* These constituted the 'first eleven' of the Malta Flotilla. Already lost were *Usk* and *Undaunted,* soon to be joined in the depths by *P.32* and *P.33* (both unnamed 'U' class submarines); but not before the last had sunk a 5,000 ton ship near Pantelleria.

Against Lieutenant-Commander Tompkinson's *Urge* would be recorded the sinking of an Italian light cruiser which was not in fact sunk. This incident is mentioned briefly at the end of chapter six and occurred off the east coast of Tunisia on 21st May. Two cruisers were attacked from long range and Tompkinson thought he had hit one, an estimate which was later confirmed by the fact that he saw—or thought he saw—his quarry, with only mast and funnel showing above the water. 'Tommo's' claim was a genuine one and, in the light of later experience, the error can be explained. The Italian escorting vessels had been indulging in their practice of lobbing depth-charges as deterrents. One of these could easily be mistaken for a torpedo hit, particularly if it exploded in line with the target, and was seen through the periscope, or even if it went off unseen; but at the time a torpedo was expected to hit. The mast and funnel effect can also be explained by mirage, a phenomenon very common in the summer months' calm weather off the north coast of Africa. Also, because of the closeness of the upper periscope lens to the water, in certain condition of haze, range of vision can be so vastly increased that one can see objects well over the horizon. This anomaly bends the line of vision, conforming it to the curvature of the earth. If the magnification effect of mirage is added, it can be understood that what Tompkinson probably saw was the upper part of one of these cruisers far away; but seemingly closer—the whole picture resembling a sunken ship.

It may be appropriate here to make a few general comments on the subject of submarine warfare. Compared to the number of days spent searching for enemy ships, actual sightings are remarkably few. An attack with torpedoes is usually the event of the month and a submarine which sinks a ship once a quarter is doing well. Therefore the reader can easily imagine the tedium of endless patrolling, a tedium accentuated by harsh living conditions and an exacting routine, in which few obtain more than a couple of hours' sleep at a time. The strain is in no way relieved by constant war with the sea and with the dangers in it, such as mines. Yet boredom or not, continuous alertness must be maintained; for a single mistake or a moment of slackness can be the death of all, with no second chance.

Indiscriminate depth-charging does have a bad moral effect on submarine crews, even though the enemy sometimes advertises his presence by it. Nobody likes the bangs! Even if distant, they constitute a reminder of what might happen. Should the submarine be below periscope depth, it is difficult to judge the distance of an underwater explosion, because variations of density, type of sea bed and many other factors affect the volume of sound carried by the sea. Knowledge of the vagary hardly improves peace of mind.

If, in addition to all the above, harbour rest periods are continually interrupted by air raids, in which the safety of personnel and the submarine are always at stake, where there is little recreational or social relaxation and when home mails are frequently interrupted, one can readily visualise the strain placed on submarine crews operating out of Malta. In addition, rations were usually poor, basically inadequate and lacked the vitamins and other ingredients essential to the re-establishment of good health after a long patrol. All these factors contributed to physical and mental disabilities which could well prove dangerous.

When suddenly and often unexpectedly, in the middle of this enervating grey drabness, would come the red flash of action at sea, the reaction had to be instantaneous, professionally skilful and completely determined.

The best boost to morale under these conditions was success; so if submariners exulted in their victories, it was an exultancy more for themselves than one over fallen enemies.

In the period from June to September 1941, the 'U' class submarines based at Malta sank eleven enemy supply ships totalling about 75,000 tons. Many ships were also damaged; and of these something should be said.

Ships very badly damaged and driven ashore or beached by their own crews were usually as good, from our point of view, as ships sunk. Unfortunately those that were damaged and made enemy harbours, regrettably the majority, did not cause the Italians as much trouble as we would have liked. They were usually quickly repaired and put into service again. However they did tie up labour, often caused a diversion and consequently the thinning out of enemy A/S forces; and a large number of damaged ships under repair in Italian shipyards could hardly have been inducive to good morale.

If we add to Malta's figure those for the Gibraltar and Alexandria submarines, the total of 116,000 tons was obviously beginning to tell on the Italians. Gibraltar's contribution was six and Alexandria's ten ships sunk in the period, totalling 41,000 tons.

The names of submarine captains were now beginning definitely to emerge: to those of Wanklyn and Tompkinson must be added Dick Cayley of the Malta brigade, Lieutenant-Commanders Miers and Nicolay from the east, and that omnipresent character David Ingram whom, in *Clyde,* we have already seen successfully battling away, from Norwegian waters to the Cape Verde Islands.

It will be seen that the average tonnage of ships sunk by the Malta submarines more than doubled that of those based at the ends of the Mediterranean. The reason lay in the size of the liners employed by the Italians as troop transports, *Conti Rossi* having already been dealt with. A result of *Upholder's* success was that the Italians changed their tactics, as *Unbeaten* discovered.

About mid-June Teddy Woodward, when on patrol in the Straits of Messina, sighted a large liner steaming down the Sicilian coast at high speed; doing a continuous zig-zag. up to 70° on either side of her line of advance. Thus at no time was the target on a steady course. Woodward tackled this problem with his mathematical brain, and fired a salvo based on a calculation which anticipated the enemy's course at the moment of the torpedoes arrival. Unfortunately *Unbeaten* was at long range and her salvo missed; but this was soon to be rectified.

Our intelligence now functioned well and, in mid-September 1941, Captain Simpson was told that the enemy intended to run another convoy of ocean liners to North Africa—destination Tripoli. From information gleaned during the previous patrols, it was anticipated that the enemy convoy would make a landfall in darkness some 45 miles to the eastward of this North Africa base. Four submarines were therefore disposed in the area, their object a concerted attack. This operation simulated a mobile patrol, although low speed precluded the real thing.

In the early hours of the 18th September, *Unbeaten* sighted the enemy convoy well to the northward and, being herself too distant for firing, made an enemy report by radio, having first attempted S.S/T without success—not surprising in view of the distance. *Unbeaten* then followed the convoy to catch stragglers.

Lieutenant John Wraith, in *Upright*, over-reached himself to the southward and met only a destroyer which would have been an easy target had *Upright's* torpedoes been the proper submarine Mark VIII's; but they were not. Only old torpedoes were available for her and, in anticipation of deep draught targets, had been set to run at 18 feet. Unlike Mark VIII's, it was impossible to alter their depth settings, once loaded into the tubes.

Upholder, which by now was converging on the convoy at her full speed of 10½ knots,* sighted the enemy at six miles, shortly before 4.00 a.m., and a quarter of an hour later fired her salvo. This attack was a difficult one for Wanklyn, since his gyro-compass had broken down and the secondary magnetic compass was apt to swing in a seaway, thus making an accurate course hard to steer. But Wanklyn, with considerable finesse, was able to overcome this disadvantage. He fired by eye, at the same time compensating for gaps which would otherwise have occurred in his salvo. Having obtained a hit each on *Oceania* and *Neptunia,* both of some 20,000 tons, Wanklyn dived and made to the westwards whilst reloading.

After a dawn, 'Baldy' Hezlet in *Ursula,* carried out a daylight submerged attack on the third ship, *Vulvania,* but underestimated her speed and missed. Half an hour later, *Upholder* again sighted *Oceania* which was stopped, and *Unbeaten* came in from the eastwards. The former had some trouble with an enemy destroyer, which Wanklyn resolved by diving under his target, now lying stopped in the water. Then he turned around and fired not only at *Oceania* but at *Neptunia* as well.

Unbeaten was now well placed; but Woodward was again to be deprived of his target. This time, not by zig-zags, but by *Upholder* whose torpedoes hit both ships just as Woodward was about to fire!

As was so often to prove the case, the hitting of troopships minimised or completed alleviated counter-attack, since enemy destroyers were too busy picking up survivors.

Both these ships sank and, in this way David Wanklyn (to include his earlier attack on *Conti Rossi*) destroyed 60.000 tons of liner shipping employed in the delivery of troops to the battlefront.

As Hitler had only recently complained bitterly to his Axis

* U-class was designed for 12 knots, but seldom achieved more than 10½.

partner about the inadequate protection of Afrika Corps reinforcements crossing the Mediterranean, these splendid successes accentuated the widening breach between the two dictators.

Captain Simpson had no intention of allowing the *Vulcania* to
remain afloat and so ordered Dick Cayley in *Utmost* to intercept the
returning vessel off Marittimo; but although sighted, *Vulcania* was
well outside range. The area around Marittimo, the adjacent islands
and the west coast of Sicily was, and was known to be, very heavily
mined; thus greatly restricting our operations, whilst the enemy
could use safe inner channels known only to himself.

During the whole period under review, a great many special
operations took place. In July, *Utmost* blazed a new trail through
the Sicilian mine barrier; making it in one go at 150 feet. Cayley sent
a signal, "Next please", before rounding Sicily and making the Gulf
of Ste Ufemia (Calabria) where he landed a folbot party which
successfully blew up a train. In August, a party from *Utmost*
dynamited a railway bridge in the Gulf of Taranto. Perhaps the most
spectacular assault was that carried out by Tomkinson's *Urge* from
which a party was landed to wreck a train in a tunnel near Taormina.
After the trap had been laid, watchers from the submarine's bridge
saw the train enter the tunnel, only to be dynamited as the engine
was emerging. This serious disruption kept the enemy busy for many
days.

As the reader will know, much of the Italian railway network
follows the coast and is therefore readily accessible to submarine
landing parties. These railways carried a great quantity of munitions
to the south, particularly bombs for Malta. There were few
alternative land routes for heavy equipment and it used to be
reckoned that, on the main west coast line, well over 10,000 tons of
war material went southwards every day in addition to a large
number of troops. Therefore to put this line out of action for only
24 hours constituted a success nearly as good as the sinking of a ship
and was well worthwhile. Of course, if one could block the line for
three days, that was an achievement out of all proportion to the risk
and effort involved.

Still viewing things from the Lazaretto staff office we now come
to the autumn and winter of 1941.

Throughout 1941, on the surface, the Maritime Services
successfully ran three convoys to Malta, from both ends of the
Mediterranean; a total of forty large and fast vessels of which only
one was lost. Additionally, aircraft, notably Hurricanes and
Spitfires, were flown into the island whenever opportunity arose.

Attacks on these convoys were frequent and heavy, fortunately only sinking the cruiser *Southampton* and a destroyer, damage to other warships apart. Malta was thus enabled to cope with air raids to the extent that a small squadron comprising two cruisers and some destroyers, known as Force 'K', Captain W.G. Agnew, was based on the island during the autumn. This squadron achieved brilliant successes, including the complete destruction of a seven-ship convoy by night, early in November. Another highlight, in December, was the sinking of the Italian light cruisers *Alberto di Giussano* and *Alberico di Barbiano* off Cape Bon; this time by Captain G.H. Stokes with only three British and one Dutch destroyer. Unfortunately, in November, the famous *Ark Royal* had been sunk by *U.81* when returning to Gibraltar after one of her Malta aircraft replenishment runs.

Here it should be mentioned that the picked German U-boats put into the Mediterranean achieved considerable success against our warships, this being an indication that their captains and crews were well trained and quite capable of carrying out attacks against the best escorted British heavy units, when the opportunity arose. My previous criticism (page 28) of German U-boats in the Atlantic therefore does not reflect on the skill or gallantry of the crews—at any rate in the early stages—but reflects rather the shortcomings of the High Command of which I will give two examples. Firstly, wolfpacks used far too much radio on frequencies which the British could D/F. This enabled us to divert convoys from German concentrations and, as in the case of *Severn,* to destroy some U-boats with our own submarines. Secondly, in the spring of 1943, Admiral Doenitz made a grave mistake by heavily arming his U-boats with anti-aircraft weapons and ordering them to fight it out on the surface with a now highly efficient and powerful Coastal Command. In the months of May, June and July, 1943, our airmen sank 28 U-boats on passage and damaged 22 more; albeit at considerable loss to themselves. These losses of well trained men were to have a marked effect upon German U-boat efficiency in the later stages of the war.

I digress, and must now return to the Mediterranean where our surface forces were to suffer grievous loss before the end of 1941. *U.331* torpedoed the heavily escorted battleship *Barham*, which blew up; later *U.557* torpedoed and sank the cruiser *Galatea*. In December, Force 'K' ran into a newly laid Italian minefield where the cruiser *Neptune* was sunk and *Aurora* (Captain Agnew) badly damaged. Another loss was the destroyer *Kandahar* which was mined and had to be sunk by her consorts. So the brilliant and dashing Force 'K' came to an early end. But this was not all; for the determined Prince Borghese and his Italian charioteers penetrated the boom defences at Alexandria and achieved a remarkably gallant victory by severely damaging Admiral Cunningham's two remaining battleships, *Queen Elizabeth* and *Valiant.* In this way the rich promise of the summer vanished into a winter gloom soon to be blackened by Japan's treacherous attack on 7th and 8th December and the immediate sinking of *Prince of Wales* and *Repulse.* These events, which caused the Admiralty to consider the abandonment of the eastern Mediterranean, further accentuated the importance of all submarine activities and those of the strike aircraft of both the Fleet Air Arm and Royal Air Force, operating from Malta.

Whilst the two last do not enter the scope of this book, these air strikes achieved a great deal of success, particularly when it is considered they were always carried out from airfields under enemy attack; the results became a cause of grave concern to the Germans, particularly to Rommel who tended personally to overrate the effects, being a most air-minded general. But in terms of war effort, when one considers the penalty of a sunken aircraft-carrier and damage to escorting ships, it might have been better had this energy been devoted to that most economical weapon—the submarine.

However, in the context of reconnaissance, Malta based aircraft were essential to many operations, including those of submarines. And at the headquarters of the Vice-Admiral commanding at Malta, a very close liaison existed between R.A.F. Coastal Command, the Fleet Air Arm, submarines and surface forces. Time and time again good intelligence followed by early air reconnaissance led to submarine success. This is something which should never be forgotten, for the seeds of good intelligence must be sown in peace time, which is also the time to equip and train airmen in the very special skills required for reconnaissance and combat over the sea.

Before giving the figures for enemy vessels sunk in the period October 1941 - February 1942, submarine armaments should be compared. Generally speaking the 'U' class based at Malta had four torpedo tubes, eight torpedoes and a twelve-pounder gun. Their speed was a cripplingly slow 10½ knots maximum which, when dived in daylight hours during the summer and zig-zagging at night, gave only a rate of advance of some ninety miles a day. The 'T' class based at Alexandria had eleven torpedo tubes, seventeen torpedoes and a four-inch gun. Their rate of advance under the same conditions would be about 130 miles a day. Of course in winter with longer hours of darkness, the mileages increased.

In these five months, the Malta based submarines sank about 54,000 tons of enemy supply shipping whilst *Upholder* despatched an enemy destroyer and an Italian U-boat, with *Unbeaten* sinking *U.374.* Also Johnny Wraith in *Upright* had a left and a right in a splendid night attack south of Taranto, sinking two 7,000-ton supply ships.

In the same period the Alexandria based submarines, mainly 'T' class, sank about 67,000 tons of supply shipping with the addition of an Italian torpedo boat, sunk by *Truant,* and the Italian U-boat *Medusa* destroyed by Lieutenant-Commander R.G. Norfolk in *Thorn.* Additionally a large quantity of enemy supply shipping was damaged.

Our patrols from Gibraltar had been thinning out during this period, the most significant achievement being that of Lieutenant-Commander J.F. van Dulm in *0.21* who, by keeping an excellent lookout, sighted and sank *U.95* in the western Mediterranean, this German U-boat having recently arrived in the area from the Atlantic. *0.21* thus became the first Dutch submarine to sink a German warship. It must have been highly satisfactory to van Dulm that he was able to make prisoners of the German captain and other survivors.

Our own losses, up to the end of 1941, amounted to only two submarines, making a total for that year in the Mediterranean of eight, comparing very favourably with the nine lost in the seven months' period June - December 1940.

Tetrarch, now under the command of Lieutenant-Commander G.H. Greenway, had, in September, a most successful Aegean patrol during which she sank two ships, one of 2,500 tons and another of 3,700 tons, in addition to other successful operations. This submarine, the exploits of which we have already followed under the command of Ronnie Mills, was now due for refit and sailed to Malta. On the last lap, she left Malta at the end of October but, alas, failed to arrive at Gibraltar. It is assumed that *Tetrarch* fell victim to a mine, probably in the tortuous waters of the Sicilian Channel.

Particularly sad to me was the loss of *Perseus,* now under the command of the gallant Nicolay who had been in the Mediterranean from the beginning, transferring from *Otus* to *Taku* where he was awarded the D.S.O., then to *Perseus* in which he sank a ship off Benghazi before sailing from Malta to undertake a patrol in the Ionian Sea en route for Alexandria. On the night of the 6th December, 1941, when off the approaches to the Gulf of Corinth, *Perseus* struck a mine on the starboard side forward and dived to the bottom. There was only one survivor, Leading Stoker Capes, whom I interviewed upon his return to England when I was on the staff at Northways in the autumn of 1943.

Capes' escape, being one of the most extraordinary in all history, deserves a special mention. The leading stoker was taking passage to Alexandria and had been given a berth in the stokers' mess which in these large submarines was right aft. When the *Perseus* hit bottom she righted herself temporarily; but flood water was rushing aft through the engine-room with what Capes described as 'a filthy scum' on it. The surge short-circuited the main motor switches, electrocuting the watchkeepers and Capes managed only with difficulty to shut the watertight door, thus isolating himself and a few others in the after compartment.

Increased air pressure had burst paint drums stowed aft and the resultant mess was greatly to hinder the escape. In complete darkness with the submarine at 360 feet and again heeling over to starboard, the chances of anybody escaping alive had become almost non-existent. Capes and one other carried out the proper escape drill, lowering the twill trunk and swiftly flooding up the compartment, with the aid of a single watertight torch.

The others were overcome by the fumes, oil and the great pressure; only Capes proved capable of exercising the enormous willpower necessary to remain alive under these terrifying circumstances. Despite the angle to starboard, he managed to flood the twill trunk, then inserted his escape set mouthpiece and opened the hatch. The only other man now alive did not follow.

There was no time to spare, for oxygen poisoning sets in rapidly when breathing the gas at such high pressures; but Capes kept his head. He used the apron attached to his escape set in order to control his ascent—this must not be too rapid because, if it is, the oxygen in both the artificial rubber lung and one's own lungs expands too rapidly and bursts the latter. In what was about a minute, but must have seemed an hour, Capes reached the surface having sighted a mine on the way up. In the moonlight he removed his mouthpiece, trapped oxygen in the rubber lung to give flotation and swam to the Island of Cephalonia which he could see.

The distance was ten miles; but his endurance and determination were such that he made it safely. There, for eighteen months, he was protected by Greek patriots, being shuffled from pillar to post in the avoidance of Italian and later German guards. His protectors passed messages which belatedly led to a rescue operation by caique. Few would believe that in those days and with such equipment Capes had escaped from this great depth. But in recent years the wreck of the *Perseus* was located and his story corroborated. This episode illustrates forcibly my earlier comment that it is only the hardiest and the luckiest who escape their ship's destruction. Capes was lucky indeed to be aft; but it was by a rugged and unparalleled determination that he came out alive.

Our next loss was that of the once mined *Triumph,* under Lieutenant J.S. Huddart, which was probably again mined near the Cyclades whilst conducting a special operation in January 1942.

Although the seemingly small figure of about 25,000 tons sunk each month in the period under review may now seem disappointing, this was not in fact the case. The German staff in North Africa, as early as September 1941, pointed out that our submarine attacks had recently been 50% successful, that they must be expected to increase and that shipping sunk could not be replaced. Admiral Raeder, Commander in Chief of the German Navy, concurred with this view, realising that if the Germans lost North Africa they would lose the war in the Mediterranean and that the consequences might be disastrous. Energetic measures were therefore taken to supply all Italian anti-submarine vessels with asdic sets and to provide instructors in their use and, more importantly, in their tactical application.

But perhaps the greatest accolade came from Admiral Sir Andrew Cunningham. When, in the autumn of 1941, the Commander-in-Chief Far East pressed for the submarines he expected but never received, the Admiralty asked for their release from the Mediterranean. In resisting this pressure Admiral Cunningham said, amongst other things: 'Every submarine that can be spared is worth its weight in gold.' That from a tight-lipped Scot is praise indeed.

Chapter 9

The Fight for Malta

MARCH - AUGUST 1942

In most of my tale so far, I personally was more on the fringe of essential operations than with them, as one would expect by virtue of my comparative juniority. From March 1942 onwards however I became much closer to the centre of the scene and therefore will be relating more events as an eye-witness. It is not my wish to over personalise the story and hope that I continue to present a balanced view.

In the Mediterranean, submarine operations, combined with those of the surface and air forces, had so deprived General Rommel of supplies that the 8th Army (continually being reinforced by the long Cape route) was able to advance, relieve Tobruk, and again enter Cyrenaica.

Although the pressure of submarine attack was kept up against the enemy's supply routes during the next three months, by many stirring exploits which I cannot relate here, achievement began to fall back as the Axis partners lashed themselves into retaliation, particularly against Malta. The picture darkens as we now approach the nadir of war, which I place in March 1942.

Looking backwards from that month it will be remembered that the Allies had lost on land—Crimea, Kiev, Odessa, Taganrog, Karkov, Philippines, Hong Kong, Malaya, Singapore and Java, with more to go. At sea the British alone had recently lost *Ark Royal, Barham, Prince of Wales, Repulse* with *Queen Elizabeth* and *Valiant* out of action at Alexandria. Cruisers lost in the same period were *Perth, Exeter and Dunedin.* Added to this was the bitter blow of *Scharnhorst, Gneisenau* and *Prinz Eugen* escaping up Channel to safety and positions of future menace.

Malta was virtually bombed out and its harbours mined up; but *Clyde, Olympus* and *Porpoise* were still running supplies to Marsaxlokk in the south of the island. At Alexandria, the 1st Flotilla had now been reduced to four submarines employed on aggressive patrols. *Trusty* and *Truant* had belatedly been sent to the Far East together with the Dutch submarines *0.23* and *0.24*.

We still continued to inflict damage; but no longer the 50% of Rommel's supplies which had been attained in some months during 1941.

Very early in March, *Unbroken* arrived at Gibraltar under my command and although destined for operations, was not yet fully worked up. As *Clyde* and *Olympus* were both on a 'Magic Carpet' run, we were for a time the only submarine alongside the depot-ship *Maidstone*. In harbour were the ships of force 'H', battleship *Rodney*, battle cruiser *Renown*, aircraft-carrier *Eagle* and a handful of destroyers.

My own thoughts were that *Unbroken* would be allowed a working up patrol from Gibraltar and then proceed to join the 10th Flotilla at Malta. But Captain Voelcker told me that the deterioration of the situation at Malta had become very serious indeed, and that the future lay in the melting pot. He added that the delay, not only to *Unbroken* but to submarines following her, would probably be beneficial as we could now accustom ourselves to conditions in the less dangerous waters of the western basin, after feeling our way with a dummy patrol off Spanish Morocco.

Thus *Unbroken* and the others gained the advantage of a longish working up period which was to stand us in good stead. It was not until 11th April that we sailed for our first really operational patrol and, by that time, things looked grim; for our three immediate 'U' class predecessors into the Mediterranean had by now been sunk. These were *P.38, P.36* and *P.39*—the last two by bombing when in harbour at Malta.

Taking Peter Churchill* and four very gallant and determined clandestine operators, we proceeded to the Riviera coast for landings. Two men were landed at Antibes and the others at Agay, everything being supervised by Peter Churchill with great expertise. He brought out with him Baron d'Astier de la Vigerie, an important resistance leader. The operators landed by *Unbroken* all reached their initial objectives, and at least two survived the war, again after torture.

Unbroken attacked a southbound ship, scoring one hit at very long range. Later, at Gibraltar, this success was confirmed by intelligence sources which stated the ship had been sunk; but there

* Captain Peter Churchill, D.S.O., Croix de Guerre, survived the war after capture and torture. He now lives in the South of France.

seems to be some doubt. After many of the alarming vicissitudes sometimes associated with the first operational patrol, we became involved with a U-boat chase by our own destroyers east of Gibraltar. At night on 1st May I attacked this Italian U-boat; but she sighted us in time to dive and avoid torpedoes. *Unbroken* made an enemy report, and then met one of the chasing destroyers, so enabling her to pin-point the enemy. Later the damaged Italian limped into Cartagena where the submarine was interned by the Spanish authorities. In contravention of international law, Franco's government allowed the crew to return to Italy. I feel that, in fairness to the Spanish Government, it should be observed that although they afforded the enemy many illicit facilities, they were under extreme Axis pressure. I feel therefore that we should be grateful to them for managing to keep the German army out of Spain and so out of Gibraltar. The Rock was indeed a powerful fortress, but I do not think it could have long lasted under heavy German assault. The results of Gibraltar falling into enemy hands could have been disastrous.

On board the *Maidstone* news was bitter. It seemed unbelievable that, after all she had done, *Upholder* had now gone, lost with all her immortal company. She had been depth-charged to destruction off Tripoli whilst attacking a convoy. It is not possible to say categorically that *Upholder* was so lost, but it does seem to be the most likely reason. Also *Pandora* had been sunk by bombing at Malta and the gallant Tomkinson, in *Urge*, had failed to arrive at Alexandria whilst on passage from Malta. *Urge* was probably mined to the eastwards of the beleaguered island.

Malta had been awarded the George Cross but that did not prevent the 10th Submarine Flotilla's evacuation to the eastern Mediterranean. In this theatre Rommel was again on the move and the situation was deteriorating, with Tobruk in jeopardy. As we know, this famous bastion was to fall and the Germans to surge into Egypt until they threatened Cairo, Alexandria and the Suez Canal. Nevertheless efforts were made to run a coordinated convoy, from the west and from the east, to Malta. The eastern part, called 'Vigorous' ran into complete enemy air and sea superiority and, despite tremendous efforts on the part of Admiral Vian, was repulsed and forced to return to Alexandria, having lost a cruiser and three destroyers. Meanwhile, at Gibraltar, a veritable little flotilla of submarines had now assembled and these were used to provide cover for the western part of the convoy, known as 'Harpoon'.

Although relatively peaceful, Gibraltar had its troubles. Italian frogmen often attacked from bases in Spain, to the existence of which Spanish authorities turned a blind eye.

Submarines were being constantly brought to the alert during rest periods because it was feared French warships from northwest African ports might break into the Mediterranean and join the French Fleet at Toulon. As force 'H' was almost continuously engaged upon varying duties, the unpleasant task of attacking the French was assigned to submarines. Although my own French ancestry led me to believe that the ships of the Third Republic would not be allowed to fall into German hands—as had been promised—I could also well appreciate that the British could not afford to take any risks. I therefore subjugated my repugnance even to the point of exhorting others that it must be done. Fortunately the French made no move during my time at Gibraltar nor, in the end, did they allow their ships to fall into German hands.

Well in advance of the actual 'Harpoon' operation, four submarines sailed from Gibraltar to offer distant cover; but as our line, from Cagliari in Sardinia to the Sicilian coast, was 180 miles long, the chances of interception were remote. On the night of the 13th June Ben Bryant in *Safari* reported cruisers steaming southeast from Cagliari, a report confirmed by *Unison* (Lieutenant A.C. Halliday) which gave me the enemy's course and speed—always supposing they did not alter these.

Unbroken was placed to cover the convoy; but as I had not been informed of the convoy's intended movements, my appreciation of the situation proved difficult. When lighthouses on Marittimo Island and the Sicilian coast started to flash, I felt encouraged; but at two o'clock the following morning, my hopes were dashed by a Malta-based aircraft's report. The cruisers were over 100 miles to the northeast of us and steaming east, having made considerable alterations of course and speed. *Unison* had attacked them from a difficult long range position and this may have alerted the Italians to their danger. The following night, again off Marittimo, we saw nothing; but heard very heavy propeller noises, close inshore and well inside a known minefield—the enemy cruisers going south for the kill.

The sea, I remember, was glassy calm with hardly any wind and, on the forenoon of the 15th June, we heard explosions for a long time and saw palls of smoke over the southern horizon. Our convoy was under attack from the two cruisers we had heard, accompanied by five fleet destroyers and combined with heavy bombing from the air. The British destroyer escorts put up a spirited fight, but could not do a great deal against the aerial attack. From this, and later from mines, we lost a total of four merchant ships out of the six sent.

On the evening of the 15th, *Unbroken* sighted the foretops and mainmasts of the two cruisers returning from their victory.

Later, in skirting the minefield, *Unbroken* almost hit a floating mine which had just broken adrift from its mooring. So perhaps it would have been impossible to attack these cruisers in any event; but I was irritated by the lack of information, which had been withheld in the interests of security, and therefore commented in my patrol report—

'It is to be noted that in my attempt to appreciate the course of action of this enemy cruiser force, I was seriously handicapped by my complete lack of information regarding the positions and movements of our own convoy and naval forces. I submit such information should be supplied in future as it is disheartening to feel the enemy probably has more knowledge of this subject than oneself.'

The Admiral at Gibraltar agreed with these feelings.

An internal oil leak into one of the main batteries caused *Unbroken* to be put temporarily out of action, so we became impotent although distant observers of the drama being enacted in Egypt. Rommel was now so close to Alexandria that the base there had to be evacuated and plans implemented to destroy the port's facilities. The *Medway* sailed for Haifa under heavy escort; but *U.372* penetrated the screen, hit *Medway* with at least two torpedoes and sank her within twenty minutes. So vanished our proudest and largest submarine depot-ship. This, for the submarines, was a disaster of the first magnitude; but there were fortunately some mitigating circumstances. Firstly, the loss of life was small; and secondly, many of *Medway's* stock of torpedoes floated clear and were recovered. Additionally the forethought of Captain Philip Ruck-Keene (Captain S/M. 1) had provided for just such a disaster by sending a large number of reserve torpedoes overland to Haifa.

The bombing of Malta had become lighter because Hitler, thinking the island permanently neutralised, transferred many aircraft to Russia. It was therefore decided at high level to re-establish the Malta submarine base. Captain Voelcker gave *Unbroken* the honour of leading the 10th Flotilla's 'Second Eleven'.

On my last evening at Gibraltar I betook myself to the Rock Hotel where I was entertained by M. Benois, the manager. Whilst watching the sun set over the Atlantic, sipping a cool drink, I reflected somewhat unhappily that we had again lost nine submarines in the

Mediterranean—this time over a period of only five months. The last had been Dick Dymott's *Olympus* which had been sunk with most grievous loss in the Malta searched channel when bringing out survivors from *P.36* and *P.39*. Only twelve were saved from a total of ninety-eight.

Whilst sad for them, I could hardly be unaware of the fact that *Unbroken* would be next up that searched channel and that all the minesweepers at Malta had been bombed into oblivion. Added to this was the unpleasant truth that every operational submarine in which I had served was now at the bottom of the sea—to wit, in order of my own service, *Grampus, Swordfish, Regulus* and *Perseus*.

M. Benois, who did not know my thoughts although he may have guessed them, refilled my glass and I was glad of it.

Without being too exact one can say that the Italians and Germans had laid something like 30,000 mines in the Mediterranean by now, most of them in the Sicilian Channel or the approaches to Malta.

The trail earlier blazed by Dick Cayley in *Utmost* was something of an impertinence to the Italians; for it passed only three miles south of Cape Granitola in Sicily and much of the route lay within ten miles of that coast; consequently the water was rather shallow. Generally speaking the deeper the water the more difficult it is to mine; but the Italians were reputed to be adept at deep water mining and had certainly done so in the central part of the Sicilian Channel. The idea behind our inshore route was that enemy convoys tended to use it, and that therefore at least some parts must be mine-free. Of course mines can be laid at varying depths and are of several types; the most usual was the moored mine which might have electrical antennae. As the mines in this northern area of the channel would almost certainly be anti-submarine mines, one could make a night surface passage in comparative immunity, but this presented dangers from E-boats.

Unbroken's orders on this occasion were to proceed through the mined area submerged. We dived in darkness south of Marittimo for the sixty-mile run at four knots, fifteen hours. We went through at 120 feet in order, as far as possible, to get below the mines which we knew to be around us because of our mine-detector.

This was a useful instrument with which to pick up the edge of a minefield and thus skirt around it; but we had to go straight through. To minimise the chances of striking a mine it is essential to keep a straight course, therefore the mine-detector was of little use in these circumstances and I had it switched off.

The passage was made without incident and that night we

Italian 7,000-ton cruiser *Muzio Attendolo* photographed in an Italian port after one torpedo hit from *Unbroken*, Autumn 1942. The target's high speed at the moment of explosion is shown by the way in which the hull's outer skin has folded back.

Safari: left to right Lt. R. A. A. C. Ward; Commissioned Engineer M. Harris; Cmdr. B. Bryant; Lt. A. N. Devlin RNR; Sub-Lt. R. S. Blackburn (lost in *Affray* in 1951). Whilst in *Safari*, Commander Bryant was awarded the DSO and two bars, Mr Harris a bar to his DSC and the others DSCs.

surfaced to run down southeastwards towards Filfla Island, near the entrance of Malta's searched channel. The snag here was that the channel had not been swept for some time; and *Olympus* had been mined in it. However, *Unbroken* arrived safely and, on the dot of sunset as ordered, surfaced half a mile off the Grand Harbour and passed the recognition signal to Castile Tower.

Twenty-four hours later, we were followed by Tom Barlow in *United;* and the next day four minesweepers arrived from the eastern Mediterranean. In charge of these was Commander J. Jerome who told me a few days later that they had swept more than seventy mines from the searched channel. Of course, as mines are bound to be placed some distance apart, there is a greater chance of missing than hitting; until providence is tempted once too often.

On the evening of *Unbroken's* arrival, we were welcomed by Lieutenant-Commander Hubert Marsham, temporarily in charge of the submarine base at Lazaretto. The complex of harbours around Valletta were all strewn with wrecks, whilst in the dockyard itself were the grotesque forms of destroyers and other vessels blasted by bombing. With the exception of one small tug, *Unbroken* for twenty-four hours was the only vessel at Malta capable of movement.

Air raids continued but were now considerably lighter than previously; and electrically-operated smoke-screen canisters had been wired up around the various harbours and particularly in Lazaretto Creek.

Although fighters were continually being sent into Malta crated, or being flown off aircraft-carriers, their losses both in the air and on the ground were continuously so heavy that they could not be expected to cope with the enormous power brought against the island by the Luftwaffe, nor could they prevent the extensive mining from the air, and from E-boats at night, which blocked the channels and had certainly claimed both *Olympus* and *Urge.*

I had been forewarned of the situation in Malta by David Ingram (still in *Clyde*), Teddy Woodward who had limped into Gibralter with *Unbeaten* and particularly by Lieutenant-Commander Boris Karnicki, D.S.O., of the Polish submarine *Sokol* which had somehow managed to fetch Gibraltar after an unparalleled record of bomb damage which I will mention briefly.

During an aerial bombardment in mid-March, the already distinguished *Sokol* was severely damaged in harbour, having about four dozen battery cells (weighing ¼-ton each) smashed and other most serious damage. With the dockyard, and indeed the entire harbour area, completely paralysed by incessant blasting, *Sokol's* crew had to do most of the work, aided only by volunteers from the submarine base and the Army. She was shuffled around between the Grand Harbour and the various creeks in an almost hopeless endeavour to avoid the bombs. Then, after a fortnight of this agony, *Sokol* was at last ready for patrol; only to be savagely attacked and, this time, have one hundred cells broken. In this attack the Greek submarine *Glaukos* was sunk.

The following day *Pandora* and *P.36* were sunk, *Sokol* being near missed. Now the remaining submarines had to dive by day whilst in harbour; and the additional strains so imposed must have been intolerable. Later *Sokol* was camouflaged and put alongside the hulk of a merchant vessel in Bighi Creek; but the Germans detected the move and bombed her in this position. Then she was surrounded by barges and again camouflaged; but the Luftwaffe again found her and attacked, sinking many of the barges but failing to damage *Sokol* any further.

All these raids were extremely heavy, varying between 70-100 bombers; sometimes four raids in daylight. A few days later the gallant submarine was again damaged, this time by splinters which punctured hundreds of holes in her casing and conning-tower; but she was now being helped by the crew of the sunken *P.39* who, being experts, were of great assistance. The Army gave *Sokol* a new camouflage; but this was soon destroyed by fire. It seemed that the Luftwaffe had an uncanny knowledge of her movements and were determined to get her. Then she lay on the bottom by day, continuing with the work at night; but this did not prevent one of her periscopes being damaged. In rough weather, *Sokol* proceeded into the Grand Harbour to change the periscope: unfortunately she fouled the boom and smashed the starboard propeller on a rock. Two days later, after a month of savage treatment, *Sokol* sailed for Gibraltar with half a battery and only one propeller.

After an extensive refit in the United Kingdom, she was taken over by her first lieutenant, George Koziolkowski, who brought her back to the Mediterranean battle in 1943.

If I remember correctly Teddie Woodward, in *Unbeaten*, after some great successes including two U-boats sunk, had to leave a part of his battery at Malta for the benefit of others. This did not seem to worry him unduly; for when I met him at Gibraltar he was sill in high spirits and kept us all amused before sailing off for home where he arrived safely.

On 22nd July, Captain G.W.G. Simpson arrived back in Malta to take up his old headquarters, now commanding a flotilla comprised of the 'First Eleven's' survivors and the newcomers from the west. In a reasonably short time the following submarines were under command—

'First Eleven'
    P.31 (Uproar)   C.O. John Kershaw
    P.34 (Ultimatum)   C.O. Peter Harrison
    P.35 (Umbra)   C.O. Lynch Mayden
    Una   C.O. Desmond Martin
                          (later Pat Norman)

'Second Eleven'
    Unbroken   C.O. Alastair Mars
    United   C.O. Tom Barlow
                          (later John Roxburgh)
    Unison   C.O. A.C. Halliday
    Utmost   C.O. Pat Norman
    Unbending   C.O. Edward Stanley
    Unruffled   C.O. John Stevens
  Lent from 8th Flotilla
    Safari   C.O. Ben Bryant
    P.222 ('S' Class)   C.O. A.J. Mackenzie
                          (the 'Black' MacKenzie)

Joe Martin was now the spare commanding officer at Lazaretto and frequently relieved other captains in order that they might have a rest. For this reason there was some chop and change; but the names given above are those most closely associated with the submarines concerned.

So it can be seen that although the demise of the 10th flotilla had been rapid, it had made an overnight recovery and was stronger than before. Also reinforcements for both the 8th and 10th flotillas were coming into Gibraltar at regular intervals.

Sometime previously the large *Clyde* had had a complete battery removed to make more room for stores. These alterations precluded offensive patrols but, now under the command of Lieutenant R.S. Brookes who had relieved the perennial David Ingram, she ran no less than 200 tons of stores to Malta towards the end of August. Soon *Rorqual* was to reappear after her refit in the United Kingdom, still being commanded by Lieutenant-Commander L.W. Napier.

Turning eastwards, we find that the 1st Submarine Flotilla's activities have been hampered by the loss of *Medway* and the transference to a temporary base at Haifa. Now they were to move into the French submarine base at Beirut in Syria—that country having been taken over by the Allies in 1941. But despite reduced numbers and the great disadvantage of constantly shifting bases, the 1st Submarine Flotilla sank over 80,000 tons of enemy shipping between March and the end of August 1942. When one remembers that the tonnage sunk usually doubled that damaged, it is reasonable to assume that about another 40,000 tons were damaged. These sinkings must have caused the greatest concern to the Axis High Command; for the ships sunk were irreplaceable and those damaged might take a long time to repair, being far from the efficient Italian shipyards.

The leaders during the period were *Proteus,* first commanded by Philip Francis then by Robbie Alexander, which sank six enemy ships. A close runner-up was Hugh (the 'Red') Mackenzie in *Thrasher* with five ships; but hot at his heels was the newly arrived Tubby Linton (whom we have seen before in *Pandora*) with his brand new *Turbulent* who had already sunk four ships in a remarkably short time. The Malta submarines in this period had sunk only some 25,000 tons, with an equivalent half that amount damaged, which is indicative of their severe losses and the effects of the terrible pounding they had suffered.

The newly arrived commanding officers at Malta were anxious to get to sea, but were delayed because plans for operation 'Pedestal' had been made some time previously and were soon to bear fruit. Despite all efforts on the surface and below it to replenish the garrison, Malta was running painfully low of food, cooking oil, aviation spirit and ammunition. Without replenishment it was feared the island must surrender, if only from starvation, within a matter of weeks. Although good food was always supplied to submarines on patrol, the base rations were largely non-nutritious and completely inadequate. To the new arrivals signs of starvation were manifest.

Wingrave Tench, later awarded the O.B.E. for his work, had somehow managed to obtain a reasonable distribution of rations throughout the island; but this obviously could not be continued if supplies ran out.

In the air, fighters were essential provided they could obtain the necessary fuel; otherwise they would be flown in at great risk only to meet destruction on the airstrips. The crux had been reached! Malta without provisions, aviation spirit and other fuels—not to mention ammunition—now had no alternative but surrender, or relief. Obviously the plans for re-establishing the 10th Submarine Flotilla at the island base had been made in the knowledge that a great convoy was to be attempted, and all our hopes became pinned on its success.

The convoy would have the most powerful escort in history; so the submarines' part might be considered a small one: nevertheless a part we had. Eight submarines were available and the plan was to place six of them on a patrol line south of Pantelleria, with one off Cape St. Vito and one off Cape Milazzo on the north coast of Sicily. The object had been laid down as the convoy's protection from attack by the enemy cruiser force always based in the Tyrrhenian Sea, usually upon Messina, Cagliari and Naples.

Unbroken was to sail early for a foray up to Capri and then down the coast of Calabria, where a train was to be gunned, and so to her billet off Cape Milazzo. When 'Shrimp' Simpson told me that *Unbroken's* patrol position would be, by day, two miles off Cape Milazzo and, by night, four miles off, I remonstrated. This was a very obvious focal point, so obvious in fact that it seemed unlikely enemy cruisers would pass anywhere near it. (And in the event no enemy cruiser did so, up to the point where they were attacked by *Unbroken* in a position 25 miles distant.) Furthermore I considered these two patrol positions so close to the lighthouse that detection was not only possible but probable. Captain Simpson informed me that the positions had been ordered by the Admiralty and could not be altered. There was therefore nothing I could do about it, except to study every patrol report I could lay my hands on, in order fully to acquaint myself with the behaviour and habits of Italian cruisers in the Tyrrhenian Sea. With the resilience of youth I then put the problem behind me and set off on the foray for which I had been allowed, given suitable targets, four torpedoes and as much 3" ammunition as I could use.

Ben Bryant, sailing in *Safari* from Gibraltar, was to take the position off Cape St. Vito which is near Palermo; so I felt my flank was well covered.

Unbroken sailed in great style on 30th July, being swept out of harbour by the ocean-going minesweeper *Rye* and escorted by fighters, a welcome change from our method of arrival. Again passing south of Marittimo, we crossed the Tyrrhenian Sea and patrolled off the Bay of Naples for a week. In a misguided effort to conserve torpedoes, I attacked a 5,000 ton ship, firing a salvo of only two and missed. If nothing else, this taught me that I was no dead-eyed Dick and that four torpedoes should always be fired at a sizeable target. As *Unbroken's* full complement of torpedoes was eight, of which I had to reserve half for enemy cruisers, this left me with only two more. To my chagrin I missed another and smaller ship with this couple, thus letting the crew down.

We then moved southwards to Calabria and, passing very close to a completely unknown minefield which could only have been laid for the purpose of protecting the railway, we approached the coast at night in the vicinity of Paola where the electrified main line literally ran along the water's edge. Sighting, and hearing, a northbound train we were amazed to see a great headlight on the electric engine. At 10.45 p.m. we opened fire on a similarly illuminated southbound train from a range of only 900 yards. The first round hit the engine and the train broke up. Within two minutes it was all over, with the train ablaze, the overhead electric cables down and signal lights out.

Unbroken withdrew from the area and made for Cape Milazzo lighthouse, 18 miles west of the naval base at Messina, arriving there in the early hours of the 10th August. Despite the most elaborate precautions on our part, *Unbroken's* presence had been detected by breakfast time.

The British were at that time uncertain whether the Italians were using coastal radar sets; but if they had been, the vicinity of Cape Milazzo would have received high priority. During the night and after diving, we had been worried by a mushy tapping noise which seemed to come from directly below the lighthouse, and thought it might be some type of detector. Conversely, it might have been only water noises or a creaking of the earth's crust; for we were in the volcanic area between Etna and Stromboli.

A patrol tug now appeared from the direction of the lighthouse, came straight towards us, dropped a pattern of five charges from 400 yards away, then returned towards the lighthouse. *Unbroken* regained her patrol position, for I thought this could be the random depth-charging of which I had been told and that therefore some good targets might be on their way. Shortly after 11 o'clock, a Cretone-class minelayer came out from Messina with a Cant seaplane. We were then depth-charged, fortunately not too accurately, for two hours before a second craft joined our opponent. By 7.15 that evening, the enemy had dropped seventy depth-charges and it was not until 10.30 p.m. that I felt it safe to surface, the submarine now being 15 miles from Cape Milazzo.

I found myself in a difficult position and the problem I had so lightly put behind me before leaving Malta reasserted itself. Our patrol position, as I had greatly feared, had become hopelessly compromised. The difficulty was further accentuated by the fact that I had challenged my orders and that they had emphatically been confirmed. I had known of only two commanding officers choosing their own patrol positions, in defiance of orders. The first was reputed to have been mined (later it proved that although undoubtedly mined, this may not have been in contravention of orders): the other had been swiftly relieved of his command and sent to repent at leisure in far distant places. Nevertheless I reflected that the object of the patrol was to intercept enemy cruisers trying an attack on our convoy, and I knew that no enemy cruiser would go near Cape Milazzo for some time—and indeed none did. Yet, if the Italians wished to leave Messina westwards, or enter it from the west, they were likely to pass within 20 miles of *Unbroken.*

The study of previous patrol reports now came to my rescue. 'Tommo' in *Urge,* had sunk the Italian cruiser *Delle Bande Nere* within sight of Stromboli some five months previously; but this cruiser had been north-bound out of Messina. Also, in 1941, Dick Cayley had sunk a cruiser and Wilfred Woods had hit another, *Bolzano,* both within sight of Stromboli on a clear day.

A glance at the chart showed that there are seven sizeable islands in the Aeolian group, northwest of Messina, and that the deep channels between them constitute a maze in which surface ships could hide themselves from the prying periscope. A further point in favour of this area lay in the fact that Stromboli's active volcano made a magnificent natural lighthouse and, being permanently lit, gave nothing away. (The sudden illumination of man-made lighthouses indicated Italian forces approaching the coast.) With all these arguments in favour, I decided to risk abandoning the ordered position and find my own amongst the Aeolian Islands. After considerable thought, I selected a spot about halfway between Panarea and Salina, the focal point of a 3-way Clapham Junction—or so I hoped. The channel between Lipari and Salina also received close cover whilst that between Salina and the more distant Filicudi was accorded a measure of attention.

With Stromboli well in sight, 12½ miles to the northeast, *Unbroken* dived in the chosen position at morning twilight on Tuesday, 11th August, by which time I reckoned the convoy somewhere south of Ibiza in the Balearic Islands. By the next afternoon it would be southeast of Sardinia, under heavy air attack, and the battleship escort would be turning back with the aircraft-carriers. Therefore I estimated that if enemy cruisers were coming out of Messina, they might do so at any time.

I did not then know that the cruisers from Messina had gone north

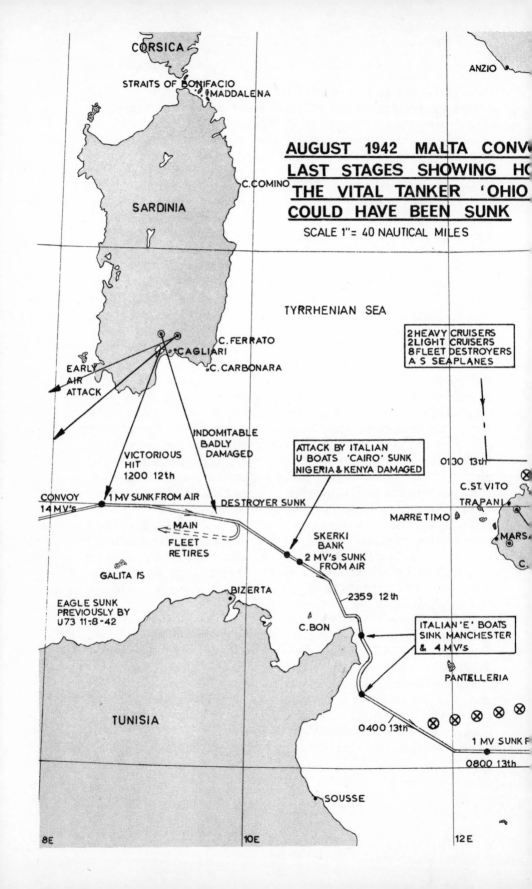

CORSICA

STRAITS OF BONIFACIO
•MADDALENA

C.COMINO

SARDINIA

ANZIO

AUGUST 1942 MALTA CONV
LAST STAGES SHOWING HO
THE VITAL TANKER 'OHIO
COULD HAVE BEEN SUNK

SCALE 1"= 40 NAUTICAL MILES

TYRRHENIAN SEA

C. FERRATO
•CAGLIARI

•C. CARBONARA

EARLY
AIR
ATTACK

INDOMITABLE
BADLY
DAMAGED

VICTORIOUS
HIT
1200 12th

2 HEAVY CRUISERS
2 LIGHT CRUISERS
8 FLEET DESTROYERS
A S SEAPLANES

0130 13th

ATTACK BY ITALIAN
U BOATS 'CAIRO' SUNK
NIGERIA & KENYA DAMAGED

C.ST. VITO

TRAPAN

MARRETIMO

CONVOY
14 MV's

1 MV SUNK FROM AIR

DESTROYER SUNK

MARS

MAIN
FLEET
RETIRES

GALITA IS

BIZERTA

EAGLE SUNK
PREVIOUSLY BY
U73 11·8·42

SKERKI
BANK
2 MV's SUNK
FROM AIR

2359 12th

C. BON

ITALIAN 'E' BOATS
SINK MANCHESTER
& 4 MV's

PANTELLERIA

TUNISIA

0400 13th

1 MV SUNK F

0800 13th

•SOUSSE

8E

10E

12E

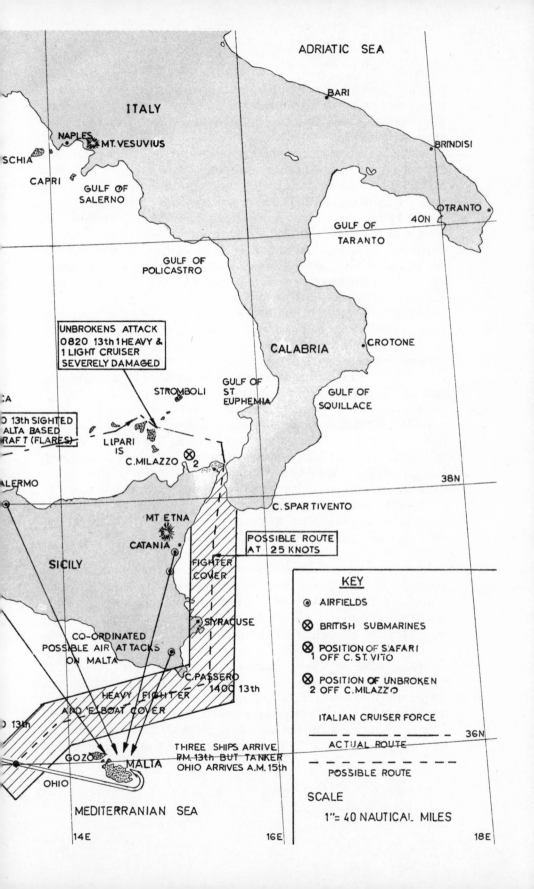

ADRIATIC SEA

ITALY

NAPLES
MT. VESUVIUS
SCHIA
CAPRI
GULF OF
SALERNO

BARI

BRINDISI

OTRANTO
40N

GULF OF
TARANTO

GULF OF
POLICASTRO

CALABRIA

CROTONE

UNBROKENS ATTACK
0820 13th 1 HEAVY &
1 LIGHT CRUISER
SEVERELY DAMAGED

GULF OF
ST
EUPHEMIA

GULF OF
SQUILLACE

STROMBOLI

O 13th SIGHTED
ALTA BASED
RAFT (FLARES)

LIPARI
IS
C. MILAZZO ⊗ 2

ALERMO

38N

C. SPARTIVENTO

MT ETNA

CATANIA

POSSIBLE ROUTE
AT 25 KNOTS

SICILY

FIGHTER
COVER

SIYRACUSE

CO-ORDINATED
POSSIBLE AIR ATTACKS
ON MALTA

C. PASSERO
1400 13th

KEY

⊚ AIRFIELDS

⊗ BRITISH SUBMARINES

⊗ POSITION OF SAFARI
1 OFF C. ST. VITO

⊗ POSITION OF UNBROKEN
2 OFF C. MILAZZO

ITALIAN CRUISER FORCE

HEAVY FIGHTER
AND E. BOAT COVER

O 13th

GOZO

MALTA

OHIO

THREE SHIPS ARRIVE
P.M. 13th BUT TANKER
OHIO ARRIVES A.M. 15th

ACTUAL ROUTE

36N

POSSIBLE ROUTE

SCALE

1" = 40 NAUTICAL MILES

MEDITERRANIAN SEA

14E

16E

18E

to join up with some from Naples. In so doing they passed at least twelve and probably fifteen miles to the east of *Unbroken's* ordered position off Cape Milazzo and could not even have been sighted, let alone attacked.

As the day passed in some anxiety, we did not know that the aircraft carrier *Eagle* had been sunk, after flying off relief aircraft to Malta, by *U.73* on the Tuesday afternoon. After that, although twice attacked from the air, the convoy arrived south of Sardinia at noon on the 12th and then came under heavy and effective air attack. In *Unbroken* we knew nothing of the convoy's progress except that we could plot its rate of advance, at 300 miles a day, and estimate that the passage of the Sicilian Channel would take place on the night of the 12th - 13th and that, on the evening of the 13th, those ships remaining afloat would arrive at Malta.

Unbroken spent the whole of the 12th at periscope depth in glassy calm, a restful day for the crew but not so for myself. In the early hours of the following morning, when on the surface under the red glow of Stromboli, we received an enemy report. A Malta-based aircraft had sighted an enemy cruiser force north of Palermo steering east at 20 knots, a course which would take them slap through *Unbroken's* ordered position near Cape Milazzo!

I felt that the flare dropped by the British aircraft would cause the Italian admiral to alter course, thus avoiding the obvious Milazzo focal point in which a British submarine had recently been detected. Navigationally, it would have been difficult for him to alter course towards the land and as such a move might also put him in jeopardy from other submarines patrolling off Cape Calava, for instance, I considered he must alter to port, a move which had the added advantage of concealment amongst the islands. It was as well for me that he did so!

In the event, *Unbroken's* chosen position proved so accurate that, about 8 a.m., we sighted the enemy cruisers (having first heard their propeller noises) on the expected bearing, coming straight for us in line ahead. As our attack developed, I found that the four cruisers were escorted by eight fleet destroyers and several Cant anti-submarine seaplanes.

Anticipating an enemy navigational alteration of course to starboard, I headed *Unbroken* in that direction at full speed, keeping deep enough to avoid detection from the air. On the other hand, if the enemy kept to his original course, *Unbroken* would still have time to whip round and fire from close range. Although the enemy's speed was estimated at 25 knots, the situation was a classic one, in which I had been well trained by Pat Steel, Bertie Pizey and those charming Wrens. At my next look I found that the enemy had indeed made a considerable alteration to starboard, putting *Unbroken* at the somewhat long range of 3,000 yards. Although considerably hampered by one of the destroyers on the screen, she passed out of the periscope's view (which she was blocking) just in time for the salvo to be fired correctly. Two cruisers were hit, both with one torpedo. The 10,000 ton 8"-gun cruiser *Bolzano* (fateful spot for her!) was severely damaged and did not again enter the war. The 6"-gun cruiser *Muzio Attendolo* of 7.000 tons had 60 feet of her bows shot off and, although attempts were made to repair her, she was soon to be bombed and sunk at Naples.

With no torpedoes left, *Unbroken* was now able to concentrate solely on her own escape; the 105 depth-charges, dropped over a period of eight hours, did no harm—except to the nerves! As so often proved to be the case, counter-attacks were less effective after a successful torpedo assault than after a failure. In the former case the escorts were busy protecting lame ducks, picking up survivors and generally more concerned with their own affairs than in killing the submarine. An additional advantage at this time of the year, previously mentioned, was the presence of density layers under which we were able to creep.

There was great elation at Malta on our return; for *Unbroken* had effected some small redress for our convoy losses which amounted to—9 merchantmen, *Eagle, Manchester, Cairo,* sunk and the cruisers *Kenya* and *Nigeria* torpedoed, both the latter by Italian submarines. Additionally the aircraft-carrier *Indomitable* was badly hit and four destroyers were sunk.

But on the afternoon of Thursday, 13th August, three merchantmen arrived in the Grand Harbour, later to be followed by one more. The convoy's most important ship, the fine new tanker *Ohio,* commanded by Captain D.W. Mason, was in deep trouble, having been so severely damaged that her decks were awash; and it was only by the tremendous efforts of her crew and helping escort vessels that she eventually arrived two days later, on the morning of the 15th August. So, by the arrival of some 30,000 tons of stores and about half that amount of oil, Malta was relieved . . . not only relieved but now enabled to provide the sinews for further attack upon the Axis powers.

Amidst a flow of congratulations, I was not asked to account for disobeying orders; but I think the strategical implications of *Unbroken's* action were overlooked. The six submarines off

Pantelleria had been hopelessly positioned; for the enemy cruiser force did not come south of Sicily. *Safari,* north of Cape St. Vito, was better placed, but too close inshore and did not in fact make contact. Nor would *Unbroken* have been able to attack the enemy, had she remained in her ordered position.

It is my contention that the enemy force of four cruisers and eight destroyers, if it had remained intact, could have proceeded south through the Strait of Messina, passed through the Malta Channel and sunk the tanker *Ohio.* Therefore I have added this hypothetical thesis to the map.*

Whilst it is true that there had been some disagreement between the Luftwaffe and the Italian Navy regarding air cover for the cruisers, that is not to say that such air forces would not have been available on the 13th and 14th August. The argument could also be put forward that the Italians did not intend to attack the damaged ships with this cruiser force. But, in war, the intention of the moment can instantly be reversed.

With only two effective cruisers, however, such a sally would have been a gamble; as the available British surface forces in the area, although inferior in strength, might well have won the day.

I think all are now agreed that without the aviation spirit and other oils carried in *Ohio,* Malta would have fallen. I have brought out this strategic implication merely to illustrate that orders are not always infallible; and that, in disregarding them, a junior commander must be not only right, but successful.

These events bring to an end our submarines' Mediterranean activities during the spring and summer of 1942, surely one of the most fateful periods Great Britain has ever faced.

* Map page 153

Chapter 10

'The Army Game' in the Mediterranean

SEPTEMBER 1942 - AUGUST 1943

The arrival of the August convoy had injected new life into Malta and this was plainly visible, even to myself who had only spent ten days there in the 'dead' time. Food supplies and kerosene became safely stored and carefully rationed by Wingrave Tench who had, after some difficulty, persuaded the Island's Government that money was a pre-requisite for fair rationing in Malta. What this meant, in effect, was that the food officials could buy out black marketeers, thus ensuring better distribution to the poor, who were in the majority.

Anti-aircraft guns now had a better supply of ammunition and the vital aviation spirit flowed to newly arrived fighters which had, for some time, included Spitfires. Although heavy air raids continued, there was a new spirit in the thousands of soldiers who had spent months filling in bomb-holes on runways, often under machine-gun and heavier attack. But the Messerschmitts now kept to higher altitudes, in protection of enemy bombers, and strafing became less frequent. Fortunately most of Malta's building materials are not inflammable; so whilst heavy bombs did enormous damage to the masonry, leaving rubble everywhere, serious fires were comparatively infrequent.

An enormous boost of morale to servicemen under these conditions is the timely and regular arrival and despatch of mail. In this we did have black periods; but by and large, the mail at Malta had been reasonable, and now improved markedly. For the submariners there were rest camps, ruggedly healthy; and we even played such games as hockey, sometimes during air raids.

As I have mentioned, the island's soft sandstone was easily excavated and thus made good shelter; on Manoel Island, the rule was to take shelter if a double-red '60-plus' raid developed. As a result, we became accustomed to smaller aerial attacks and to heavier ones some distance away. One could soon estimate where the heat was falling—at this time mainly on the airfields—and take cover, as from rain, when the cloud came your way. In this manner interference with work and play was minimised.

The staff at the Submarine Base had always been small, partly because the more important defects had to be made good in the dockyard and partly through sheer lack of accommodation. Our principal supporter was Commander (E) Sam McGregor who described himself as Garage Manager; such a good one that one could turn over a defective submarine to him as easily as one could garage a car for repair—with the difference that we could trust our garage manager. Lieutenant-Commander Giddings, as first lieutenant, looked after the domestic side of the base; kept an eye on Zara, the wardroom messman, and controlled the piggery—a vital concern which provided much of the meat ration. The beer had to be made from onions and most spirits were in short supply. But some local bars had ingeniously obtained large quantities of looted service rum which, when mixed with the local ambite, made for spontaneous gaiety, usually followed by severe hangovers.

Despite frantic efforts by Germans and Italians to improve their anti-submarine efficiency, the 10th Flotilla had a six months' respite from losses between May and October 1942. Nevertheless the enemy had made considerable advances and was to catch up with us later. But the First Flotilla was not so lucky, and it will be convenient here to deal with their activities during the latter half of 1942.

The drive and initiative of Captain Philip Ruck-Keene quickly resulted in a first class base at Beirut, one which disposed splendid recreational facilities and many venues of entertainment—not without evoking some envy from officers and men of the less fortunate 10th Flotilla. Although personally I was quite happy with Malta, finding friends to stay with, some sailing, tennis and the occasional game of hockey.

In the period some 33,000 tons of enemy shipping was sunk by submarines of the 1st Flotilla, with about half that amount damaged. There were ten ships sunk, including a tanker of 10,000 tons despatched by Lieutenant L.W.A. Bennington in the minelayer *Porpoise* off the North African coast. Bennington had previously had some very fine patrols and, on one occasion, had been seriously damaged by an Italian destroyer, eventually making Port Said under the escort of Hunt class destroyers called out by radio. As the newer battery cells were toughened to withstand shock, the cracking of cells became a good yardstick by which to measure damage. On this occasion, *Porpoise* had about half her electric cells smashed; only three submarines are known to have survived more. When *Sokol* broke 100 cells in harbour at Malta—just less than half the 224 carried—a 1,000-kilo bomb had exploded only five yards from her. This is perhaps illustrative of the pounding a submarine can take, provided always that her pressure hull is not actually holed.

It might be as well for me to mention at this point that the post-war analysis of British submarine attacks was conducted by reference to enemy records. Frequently and especially in the case of the Japanese, no record existed, so the true result became confused. This point must be brought up, because many submarines were not credited with the results they had actually achieved. For this reason, all figures mentioned in any part of the present work should be considered the absolute minimum as regards sinkings, whilst ships damaged and small ships sunk are often omitted altogether. Naturally some claims were made erroneously but I think always in good faith, for there was usually a perfectly adequate explanation. Later in the war, British submarines were supplied with torpedo firing pistols which worked on, roughly speaking, a magnetic principle and with these we suffered many premature explosions. I personally know from experience how galling such a mishap can be to all in the submarine, and they were not always easily recognisable as torpedo failures.

During the autumn of 1942, Malta frequently became used as an advance base for the 1st Flotilla's submarines and some of the successes mentioned were achieved by operations from Malta, notably two sinkings by Tubby Linton in *Turbulent* which have been included.

As the *Maidstone* remained at Gibraltar, the 'S' class submarines of the 8th Flotilla used in Malta throughout the autumn, until their new base at Algiers was established. In this way, the balance of achievement shifted visibly to the central Mediterranean where the 'U' class and 'S' class submarines sank at least 24 ships of some 80,000 tons in the last four months of 1942.

In addition, *Splendid* (Lieutenant I.L.M. McGeoch) sank the 1,600-ton Italian destroyer *Aviere,* north of Marittimo in December. In November Lieutenant Michael Lumby, commanding *Saracen,* scored three torpedo hits on the Italian U-boat *Granito,* north of Sicily and sent her to the bottom. Apart from a success by *Unbending,* the only other enemy warship sunk in this period was at the hands of Lieutenant-Commander George Colvin in *Tigris* who sank the Italian U-boat *Porfido,* off Bone early in December.

The German and Italian High Commands acknowledged that British submarines operating from Malta were mainly responsible for that diminution in Field-Marshal Rommel's essential supplies, to which they attribute his defeat at El Alamein and eventual evacuation from North Africa. Thus the enemy, having failed to subdue Malta, were now prepared to admit that it became the biggest thorn in their side, not only at the hands of our submarines but also from Fleet Air Arm and Royal Air Force strikes against Axis shipping. Too late did the Germans appreciate that aerial bombardment alone could not immunise Malta's dockyards and air maintenance workshops. For although the buildings were wrecked and civilian personnel temporarily demoralised, the dockyard's machinery had regained 80% efficiency by November.

Notwithstanding close cooperation in the past, the submarine staff office at Malta now became completely dominated by a great map showing our Army's position in North Africa. Commanding officers returning from patrol made a beeline for this map to see how the Eighth Army fared. It seemed to us that advance or retreat were both inexorably linked to our achievements or failures. In this, we may have tended to overlook the feats of others; but the tendency did no harm and certainly improved our determination.

Omitting many praiseworthy patrols, I must come now to an attack on a most important enemy convoy which took place on 19th October, or four days before the opening of the Battle of El Alamein. A convoy had assembled, probably at Palermo, and sailed westwards past Cape St. Vito on the afternoon of the 18th October.

Safari, Utmost, Unbending and *Unbroken* were ordered to positions* between Lampedusa and Pantelleria, whilst *United* received orders to come up from the south, on the convoy's probable path. The convoy was composed of four cargo vessels and a tanker, the former loaded with motor vehicles and tanks. 'Shrimp' Simpson signalled from Malta that its destruction could make 'all the difference' to the war in North Africa. This exhortation primed us for an all out attack; something which would be necessary since the convoy was escorted by eight crack destroyers which were reckoned the enemy's best anti-submarine team. (It is interesting to compare this heavy escort with the usual situation in the Atlantic where a large Allied convoy of perhaps thirty ships might, with a great deal of luck, have equivalent protection. But in the Mediterranean we usually faced two escorting destroyers *for each supply ship*!).

Ben Bryant, in *Safari,* sighted a mast, but this did not belong to

* See map opposite

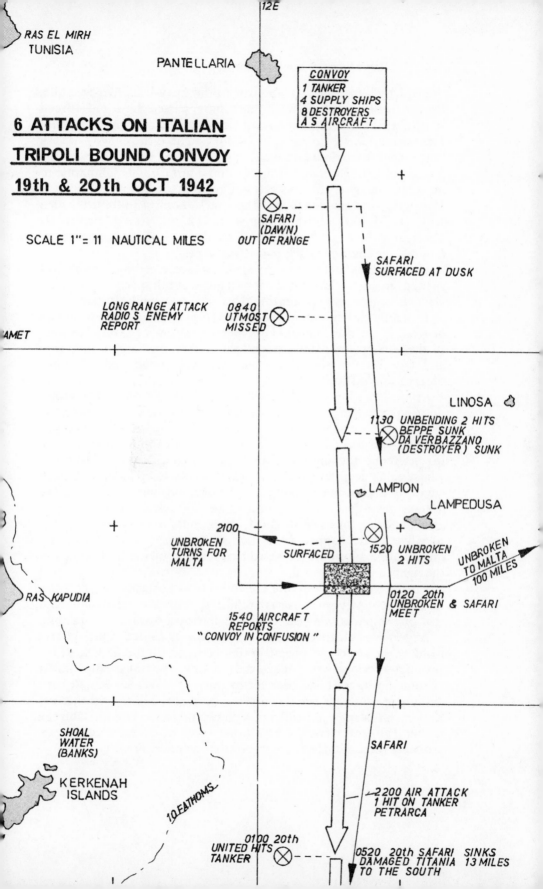

RAS EL MIRH
TUNISIA

PANTELLARIA

12E

CONVOY
1 TANKER
4 SUPPLY SHIPS
8 DESTROYERS
A S AIRCRAFT

6 ATTACKS ON ITALIAN
TRIPOLI BOUND CONVOY
19th & 20th OCT 1942

SCALE 1"= 11 NAUTICAL MILES

SAFARI
(DAWN)
OUT OF RANGE

SAFARI
SURFACED AT DUSK

LONG RANGE ATTACK
RADIOS ENEMY
REPORT

0840
UTMOST
MISSED

AMET

LINOSA

1130 UNBENDING 2 HITS
BEPPE SUNK
DA VERBAZZANO
(DESTROYER) SUNK

LAMPION

LAMPEDUSA

2100

UNBROKEN
TURNS FOR
MALTA

SURFACED

1520 UNBROKEN
2 HITS

UNBROKEN
TO MALTA
100 MILES

RAS KAPUDIA

0120 20th
UNBROKEN & SAFARI
MEET

1540 AIRCRAFT
REPORTS
"CONVOY IN CONFUSION"

SAFARI

SHOAL
WATER
(BANKS)

KERKENAH
ISLANDS

10 FATHOMS

2200 AIR ATTACK
1 HIT ON TANKER
PETRARCA

0100 20th
UNITED HITS
TANKER

0520 20th SAFARI SINKS
DAMAGED TITANIA 13 MILES
TO THE SOUTH

the convoy which was out of sight to the eastwards. After a while, Bryant realised the convoy must have passed him and turned southwards to give chase. About nine o'clock in the forenoon, Lieutenant J.W.D. Coombe, in *Utmost,* sighted the convoy at very long range. A salvo was fired but missed. Taking a suicidal risk in the face of escorting aircraft, John Coombe surfaced his submarine to make an enemy report. As a result Lieutenant Edward Stanley in *Unbending* was enabled to get in an attack at only 1,000 yards which sank the 4,500 ton ship *Beppe* and 2,000 ton destroyer *Da Verazzano.* Stanley then dived under the convoy, an action which reduced the counter-attack to ineffectiveness.

Five minutes after *Utmost's* signal was received in *Unbroken,* I sighted smoke to the westwards and ran in at full speed. The convoy was executing a very elaborate and broad zigzag; whilst its destroyers were madly dashing about, all over the place, and Cant seaplanes hovered in the sky, almost like spiders on the end of a strand of web. In the convoy were four vessels—the tanker, one large supply ship and two smaller ships; but the sea was rough and periscope observations difficult.

Unbroken soon found herself in an unenviable position with a destroyer charging down on her, a Cant seaplane overhead and the necessity to use a large amount of periscope. We fired a long-ranged salvo of four torpedoes, on the swing and with about five feet of the big periscope sticking up in the air, like a lamp-post. My last sight, whilst going deep, was that of a seaplane in a steep bank with a full view of the pilot in his cockpit, and a dropping marker-flare. As the nearest destroyer was now only some 300 yards (or 18 seconds) away, heading for us at 30 knots, there could not be much doubt as to what would happen next. But she over-ran us: there were no immediate explosions. We heard two torpedo hits at approximately the right time and interval.

During the next hour the convoy was not attacked again; but a R.A.F. reconnaissance aircraft reported it to be in confusion, and that one ship was being escorted by a destroyer towards Lampedusa.

At ten o'clock that night, Tom Barlow in *United* sighted flares from an air attack and went in to score a hit on the tanker, which although previously torpedoed did not sink. The Italian ship *Titania* of some 5,000 tons had been hit by one of the attacks: Ben Bryant, dashing southwards on the surface by night, fell in with her off Kerkennah Islands and sank her with two more torpedo hits. But the tanker *Petrarca,* about 3,500 tons, survived at least two hits— probably three—and later managed to stagger into Tripoli.

From all causes, the Italians estimate that, in August 1942, Rommel lost 25% of the supplies, ammunition, tanks and motor transport and 41% of the fuel sent to Africa. In September the lost tonnage dropped to 20% of the total sent; but in October it rose to a staggering 44%, of which the lion's share fell to submarines.* No army could stand this and Rommel, despite his great generalship, found himself unable to overcome such a crippling disadvantage.

The 10th Flotilla then, had had its successes before Trafalgar Day of 1942; whilst Lynch Maydon in *Umbra* was to destroy a large vessel in Khoms Roads on 23rd October—the very day that the battle of El Alamein commenced. This was, for those days, the enormous supply ship *Amsterdam* of no less than 8,670 tons which was festooned with motor transport and carried tanks in her holds.

Unfortunately, of the convoy comprising one tanker and four supply ships, the tanker and one other vessel made Tripoli. This was not satisfactory from our viewpoint and deserves a little more attention. The beginnings of this convoy were reported by reconnaissance aircraft operating from Malta and we therefore did not get that length of warning now usual from an intelligence source. It resulted that a very rapid and completely unexpected concentration of submarines had to be effected. *Utmost* and *Unbending*, both returning to Malta from successful patrols, were diverted without much difficulty and *Safari* was sailed to her position direct from Malta. *Unbroken* and *United*, off the coast of Africa, were ordered northwards to meet the convoy. The route which the convoy would have to follow was fairly obvious from the configuration of land, the positions of known minefields and our past experience of Italian movements.

It will have been noticed from my account of the action that we were receiving fairly regular air reconnaissance, although not without cost. In view of this it might have been better to concentrate the submarines more closely together, rather than placing them about twenty miles apart.

In these very confined waters, there could be no suggestion of using mobile patrol communications; firstly, because transmissions on asdic would certainly have been picked up by the highly efficient Italian destroyers. Secondly, the radio mast carrying H/F equipment had been removed to reduce topweight. Therefore, in order to make an enemy report, it was necessary to surface and use the main aerial, as *Utmost* did.

The most disappointing aspect of the operation was our failure to

*The Italian Navy in World War Two, by Commander M.A. Bragadin

sink the Italian tanker *Petrarca* after certainly two and probably three torpedo hits. (On the night of 19th October the convoy was successfully attacked by aircraft which probably resulted in the tanker being hit).

Whilst the submariners could usually sort out their claim differences with the Fleet Air Arm, this frequently proved impossible with the Royal Air Force. They tended markedly to overclaim, thus confusing the issue. Some reports suggested only a total of four ships in this convoy; but this is not so. After Edward Stanley had sunk the *Beppe,* I personally sighted the tanker and three other ships, making the total five on that part of the route between Marsala and Lampedusa.

As *Unbroken's* attack put the convoy in confusion, it seems reasonable to suppose that we did in fact score the two hits claimed—one on the tanker and one on a supply ship. This supply ship was seen being escorted back to Lampedusa. Now the convoy was reduced to the *Petrarca* and two ships of which one, *Titania,* was sunk by two torpedo hits from Ben Bryant. The ship sunk in Khoms Road by *Umbra* had nothing to do with this convoy; so it can be seen that two ships of the five got in. Annoyingly the tanker, despite heavy damage, was able to discharge her valuable cargo which was sent to the front.

As expected by all on board, *Unbroken* was severely hammered, certainly by two and probably by all three destroyers on the convoy's port side. Although the counter-attack lasted only a quarter of an hour, with perhaps two dozen depth-charges being dropped, the ensuing damage proved some of the worst in the whole war, 124 battery cells being smashed from a total of 224.

Unbroken was put completely out of action, developing a serious battery fire which could not be extinguished. After darkness we surfaced in calmer water and limped towards Malta, unable to dive; being met by Lieutenant John Peel, R.N.V.R. in *M.L.121* and a fighter escort on the following forenoon. About two o'clock that afternoon we arrived alongside the base with smoke billowing not only from the conning tower, but from the forehatch which had had to be opened. *Unbroken* was immediately docked and, when she settled on the chocks (thus imposing new strains), the rivetted seams amidships opened up and flooded No. 2 battery with salt water. It is therefore reasonable to suppose that had we bottomed after the counter-attack, or had the sea been very rough, the same might have happened.

Unbroken's escape was undoubtedly due to the enemy destroyers, which must have anticipated further attacks by our submarines, dashing off quickly to protect and cosset the remnants of their connvoy. Captain Simpson, in his covering letter to my patrol report, criticised *Unbroken's* avoiding actions; but as we were already pin-pointed, salvation probably lay in the choice of a depth at which the enemy's charges did not explode. One of these actually landed on the fore casing, only to roll off and explode beneath us.

Had it been possible to concentrate the submarines more closely, the convoy's destruction might have been completed. Attacks in rapid succession would have thrown the entire Italian force into complete confusion, whilst their destroyers would have had to cope with more than one British submarine at a time.

The damage to *Unbroken* took nearly a month to repair, therefore we were unable to join the large number of submarines which covered the Allied landings in North Africa, operation 'Torch'. Nevertheless, whilst nursing wounds, we were most gratified to hear that after almost a fortnight's hard fought battle, the Eighth Army had Rommel on the run.

About this time Lynch Maydon returned from patrol with a German Luftwaffe pilot whom he had fished out of the sea. As usual, I joined the welcoming party and watched the prisoner's face as he stepped ashore, for he was not blindfolded. In sight at the time, were about eighteen British submarines awaiting 'Torch'. This young German pilot, whose squadron had taken part in the 'annihilation' of Malta, could not believe his eyes—such was the measure of our rapid resurgence.

Malta had been lent submarines from the 1st Flotilla, including *Thrasher* commanded by the highly successful Hugh ('Red') Mackenzie and later *Turbulent* with the great Tubby Linton. Throughout 1942 the areas of submarine operational command between the 8th, 10th and 1st flotillas were varied to meet circumstance; but the tendency became that Malta, being at the pivot, controlled the majority.

For 'Torch', five submarines were placed around Toulon to watch the French Fleet and six others patrolled off the Algerian Coast. To look after the Italian cruisers, we had two submarines south and three north of Messina, five more on a patrol line stretching northwestwards from Marittimo and two off Cagliari. All twenty-three submarines sailed from Gibraltar or Malta early in November.

Bill Jewell in *Seraph* had previously landed a mission under the American General Mark Clarke on the coast, not far from Algiers, re-embarking them after their parley. Then *Seraph,* nominally under the command of Captain Wright, U.S.N. and flying American colours, embarked General Giraud, his son and some officers from a point near Hyères on the Cote d'Azur whilst *Sybil* (Lieutenant E.J.D. Turner) carried out another political operation; the object of all these being to soften opposition from the French in Algeria, and this proved successful.

The French Fleet at Toulon made no effort to interfere with the British and American invasion convoys. Nor, more surprisingly, did the Italian Fleet make any move; a lapse which probably arose through disagreement between Germans and Italians about the objectives, the former believing French Northwest Africa to be the Allies' target. But it was chiefly Algeria; here our submarines had a novel role in acting not only as beacons for the assault forces in the offshore approach, but also by landing small parties in folboats which successfully guided the invaders right into the beaches.

The landings took place during the early hours of the 8th November; and, on the following day Vichy France—presumably as a sop to the Germans for the inactivity of their fleet—granted our enemies the use of Tunisian ports; but this did not prevent the Germans invading the whole of unoccupied Southern France two days afterwards.

The race for the great ports of Bizerta and Tunis now began. The Germans, taking advantage of the fact that the Allies were slow to establish themselves in Algeria, rushed massive reinforcements to Tunisia by air; and so gained the advantage. Nevertheless our invasion of Algeria resulted in Malta becoming much closer to points of departure for the relief supplies which were still necessary. It provided us with a base at Algiers for the 8th Submarine Flotilla and eventually enabled the allies to catch the German North African armies between two fires.

The fast minelaying cruisers *Manxman* and *Welshman* continued to supply Malta, sometimes accompanied by destroyers. As previously mentioned, the submarine route through the Sicilian Channel minefields passed only three miles south of Cape Granitola. One night when westbound in this vicinity, I had met *Welshman* coming in the opposite direction at the best part of 40 knots. The night was calm and we heard her boiler fans from our bridge when she was yet some miles off. Later I mentioned to Captain Simpson that the continual use of this route by both submarines and the fast minelaying cruisers would eventually lead to compromise. An alternative route was discussed but not immediately implemented.

Unbroken, sailing on the 15th November for patrol off the north coast of Sicily, had a most uncomfortable time; being harrassed and bombed, although not depth-charged. Some 2,000 aircraft on the German air ferry run to Tunisia were sighted during this patrol and we were continually hunted by enemy A/S vessels, who were now lashing themselves into a fury of retaliation.

On the route between Palermo and Tunis, we kept an average of about five submarines for a whole month, resulting only in damage to four ships and the sinking of two. Lieutenant J.D.W. Coombe in *Utmost* reported a successful attack and that he was returning, having expended all torpedoes. *Utmost* was unfortunately rammed by the Italian torpedo boat *Groppo* and sank with all hands.

In the meanwhile, *Unbroken* had been so harried that I thought it advisable to report the matter. Withdrawing to seawards, I did so, even going so far as to suggest that naval ciphers might have been broken. Although ours were meant to be secure, I had recalled that we often deciphered enemy signals and it seemed logical to suppose that the enemy might do the same to us. (In this I may well have been correct; for our ciphers were compromised far more frequently than we thought at the time). My suggestions were not accepted and I was given a patrol position very close to the first one. But when it was realised *Utmost* had been lost and *Unbroken* was now due to return from patrol, we were ordered to take the route previously discussed with Captain Simpson.

This meant getting down into the middle of the Sicilian Channel, putting the Skerki bank astern, and heading for a point close to Pantelleria. Once there, we could use the enemy convoy route to the southward and come roundabout to Malta. The first part of our new route lay down the deep gully which runs southeastwards through the Sicilian Channel, and was known to be heavily mined. In previously talking the matter over with Captain Simpson, we had concluded that these minefields were probably rather old and that natural wastage would have thinned them out. The theory proved correct; for although *Unbroken* set off a mine in her wake, the passage was made without incident, and we were to be followed by many others.

Malta continued to be bombed, although the raids were becoming much lighter. Whilst our morale remained high in the face of these and of the ever increasing enemy anti-submarine activity, there were some personal problems of both officers and men which could bear examination.

Even with submarine pay added, the total emoluments of chief and, petty officers and men remained dismally low, a fact which came increasingly to the notice of commanding officers; particularly in many cases where families at home had been bombed out and were not only homeless, but in desperate financial trouble. It was of course quite impossible to pay the men for their services; nevertheless something should have been done much earlier in the war to alleviate this distress.

An increase in submarine pay would not have been out of place when one considers that the chances of survival of these men were even. This one in one chance compared most unfavourably with that of the navy in general, where the chances ran out at 10 to 1 against being killed. Also when it is considered that the men's families, as indeed the officers', were entitled to a death pension of approximately one-third pay; this to me seemed a savage and unnecessary insult.

Considering it to be my duty, I had a lengthy conversation with Captain Simpson on this subject; but he said that nothing could be done, giving all the usual official reasons. Although a great admirer of Captain Simpson in many ways, I told him that if I ever received a decoration I would do something about it. In reply he gave me a friendly warning that any such attempt would ruin my naval career and that I would be most unwise to try anything of the sort. Whilst I realised Captain Simpson's prediction was quite correct, I thought his attitude, and indeed the attitude of all above him to the top of government, was utterly wrong. And so it proved, when in the summer of 1945, the Service vote chucked the rump of that government out.

Although the British Government were now responsible for paying Dutch, Norwegian, French, Belgian, Polish and other armed forces, the British men were by far the lowest paid; in some cases the difference was staggering. Most of the submarine ratings in the Mediterranean had 'stood by' the final stages of their submarines' fitting-out in the building yard. They had therefore seen at first hand that even unskilled workmen were being paid five times as much as themselves; whilst the former lived at home with their families at comparatively little risk—and frequently struck for more money The pay of an able seaman torpedoman, including all submarine allowances, was then about 10/- a day. If he was killed, which was likely, his family would receive about one-third of that amount.

It so happened that my own upbringing and education had been far more widely based than that of the average naval officer: therefore I was able to see this situation more objectively than most, and it appalled me.

By this stage of the war, most commanding officers of the smaller submarines, indeed sometimes of the larger ones, were lieutenants. It had long been established in the Navy that a lieutenant would serve eight years, whereupon he became a lieutenant-commander ('Senior Lieutenant') and would have to wait a further four years before even entering the zone for promotion to commander. This rule was rigorously applied in war; although the Fleet Air Arm had managed to overcome it by arguing that Naval Air squadron-leaders must have parity with the Royal Air Force, which was now promoting some officers to Group Captain at my own age of 28, as they had promoted the famous Wing-Commander Pickard who I later met.

In talking over this situation with my contemporaries at Malta, we foresaw that we could remain commanding officers of submarines, bearing responsibilities out of all proportion to either age or rank, for the duration of the war, without even entering the promotion zone.

Before my time at Malta, Lieutenant-Commander Tompkinson had brought this issue to the fore by requesting the award of seniority, in lieu of a decoration for which he was being recommended. He got his seniority; although the request was looked upon askance, and a warning issued that the grant in his case was not to be taken as a precedent.

In the meantime R.N.R. and R.N.V.R. officers were being given acting rank, thus being promoted above our heads. In this way, the permanent R.N. officers commanding submarines—whose parents had paid heavily for their education and naval training—were being rapidly relegated to the position of 'they also served'.

It would be pretentious to maintain that captains, officers and men were not anxious to receive the decorations for which they had been recommended. Naturally they wanted them; for these were the outward signs of success in the arduous combat for which they had been trained—and they wanted them before being killed! (Most of these honours could not be awarded posthumously). At home, recommendations went through in a few weeks; in the Mediterranean, it took months. There were of course administrative reasons; but it was not nice to think that those in the forefront of the battle were at the rear of the honours queue. After discussing all this with Lynch Maydon and others, I decided that, if the opportunity arose, I also would request seniority. From the viewpoint of the satisfactory performance of duty, it mattered little whether a submarine commanding officer was a lieutenant, lieutenant-commander, commander or post captain; but pay was now becoming a matter of urgency to officers, the higher the rank the more one received.

Traditionally naval officers were not expected to ask favours; but it was reasonable to hope that, in these particular circumstances, they might be accorded. There was naturally some jealousy amongst the more pedantic of officers and men who had not joined the Fleet Air Arm or submarines, but that had been a matter of their own choice.

I have mentioned this subject because the tendency in official records, particularly those of the Admiralty, is to gloss over any distress caused by default of the establishment; but if we are to learn from the past, such faults must be exposed, lest they be repeated unwittingly. Also the fact that such personal affairs were discussed by both officers and men shows that we had our private and human anxieties and were not of that navy once so wittily described by Mr. Winston Churchill as 'rum, buggery and the lash.'

I do not think that these matters particularly affected our morale; for the pressures at sea tended to make us all seek as much relaxation as possible in harbour and to subjugate our worries.

For several reasons, the use of the gun by submarines based at Malta had been limited. Firstly, the earlier 'U' class to arrive there had only a 12-pounder, *Unbroken* being the first to be armed with a 3"- gun. Secondly, a gun action on a small target would compromise the submarine's position in a given area, which enemy convoys could then avoid. Lastly, the enemy's complete domination of the air made such attacks dangerous. Whilst Italian bombing efforts on Malta were not particularly accurate, their anti-submarine Cant seaplanes and other aircraft proved both efficient and omnipresent. On patrol, hardly a day passed without sighting many Cants. These aircraft would report the submarine's position thus bringing up A/S craft. When escorting convoys the Cants would try to mark the submarine for the destroyers to pounce upon, as one had done to *Unbroken.* These air patrols interfered considerably with our activities by putting the submarine deep and preventing use of the periscope. Good targets were missed thereby; for asdic listening watch could be unreliable in detecting the slow propeller beats of smaller cargo vessels, and water conditions of varying density aggravated this disadvantage. Naturally one stayed deep for as short a time as possible. But it would have been bad practice to gun a small schooner and then suffer consequences which would result in the loss of a fine target.

The first of the new and improved 'S' class submarines,*Safari* (P.211), had been nursed through the later stages of her building by

Ben Bryant, a gunnery enthusiast. These submarines were larger than their predecessors, carried an extra torpedo tube in the tail, making the total seven tubes and thirteen torpedoes—and a fine 4" gun. They could make 15 knots on the surface. This gave them a great advantage over the 'U' class, a point illustrated in the convoy attack where Ben Bryant, having failed to sight on the first day, was able to catch up and sink a ship before the following dawn. Those extra four knots gave a double chance of attack; and this is analogous to having two submarines, in lieu of one. *Unbroken's* success against the electric train in Calabria had redrawn attention to the possibilities of gun action and Ben Bryant waxed enthusiastic, demanding all details.

After covering operation 'Torch', *Safari* was sent to the Tunisian coast where she immediately sank the Italian brigantine *Bice* by gunfire. A few days later, further east, she destroyed five or six small vessels in roadsteads by gun and torpedo. Then, off Naples in January, *Safari* sank two schooners and a 1,200 ton vessel with her gun and another of 6,000 tons by torpedoes. So after his long campaigns in Home Waters, a revived Ben Bryant began to sweep the Mediterranean as van Tromp had once swept the English Channel.*

I have, I hope, shown how close was the submarine liaison with the Army, firstly before the battle of El Alamein, secondly during it and now in the 'Torch' period. This close liaison continued, our main duties now being two-fold. The first was the obvious one of destroying enemy vessels frantically taking supplies to Bizerta and Tunis for the massive German build-up there. The second was less obvious and arose because there then existed no railway and only inadequate roads between Sousse and the Benghazi-El Agheila area in Cyrenaica, Rommel's main supply base. Consequently the enemy made use of every conceivable ship, coast crawling in the shallow waters along this 500-mile stretch of beaches, and using even the smallest of roadsteads in which to disembark supplies for further conveyance by lorries. And, as Rommel's precipitate retreat began, coasters and larger vessels reversed their direction, now carrying equipment and troops to the strongholds behind the Mareth Line.

The 8th Flotilla was established at Algiers under the command of Captain 'Barney' Fawkes who had, in July 1942, relieved Captain Voelcker in the *Maidstone*. But the operational command of 8th, 10th and 1st flotilla submarines continued to be highly coordinated, under control of the Commander-in-Chief Mediterranean.

When the time came for the Germans to evacuate Tripoli, their ships kept so close inshore that submarine attack with torpedoes was

*Commander B. Bryant DSC was awarded the DSO and two Bars in *Safari*.

difficult; but our aircraft from Malta, now even sometimes escorted by fighters, were causing heavy casualties. By mid-January, the scuttle from Tripoli had reached the point where the Germans were grossly overloading all ships and craft with retreating soldiers, in the hope that they would fight again behind the Mareth Line—as indeed they did, causing great casualties in our armies.

There is a spot, off Djerba Island, where the 10-fathom line (60 feet) runs within three miles of the beach. Here *Unbroken* torpedoed the 6,000 ton ship *Edda* which was creeping along on her own, escorted by two torpedo boats. The *Edda*, grossly overladen with men of the Afrika Corps (by some estimates 5,000) sank like a stone. The counter-attack was brief and only a token; for the escorting vessels were busy picking up survivors. Also one of our torpedoes had a gyro failure and circled. This mishap deterred the Italians and frightened us.

During the period of German build-up in Tunisia, supply ships were considered so important that our submarines frequently had orders to sink only those that were southbound and not to attack any enemy warships.

Submariners were therefore not only surprised but distressed by a chain of events I will now relate briefly. Immediately after the successful attack by Prince Borghese on the British battleships *Queen Elizabeth* and *Valiant* at Alexandria, Mr. Winston Churchill demanded that we should conduct similar operations. As a result, 2-man torpedoes with detachable warheads, known as chariots, were developed; the 'T' class submarines *P.311, Trooper* and *Thunderbolt* being converted to carry and launch them. A plan to attack Italian battleships in Taranto harbour (although these were at Naples) was evolved and reconnaissance demanded. Taranto was known to be very heavily mined and its closer approaches barred to British submarines. Therefore we had little recent information about that area. Such became the pressure that the *Traveller* was chosen for this reconnaissance; a most unhappy choice, since a large submarine is much more easily detected and mine-prone than a small submarine. Furthermore her captain, Michael St. John, had just been placed on the sick list with dysentery. Nevertheless *Traveller* was sailed for the Taranto reconnaissance under the captaincy of the experienced Lieutenant-Commander D. St. Clair Ford, properly the commanding officer of *Parthian* which had recently been refitted in the U.S.A.

Traveller did not return from this patrol, having almost certainly been mined.

Lieutenant-Commander Dick Cayley, D.S.O. in *P.311* was now

ordered to attack, with chariots, enemy cruisers in Madellena harbour which was also known to be heavily mined. *P.311* did not return.

A very gallant and successful attack was made at Palermo by charioteers from *Trooper* and *Thunderbolt,* causing the sinking of the small cruiser *Ulpio Traiano* of some 3,500 tons and damage to the 8,500 ton liner *Viminale,* this last later being torpedoed by *Unbending* when under tow to Messina; but survived until July when whe was sunk by our air and surface forces.

Thunderbolt made her second attack on Tripoli harbour with the intention of destroying blockships before they could be sunk in their designated positions. This attack proved partly successful, one of the blockships being sunk.

Lieutenant R.T.G. Greenland, R.N.V.R., and Lieutenant R.G. Dove, R.N.V.R., were awarded D.S.O.'s for the Palermo attack, Leading Signalman A. Ferrier and Leading Seaman J. Freel both received the Conspicuous Gallantry Medal. There can be no doubt of the bravery and skill with which these operations were conducted; but there is considerable doubt as to their desirability. Two 'T' class submarines were lost and two more diverted from their main function which, at this time, was to sink enemy supply ships southbound. Also two 'U' class submarines had been diverted from more important duties, in order to bring out the chariot crews, after completion of their missions.

This is a criticism of the higher direction of naval warfare in London, whose object could only have been the propaganda value of spectacular success. People at home would not have known that, with the exception of the Tripoli attack, the targets had become of secondary importance.

A matter which may have puzzled the reader is the question of numbers or names for our submarines. During the First World War, all submarines carried numbers and old-fashioned submariners preferred them: numbers survived in the 'L' and 'H' classes. But as the vessels became bigger, they were given names and this practice continued for most submarines laid down in peacetime. In the Second World War, submarines under construction were given numbers as a matter of convenience. When, in the autumn of 1942, we started making things boil in the Mediterranean, Mr. Winston Churchill decided that all submarines should have names; and I think most of us were glad of it. Therefore names quickly replaced the original numbers although some, such as *P.311, P.222,* and *P.48,* did not survive long enough to adopt them. This last, under the command of Lieutenant M.E. Faber, was lost on her third Mediterranean patrol during operation 'Torch', being sunk on Christmas Day by the Italian torpedo boat *Audace,* near the island of Zembra. In mid-December, Lieutenant-Commander A.J. (the 'Black') Mackenzie took *P.222* on her fifth patrol, this time to the Naples area. The Italian torpedo boat *Fortunale* depth-charged a British submarine off Capri at that time; this is thought to have been *P.222,* which did not return.

The loss of *Utmost,* off Marittimo towards the end of November 1942, was to herald the grimmest sinking rate of all. In a period of five months, we lost no less than eleven submarines in the Mediterranean, reflecting a savage assault by both Axis partners. Of these, seven were sunk by depth-charge attack: the remaining four are presumed to have been mined. There was now no 'early stage amorphism': captains and crews were war-experienced and highly trained; these losses were hard to bear, reflecting, as they did, our enemies' exceptional proficiency in anti-submarine tactics.

It had long been held amongst submariners in the Mediterranean that one got sunk in the first few or the last patrols, and this was frequently so. In the beginning they were not, as it were, properly played in: at the end, they were played out. Very few lasted longer then twelve months and that period became the unofficially accepted duration of an operational tour in this area. We therefore set our sights on twelve months of survival and success; feeling that, by the thirteenth month, we should have a single ticket to Gibraltar.

Lynch Maydon, after a splendid career of destruction, was due to sail for home in mid-January. He did so after a stirring last patrol in the Gulf of Hammamet. This caused me to think about *Unbroken's* return which I reckoned should be due in April. Therefore, I was somewhat dismayed when 'Shrimp' Simpson told me that operational tours had been extended by three months.

Of the 10th Flotilla's commanding officers following me into the Mediterranean, Tom Barlow had been relieved by John Roxburgh; Harry Winter by Edward Stanley and John Halliday by Antony Daniell: whilst John Coombe (*Utmost*) and Michael Faber (*P.48*) had been killed. The remainder had entered at least four months later—excepting Ben Bryant who properly belonged to the 8th Flotilla. So I pointed out to 'Shrimp' that *Unbroken's* crew had been very roughly handled, that they expected to serve a year in the Mediterranean and that any prolongation would have a very bad effect. We both knew that other submarines had been lost during such extensions, including Wanklyn in *Upholder;* but, in these earlier cases, necessity had been the overriding factor. Now, with the Eighth Army on the outskirts of Tripoli and the tide of victory starting to flow, I did not consider such a prolongation of the agony justified: and I said so. 'Shrimp' suggested that I allow a spare C.O. to do a patrol in *Unbroken* and take a rest for myself. This I considered unfair on the crew and I made it unequivocally clear that *Unbroken* did not go to sea without me until I was properly and permanently relieved. 'Shrimp' said he could do nothing about the extension which had been 'ordained'. Eventually I told him I was good for four more patrols and would like to make early arrangements for a new commanding officer after that, come what might. It was agreed, therefore, that the efficient and amiable Lieutenant B.J.B. Andrew should come to sea 'additional' in *Unbroken* for one patrol to aquaint himself with the submarine and her crew. Later, in April, Andrew would relieve me. This arrangement worked excellently, but I was lucky that a spare commanding officer of this calibre was available. Anyhow, my thoughts were that somebody in London was flogging the willing horse to death.

About the time that Tripoli fell, Captain Simpson was relieved by Captain G.C. Phillips, D.S.O., of North Sea renown in *Ursula*. This happily coincided with an announcement that British submarines in the Mediterranean had sunk a million tons of Axis shipping and that those operating from Malta were responsible for half of it. Although in the light of later information, this claim was somewhat exaggerated, if severely damaged shipping is included, the figure comes out about right.

Captain Simpson had proved himself a brilliant tactical strategist whose leadership inspired all, as evidenced by the destruction of some half-million tons of enemy supply shipping mainly by a handful of small and very slow submarines under the most adverse conditions of war. His award of the C.B.E. seems an inadequate recognition of this great service.

As targets decreased along the North African coast and our aircraft were now ploughing into all enemy shipping in Tunisian waters, the centre of submarine operations shifted to the Tyrrhenian Sea, which had been placed under the operational control of Captain 'Barney' Fawkes at Algiers. 'T' boats from the eastern Mediterranean were sent ot reinforce the 8th Flotilla and the 'U' class, operating form Malta into the Tyrrhenian Sea, fell under Captain Fawkes' sea command. No complications arose through these changes, for procedures were standardised and cooperation complete.

The 10th Flotilla's youngest commanding officer, John Roxburgh in *United,* sank the Italian destroyer *Bombardiere* of 1,700 tons in mid-January north of Marittimo. Roxburgh's target was in fact an escorted merchant ship, but the destroyer crossed the line of fire and met an unexpected end. Several Italian destroyers were sunk in this manner—an occupational hazard of some magnitude when on escort duty in the face of British submarines! On a later patrol in June, off Cape Spartivento, Roxburgh scored two hits on a German liner of 5,000 tons which broke up and sank immediately. He then proceeded to score three hits out of four on the Italian liner *Obia* of 3,500 tons, sinking her too. Later again, whilst on a patrol line across the entrance to the Gulf of Taranto during the invasion of Sicily, John gained two hits out of four on the large Italian cargo-carrying submarine *Remo* which sank rapidly. Enemy officers and men on her bridge were rescued, including the captain. In September 1943, *United* returned to the United Kingdom after sixteen months in the Mediterranean under her two captains, Tom Barlow and John Roxburgh, the latter having sunk a destroyer, a U-boat and much valuable shipping with great economy of torpedoes. He later gave me a much needed refresher course on the attack teacher at Rothsay before joining his next submarine for operations in Home Waters and the Far East.

My own last patrol in *Unbroken* took me to the Gulf of Squillace, a bight out of the ball of Italy's toe. Here we torpedoed a large tanker of 9,000 tons which suffered an internal explosion and had to beach herself—and remained out of the war.

By this time the German forces in North Africa had surrendered and preparations were going forward for the invasion of Sicily. The 8th Flotilla now had five 'T' class and seven 'S' class submarines, assisted by the Dutch *Dolfijn* which was British 'U' class. In the 10th Flotilla were eight 'U' class, shortly to be reinforced by *Ultor, Uproar, Unruly, Sokol* and *Dzik,* the last two being Polish manned 'U' class submarines. *Rorqual* was based on Algiers and *Regent* had arrived at Malta after her retit in the U.S.A. *Parthian* was the only British submarine at Beirut, aided by the Greek *Papanicolis. Osiris,* three Greek and one Yugoslav submarine, *Nebojsca,* were refitting.

Our further losses in March proved quite shattering; for *Tigris* (George Colvin) is thought to have been mined near the island of Zembra, according to a report from an Italian aircraft which saw an explosion. *Thunderbolt* (ex *Thetis*), which had been under the command of Lieutenant-Commander Crouch throughout the war, was almost certainly sunk by an Italian corvette *Cicogna* with depth-charges off Cape St. Vito. These submarines had most

Commander J. W. Linton VC DSO DSC.

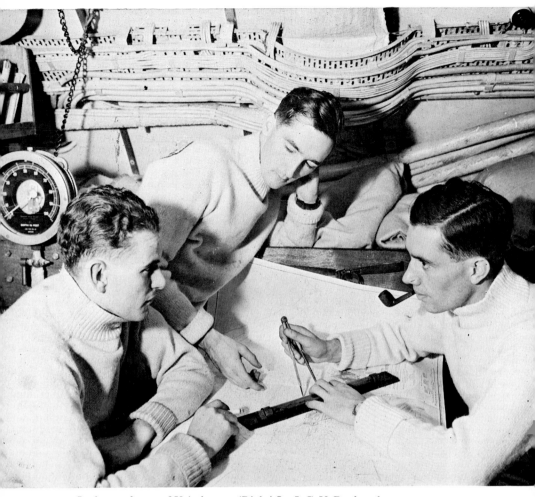

In the wardroom of *United*, 1943. (Right) Lt. J. C. Y. Roxburgh DSO DSC; (centre) Lt. J. M. C. Fenton DSC; (left) Sub-Lt. P. G. Evatt RANVR.

experienced commanding officers and their loss was keenly felt, personal friendships apart.

But worst of all was the sinking of Tubby Linton's *Turbulent* by depth-charges from A/S craft off the coast of Corsica; although he was originally thought to have been mined in the approaches to Madallena. Tubby Linton who was credited with 90,000 tons of enemy shipping sunk, in both *Pandora* and *Turbulent,* in addition to the large destroyer *Pessagno,* was much beloved by all submariners and particularly by the less experienced and younger commanding officers to whom he would give fatherly advice; but only if asked. He was posthumously awarded the Victoria Cross for his great services during 1942. Tragically, this was to have been his last patrol before *Turbulent* returned to England for refit, As in the case of Wanklyn, submariners found the news difficult to believe; but when it was established beyond all doubt, even those who had never known him were greatly saddened. In April the well-refitted *Regent,* captained by Willy Knox, was presumed mined off Monopoli in the Adriatic. In the same month, we were to lose two 'S' boats of the 8th Flotilla.

The ex-Greek destroyer *Hermes,* now manned by Germans, had the reputation of being a crack anti-submarine vessel. Lieutenant I.L.M. McGeoch. in *Splendid,* encountered this German warship close off Capri and, unfortunately, mistook her for an ex-Yugoslav destroyer in Italian hands. *Hermes* sighted *Splendid's* periscope and immediately made asdic contact. After about an hour's accurate and well-planned depth-charging, the submarine was forced to the surface, coming under gunfire. She manned her gun; but the German fire proved murderous. A little later, *Splendid* abandoned ship, amidst a hail of shells and heavy automatic bullets. Her captain, first lieutenant and twenty others were rescued. Ian McGeoch, who had a badly injured eye, made a determined and fantastic escape through Switzerland and France via Spain to England where he arrived in the middle of 1944.

Three days later Lieutenant J.H. Bromage in *Sabib,* destroyed a tug off Cape Vaticano in Calabria and then moved across towards Cape Milazzo where he sank a well escorted 1,500 ton vessel; but almost broke surface after firing his salvo. The Italian corvette *Gabbiano* delivered a severe and accurate depth-charge attack which forced *Sabib* to the surface. Realising his submarine was uncontrollable, Bromage ordered her to be scuttled and ship was abandoned. German aircraft gunned survivors in the water, killing one of them. All the others were rescued.

During the invasion of Sicily (operation 'Husky') which took place at midnight on the 9/10th July, five British submarines were stretched on a patrol line across the entrance to the Gulf of Taranto, in case Italian battleships came out; but they did not. Three more were placed north of the Strait of Messina and seven submarines patrolled off the landing beaches to act as navigational beacons, both for the incoming convoys and the actual landing craft.

Previously much beach reconnaissance had been done by Combined Operations Pilotage Parties (C.O.P.P.) along the shore, these being conveyed there by submarine. This activity included search for underwater obstacles, mines and the general clearance of the beaches' seaward approaches for use by assault craft. These preliminary operations were rapidly becoming more advanced, until they eventually reached their peak of expertise in the invasion of Normandy.

Other submarines continued normal aggressive patrols in the Gulf of Genoa and along the French coast, for the Germans were taking over more and more French merchant ships.

Our chapter of losses is not yet complete for, in August, *Parthian* was sunk, presumed mined in the southern Adriatic. Under Michael St. John (sent to her after the loss of *Traveller*) she had achieved her successes; but he had now been relieved by Lieutenant C.A. Pardoe, R.N.R. Leaving Malta in mid-July, *Parthian* was ordered to make a brief patrol in the southern Adriatic on her way to Beirut, but failed to arrive. Thus was lost this fine old submarine from the China flotilla which had so distinguished herself in the early days of the Mediterranean war, under Lieutenant-Commander 'Bim' Rimmington.

There were now more British submarines operating in the Mediterranean than at any time previously, and we enjoyed the cooperation of many French submarines which had joined us, notably the *Casabianca* which, under the command of the well known Capitaine de Corvette de l'Herminier, was to carry out so many successful special operations; particularly in the liberation of Corsica.

It is now time to leave the Mediterranean theatre which we have seen through many vicissitudes in three years of war. The pressure of our submarine operations was to continue for a long time yet, mainly in the Aegean; but the *effect* no longer had the impact of those vital days between the summers of 1941 and 1943.

With the tide of victory running strongly in our favour it is easy now, and much safer, to fly back to London and see how things are shaping at home.

Chapter 11

Operations in Home Waters

MARCH 1942 - AUGUST 1943

There used to be a ditty amongst submarine crews in the earlier days of the war entitled 'Twelve Little "S" Boats'. We started the war with a round dozen of these submarines and the reader will remember that those in the Mediterranean were swiftly recalled for operations in the North Sea. The ditty portrays their misfortunes. These were serious: with the loss of *Swordfish* in the Bay of Biscay in November 1940, only three 'S' boats remained—Ben Bryant's *Sealion* with *Seawolf* and *Sturgeon*; for George Colvin's *Sunfish* had been very badly damaged by bombing and, after extensive repairs, was handed to the Russians in 1944, together with *Unbroken*, *Unison* and *Ursula*. *Sunfish* sank whilst on passage to North Russia, presumably by submarine accident.

These severe losses of our small submarines in Home Waters could not be made good, because all new construction was so urgently required in the Mediterranean. Therefore in this period, the long western coastline of Europe did not receive as much attention as we would have wished. This coast stretched from Portugal to North Cape; but we were greatly concerned with the prevention of blockade-running into French Biscay ports, our patrols sometimes being reinforced by submarines going to, or returning from, Gibraltar.

In the whole seventeen months under review, we sank only five ships totalling about 20,000 tons and damaged two more. One of the latter beached herself after being torpedoed by the French submarine *Junon*, off the west coast of Norway in October 1942. On the following day Capitaine de Fregate Querville sank a 5,000 ton vessel in the same area. As the Norwegian submarine *Uredd* commanded by my friend Lieutenant R.O. Røren, Royal Norwegian Navy, had sunk the German ship *Libau* 3,700 tons in the same area and only three days previously, one could almost say that October

1942 was the highlight of the whole period. *Rubis* of course continued to lay her mines and claim victims.

During August of 1942 the Admiralty requested United States submarines for the western Mediterranean, but the Americans rightly declined on account of the size of their craft—1,800 tons, about equivalent to the British 'O', 'P' and 'R' classes. The Americans did however send over Subron 50, consisting of five Gato class submarines, armed with ten 21" torpedo tubes, two 5" guns and anti-aircraft weapons. These covered the Atlantic side of 'Torch' convoys and later carried out operations in the Bay of Biscay where successes were difficult to obtain. Nevertheless Lieutenant-Commander Davidson, U.S.N., in *Blackfish,* sank an A/S vessel whilst the *Shad* (Lieutenant-Commander McGregor, U.S.N.) damaged a 6,500-ton blockade runner, both early in 1943. After six months operations, Subron 50 was withdrawn for Pacific duties at the request of Admiral Stark who commanded the American Naval Forces in Europe.

In the period between August 1942 and April 1943, the British had three successes in Home Waters against U-boats. Lieutenant Michael Lumby, in *Saracen,* on her first war patrol, received information of U-boats outwardbound from Norway into the Atlantic. Already being north of the Shetlands, Lumby shifted his patrol to intercept. Two days later, taking the wise precaution of remaining submerged as long as possible, Lumby caught *U.335* surfacing for her night's run westwards; and promptly sank her, rescuing one member of the crew.

In April 1943 Lieutenant D.S.R. Martin in *Tuna,* again acting on intelligence, was quickly despatched to the vicinity of Jan Mayen Island to deal as best he could with a hornet's nest of U-boats. On this occasion, *U.644* surfaced too early and Martin sank her. Next day Martin chased another U-boat but this one dived too soon for him to attack. A short while later, Martin had an underwater encounter with this, or another U-boat, but no attack was possible.

In the following week, *Tuna* fired a salvo from very long range at *U.302,* but the enemy spotted the torpedo tracks and dived. These activities caused great concern to the German U-boat Command, whose object was to attack our P.Q. convoys bound for North Russia. They now found themselves faced not only with the increasing power of R.A.F. Coastal Command, but also with our submarines.

The U-boat tracking room at the Admiralty had, by 1943, become most proficient and was able to indicate accurately the routes used by U-boats, partly because the enemy transmitted too much. Therefore our submarines were sent on anti-U-boat patrols between the coast of Norway and Iceland. Unfortunately the Germans managed to break some of our ciphers and many areas were compromised, resulting in wasted effort. However a German Staff mix-up came to our rescue; for Robbie Alexander in *Truculent* sank *U.308* early in June: and here ends our success story for the long period under review.

These sinkings were hardly commensurate with our own submarine losses, unfortunately not all attributable to the enemy. *Unique*, under the command of Lieutenant E.R. Boddington, was bound for the Mediterranean in October 1942, but had orders to patrol for a short while off the north coast of Spain, where we were having a lot of trouble with blockade-runners. When crossing the Bay of Biscay *Ursula*, under similar orders, heard underwater explosions and assumed that *Unique* was being attacked. The Germans seem to have made no claim, but records are seldom infallible. Unfortunately *Unique* did not arrive at Gibraltar and it must be assumed that these explosions destroyed her.

In November 1942 *Unbeaten,* commanded by Lieutenant D.E.O. Watson, carried out a successful landing operation near Vigo and was then ordered to patrol off the north-western corner of Spain. Later she was told to intercept a blockade-runner already attacked by Coastal Command. *Unbeaten* sighted and reported the enemy vessel and was later ordered to leave patrol and rendezvous with one of our submarine escorting vessels off Bishop's Rock. She did not arrive.

On the 11th November an aircraft of Coastal Command reported a successful attack on a northbound U-boat. The position given was very close to *Unbeaten's,* the latter being well within her bombing restriction area and having every right to be on the surface by night—when the attack was made. Coastal Command instituted a Board of Enquiry, the report of which I later read, when one of my duties at Northways was the imposition of bombing restrictions for the safety of our submarines. The Board of Enquiry had cannily come to no definite conclusion; but it was the general view at Northways that *Unbeaten* had been sunk by our own aircraft.

This view was heavily enforced by the fact that *Sealion*, returning to England from a previous patrol, was severely attacked by a Coastal Command aircraft, although she managed to return safely. These matters will be amplified in the next chapter where I deal with bombing restrictions.

Near Bodo on the Norwegian coast, just inside the Arctic Circle, was a power station which supplied a very important inland mine, producing, amongst other things, pyrites. Lieutenant Røren's *Uredd* was chosen to land a party with the object of blowing-up this power station. *Uredd* had to skirt a known minefield, near which there was thought to be a gap. But the enemy had filled the gap and *Uredd* did not return. This Norwegian 'U' class submarine had been built alongside *Unbroken* at Vickers' yard in Barrow, her number being *P.41* whilst ours was *P.42*. *Uredd* had a remarkably fine commanding officer and an efficient, determined crew. Her loss was keenly felt by myself and by all other British submariners.

But we had our own tragedies in this period. The ex-Turkish submarine *P.615* was sunk by *U.123* off Freetown in mid-April 1943. This now British submarine was at the time being escorted by a motor minesweeper and both were on a steady course and speed. the minesweeper's asdics being relied upon for safety.

The improved 'U' class submarine *Vandal,* on independent working-up practices in the deep waters of Kilbrannan Sound was last seen leaving Loch Ranza in the Isle of Arran during the forenoon of the 24th February 1943. Her loss must be attributed to submarine accident or a failure in material.

Only three months later, *Untamed* was exercising off Campbeltown with an Escort Group. She did not surface on time and the A/S yacht *Shemara* quickly located her on the bottom, in about 150 feet of water. Rapid salvage operations were put into effect; but were so hindered by tides that all hope for the crew had to be abandoned. On eventual lifting, it was found that incorrect drill in raising the log had caused the disaster. These logs were a necessity to accurate navigation and, when lowered, protruded an impeller into the sea. As the submarine proceeded forwards through the water, the revolutions of the impeller were recorded, thus giving speed; but, much more importantly, the distance run. *Untamed* was refitted and later went to sea under the name of *Vitality*.

Much earlier, in June 1942, the ex-American submarine *P.514*, on A/S training duties with the Canadian Navy, was unfortunately rammed and sunk by one of our own escort vessels off the coast of Newfoundland.

Another ex-American submarine, now the Polish *Jastrazab,* was lost in May 1942 by a navigational error; after becoming involved with A/S vessels escorting one of our own North Russian convoys. These convoys were subject to attack by the Luftwaffe, by U-boats and by German surface forces; so it was against the last that we deployed our submarines. But their safety lay in accurate navigation;

because our destroyers had to be free to attack German U-boats.

Although the Commander-in-Chief of the United States Navy, Admiral King, had complained at being deprived of these old 'pig-boats', his objections were based more on prejudice than practicability. These were of the 'Reluctant Dragon' type, so derided in our training flotilla. As the log had caused *Untamed's* end; so the lack of one contributed largely to the loss of *Jastrazab,* which was nearly one hundred miles out of position, the weather having precluded astronomical observations for nearly a week. Two of the escorting vessels from our convoy detected and attacked the Polish submarine, blowing her to the surface. Then recognition was established, and all the crew except five rescued. *Jastrazab* was so badly damaged that she had to be sunk.

No less than twelve British, one French and several Russian submarines were deployed for the protection of the ill-fated convoy P.Q. 17, at the end of June and the beginning of July 1942. In mid-summer these convoys were most definitely not worth the risks involved, a matter which had repeatedly been represented to the Admiralty by Sir John Tovey, Commander-in-Chief Home Fleet. Nevertheless the political climate in Great Britain was such that our terrible losses had to be endured. It is an incontestable fact that a section of the factory-working population of this country, ably abetted by many trade-unionists, were more interested in the fate of 'brotherly' Soviet soldiers than they were with that of sailors in the Royal and Merchant Navies whose blood was apparently expendable.

The returning convoy P.Q. 13 was to come westwards at the same time, thus also being protected by the British covering force which included the Home Fleet, its cruisers, destroyers and numbers of other escorting vessels.

Sir Max Horton informed submarines that German heavy forces might leave Trondheim and Narvik in an attempt to intercept one or both of the British convoys near Bear Island; for ice conditions were (incorrectly) thought to prevent sailing north of this. This appreciation was largely right; for, on the afternoon of the 3rd July, the super-battleship *Tirpitz,* the pocket-battleship *Scheer* and the heavy cruiser *Hipper* anchored in Alten Fjord; *Lutzow* having previously run aground, thereby putting herself out of the action. From intelligence sources, the Admiralty appreciated that the enemy's heavy force was in the vicinity of Alten Fjord and would make a sally. As this intelligence could not be confirmed by reconnaissance, the fleet at sea were not informed. (This omission seems reprehensible to me, since intelligence reports are graded for the likelihood of the event and the reliability of the reporting agent. Therefore I feel that the Commander-in-Chief Home Fleet should have been given this intelligence report. He could then have used his discretion upon what action to take). On the afternoon of the 5th July, *Tirpitz, Hipper, Scheer,* and a heavy destroyer escort sailed from Alten Fjord northwards, then eastwards.

But on the previous evening, because of the threat of the enemy force then at anchor in Alten Fjord, the Admiralty had ordered the, so far entirely successful, convoy to scatter. The enemy force was thought to have sailed that day for an attack on the convoy at dawn on 5th July, although the convoy was over 400 miles from Alten Fjord. The scatter signal, and those preceding it, constitute a classic in the annals of inept communication. Only two things were clear to those at sea; firstly that the cruiser force was to withdraw to the westwards; secondly that the convoy had been ordered to scatter, owing to the threat of surface ships. There was no amplifying information, and no indication of the whereabouts of the enemy battle-force.

To Admiral Hamilton and Commander J.E. Broome, Senior Officer of the close escort, the Admiralty's signals could have only one meaning—that *Tirpitz, Scheer, Hipper* and even *Lutzow* would at any moment appear over the horizon with a large force of destroyers. Admiral Hamilton had not been given even the latitude to stand and fight. He had been clearly and unequivocally commanded to withdraw his cruisers westwards at high speed. He therefore took Commander Broome's six destroyers into his own squadron of two British and two American cruisers, thus giving the combined force at least a chance of a destroyer torpedo attack against an overwhelming enemy.

P.614 and *P.615,* British ex-Turkish submarines, were also with Commander Broome's close convoy escort; and these took up positions in an attempt to cover the scattering convoy, having been told that enemy heavy ships were in the vicinity. In fact, the German battle-force was still at anchor in Alten Fjord.

All naval personnel seethed with rage at the Admiralty's orders, but had to obey them. Admiral Hamilton has been criticised for taking Commander Broome's destroyers with him to the westward. However the Admiral expected, at any moment, to meet a vastly superior enemy force; and suffered the additional disadvantage in that he faced the prospect of having to sacrifice two American cruisers with his own.

The convoy was now wide-open to attack from U-boats and aircraft, being protected only by a few small escorts and anti-aircraft vessels. The Germans created havoc, sinking twenty-one ships: only thirteen of the original thirty-six arrived, after a gruelling time and great gallantry on the part of the small escorts remaining in the action.

In my view, to suggest—as has been suggested—that Commander Broome should somehow have stayed with the convoy, displays ignorance—or worse. No one could have disobeyed these Admiralty orders. (My personal opinion should carry weight here, because some consider me an expert on the interpretation of Admiralty orders!)

We left the *Tirpitz* and her consorts steering eastwards at 20 knots on the afternoon of 5th June. The enemy force was sighted by the Russian submarine *K.21* which attacked *Tirpitz,* claiming two hits. The claim was, in fact, incorrect; but *K.21's* enemy report, received by the Admiralty that evening, provided the first tangible evidence that the German force was at sea.

An aerial report followed and, that evening, Lieutenant C.E. Oxborrow in *P.54,* sighted the *Tirpitz* and attempted to attack. But the enemy had complete mastery of the air and this, combined with *P.54's* slow surface speed, allowed the super-battleship to escape. By now the Germans realised that their position was known; that submarines were in the area and that, if they proceeded north after the convoy, they might have to face attack by aircraft from the fleet-carrier *Victorious* which was with Admiral Tovey's main force. Furthermore, the German admiral must have known that P.Q. 17 was already being cut to ribbons and, consequently, the further risk to his valuable force would be unjustifiable. He therefore returned to the protection of the fjords, ensuring on the way that *P.54* was attacked by his destroyers, fortunately without success.

There are, in my view, three lessons to be learnt from the *P.Q. 17* calamity. Firstly to subjugate military to political considerations in war involves grave risks. Secondly distant staffs must confine themselvs to giving information intelligently to the commanders on the spot: not to giving them orders. Thirdly, and insofar as submarines were concerned, the naval staff in peacetime had failed to appreciate the value of speed. Had this last been incorporated in a firm 'staff requirement', our submarines would have had it, with damaging consequences to all enemies.

The reader may well ask why the large numbers of British and Allied submarines did not achieve more in their activities. One reason was that the German heavy units' long delay in Alten Fjord resulted in most of the patrol positions being too far to the westward. The overriding factor, however, lies in the immensity of the ocean. In this case, the total area covered by four days' operations on both sides amounted to a million square miles. Given visibility of ten miles, the area covered from a submarine would be about 300 square miles, and even this is exceptional.

Here I must bring to a close the disparate and not particularly rewarding efforts of our submarines in Home Waters during the long period between March 1942 and August 1943, having deliberately ended on the note of threat imposed by German heavy ships in Norwegian waters; for this threat has again come very much to the fore by the beginning of the next chapter.

Chapter 12

Home and Mediterranean Operations

AUGUST 1943 - MAY 1945

In November 1942, Admiral Sir Max Horton had handed over his command to Rear-Admiral Barry who became Flag Officer Submarines. Admiral Horton relieved Admiral Sir Percy Noble as Commander-in-Chief Western Approaches where his main concern was the Battle of the Atlantic, that ever-continuing struggle to ensure the life-blood with which to wage war, and indeed to live at all.

In August 1943 after a long* period of leave, I myself was appointed Assistant Staff Officer Operations at Northways, by which time our total submarine strength had reached its optimum of nearly 100. The now enormous training demands of the ocean escorts were satisfied by thirty submarines, whilst we had the luxury of half a dozen for our own practice purposes. Other submarines were refitting or working-up, and there were nearly forty on the stocks. About fifty British submarines were immediately available for operations, disposed as follows:

Home Waters - 16, of which 6 were destined for foreign service
Mediterranean - 32 of which 6 were to go to the Far East
Colombo - 1

My routine duties were to be the operational control of bombing restrictions in Home Waters and, on the administrative side, the analysis of former and current patrol reports with a view to future improvements in all fields. Thus I studied all such reports up to November 1943.

Submarines in Home Waters were operated directly from Northways and, in this, we had two main areas; Northern Norway and Biscay. The latter work was mainly the safeguarding of submarines on passage to and from Gibraltar. In Northern Norway, the emphasis lay on the blockade of *Tirpitz*, for which a snug lair had been made at Kaa Fjord in the inner-most reaches of Alten Fjord. In

* The first in five years

choosing this berth, the Germans had made attack by our submarines impossible and *Tirpitz* was out of range of shore-based aircraft. Even reconnaissance from North Russia proved extremely difficult. We still maintained anti-U-boat patrols and continued the frustrating attempts to penetrate the Norwegian Leads in order to sink supply shipping.

In February 1943 the presence of *Tirpitz, Scharnhorst* and *Lützow* in Alten Fjord, combined with a serious crisis in the Atlantic, eventually decided the Government that the North Russian convoys must be suspended temporarily; at any rate until our midget submarines could cripple the enemy heavy units.

Over a considerable period, plans had been formulated for the construction of a miniature submarine which could cut through nets and yet carry sufficient high explosive to destroy the most heavily armoured ships. The 'X' Craft had been the result. They were proper submarines with four-man crews, having a 'wet and dry' chamber, through which a frogman had access to the sea for the purpose of cutting nets. He could then return to the midget. About 40 tons, their main difference from a real submarine lay in their armament. This consisted of two 2-ton charges which could be released under the keel of an enemy ship, sink to the bottom, then explode by timing mechanism.

I had not long settled into Northways before becoming intimately involved with the planned attack by 'X' Craft on *Tirpitz, Scharnhorst* and *Lützow*. In September 1943, the main power of our battlefleet and its associated aircraft-carriers had been sent to the Mediterranean for operations against Italy. Therefore, before continuing the story, it is pertinent to summarise the strength of a weakened Home Fleet under Admiral Sir Bruce Fraser.

The 'X' Craft operation was called 'Source' and took place on the night of 21st-22nd September. On this night the Home Fleet was disposed as follows:

At Scapa Flow Flagship, *Duke of York*, 14" guns and modern
Old British battle-cruiser *Renown*.
Light aircraft-carrier, U.S.S. *Ranger*.
At Havalfjord (Iceland) - Modern British 14"-gun battleship *Anson*.

Also under command were the United States 8"-gun cruisers *Augusta* and *Tuscalusa*, five British 8"-gun cruisers and seven light cruisers. There were about twenty-seven destroyers altogether.

It will be seen that the Home Fleet was not concentrated and it should also be observed that it was hardly a match for the three

German ships, because it was known that *Tirpitz*, like *Bismarck*, was probably unsinkable by gunfire. *Renown* was even more likely to blow up than *Hood;* and *Duke of York* by herself was no match for *Tirpitz*. Also the *Ranger's* strike capacity was limited.

At Northways, Commander G.P.S. Davies had the staff duty of operating 'X' Craft and had written the orders for 'Source' in rough. He then took some much deserved leave, after I had been given the job of checking and fairing-off the orders. This I did; and such was their secrecy that they were typed by the Paymaster Commander in person. Davies returned, but soon left for Loch Cairnbawn, whence the six 'X' Craft, towed by parent submarines, set out on 11th September with a thousand miles of ocean passage before them. 'D' Day was, for this operation, two days before the intended attack, and had been fixed for 20th September. All submarines at sea were very much my affair, and I watched over these with special attention because of the supreme importance of their object.

We had made arrangements with the Russians for special reconnaissance and had flown Spitfires to North Russia for that purpose. On 14th September, aircraft confirmed the presence of *Tirpitz* and *Scharnhorst* in Kaa Fjord and of *Lützow* in Lange Fjord (all in the Alten Fjord complex), at their usual heavily protected berths. We also received photographs flown by Catalina from North Russia, and full details of a photographic interpretation were signalled to the parent submarines, in which the 'X' Craft's operational crews were accommodated—the passage crews being, at that time, in the 'X' Craft. The Target Plan was also signalled—*X.5, X.6* and *X.7* to attack *Tirpitz; X.9* and *X.10* to attack *Scharnhorst* and *X.8* the *Lützow*.

On 19th September, we received a signal from *Seanymph* reporting the ordered scuttling of *X.8* because of serious defects. This meant that the pocket battleship *Lützow* would not be attacked. It was not known at Northways that *X.9* had been lost on the 16th September, because a report from *Syrtis*—the parent submarine—suffered a communication failure, and was not received until 3rd October.

By 2000 G.M.T. (8 p.m.) on 'D' Day, the actual position was that *X.5, X.6, X.7* and *X.10* had left their parent submarines with operational crews on board and were proceeding independently towards the minefields off Soroy Sound, through which they had to pass before reaching Alten Fjord. Their orders were to remain in Alten Fjord during the night of 21st-22nd and not to attack before 0001 G.M.T. on 22nd September. In fact, the commanding officers of *X.5, X.6* and *X.7* had agreed not to attack the *Tirpitz* until first light. (I imagine that Lieutenant K.R. Hudspeth, R.A.N.V.R., in *X.10*, intended to attack *Scharnhorst* at the same time; but in the event mechanical trouble put him out of the race).

At Northways we thought we had three midget submarines to attack *Tirpitz* and two for *Scharnhorst.* The weather prevented any further photo-reconnaissance. To add to our troubles, the Germans were showing signs of activity. On 8th September, *Tirpitz* and *Scharnhorst* had bombarded Spitzbergen. Furthermore the First Sea Lord, Admiral of the Fleet Sir Dudley Pound, had suffered a stroke and was on the sick list.

On the night of 21st/22nd September, the Duty Staff Officer at Northways was Commander R.L.S. Gaisford, the Staff Officer Operations and my immediate superior. Captain S.M. Raw, C.B.E., R.N., Chief of Staff was not in the building; but Admiral Barry was of course there.

Because of my unique position as the only heavily war experienced submarine commanding officer in London, and because I felt I owed it to those at sea, I had made it a practice never to leave the building except for the shortest periods and for enforced 48-hour periods of leave every fortnight; so I was asleep in my usual place, a camp bed in one of the administrative offices.

Shortly before midnight I was awakened. "The Admiral wants you in the Operations Room now . . . right away." I went there immediately, in pyjamas and dressing gown, to find the Admiral in the same attire.

Rear-Admiral Barry told me that a report had just been received from a reconnaissance aircraft which had got through at dusk: '*Tirpitz* was in her berth; but *Scharnhorst* and *Lützow* had left their's and could not be found.' (The delay in the receipt of all these reports was because the aircraft had to return to its North Russian base; and the signal then had to be passed to the naval authorities for enciphering and transmission).

Admiral Barry also informed me that the Home Fleet was raising steam and might be sailing at that very moment. He added that the Commander-in-Chief Home Fleet had urgently requested the Admiralty to *cancel our operation!* Furthermore the Naval Staff at the Admiralty wished to comply with this request, but had suggested a postponement, as opposed to cancellation. They wanted Admiral Barry's views. The Naval Staff had also suggested that *Tirpitz* might have sailed after dusk. Admiral Barry asked: "Mars, what would you do?"

I was stunned. I could understand that Admiral Fraser wished British submarines out of the way, so that his destroyers could be fully effective against U-boats, and that no one wanted to risk lives by 'X' craft attacking empty berths. Nevertheless, that there could be any doubt whatsoever meant, to my mind, vacillation—or worse. My reply was forceful and ran as follows:-

As the *Tirpitz* was there at dusk, she would be there when we attacked, at dawn—only six hours ahead. No one, I suggested, would risk the navigational hazards of taking a 60,000 ton battleship down Alten Fjord at night, except in dire emergency. I illustrated this by reference to the chart, which I knew like the back of my hand.

Secondly, I was glad we now had but one target, *Tirpitz*. I had always held the view that only three of the six 'X' Craft would penetrate the formidable defences and had never liked the plan of splitting them up.

Thirdly, the operation could not be postponed, only cancelled, and perhaps not even that at this very late stage. An attempt at cancellation might lead to confusion.

Fourthly, operation 'Source' could never be remounted for many reasons, security being one of them.

Fifthly, as regards the Home Fleet, the extra delay in clearing the area* (which they might never use) would be marginal and I could guarantee that no British submarine would embarrass their operations. I pointed out that this would involve sinking any 'X' Craft that might return to its parent submarine, after taking off the crew; but I did not think any would return.

I finished by saying: "And if that is not enough sir, please remind the Naval Staff that we cannot afford another Bismarck". Richard Gaisford heartily endorsed my opinions, and Admiral Barry left for his office, from which he telephoned the Admiralty on his personal closed line. Within a quarter of an hour the answer came back. "The operation is to proceed. Target for all 'X' Craft— *Tirpitz.*"

There is no mention of this episode in the gazetted despatches, nor will it be found in any of the war diaries concerned; for that would not be politic. In retrospect, my conclusion is that, because of my close familiarity with the operation, I was able to give Admiral Barry an instant and telling argument to put forcibly to the Admiralty, which seemed to be in a state of confusion. Also I now feel that someone, somewhere, wished to claim a classic naval victory through battle squadrons meeting at sea; not realising that it could easily have been a disastrous defeat.

* See map page 200 which demonstrates the enormous area taken up by operation 'Source'.

The result of the gallant attack by Lieutenant Donald Cameron, Lieutenant Godfrey Place and their men is well known and has been most graphically described by Thomas Gallacher in his story *'Twelve against the Tirpitz.'* Not to be forgotten is Lieutenant Henty-Creer, the men of *X.5* and those killed in *X.9* when the tow broke. This great and successful attack most surely be the most courageous epic in all history since David slew Goliath.

The severe damage to *Tirpitz* removed overnight the greatest danger we then faced at sea. Several months later, the *Tirpitz* was twice attacked by carrier-borne aircraft of the Fleet Air Arm which kept her out of action until she crawled away to Tromso in October 1944; only to be destroyed there on November 12th by the Royal Air Force, using special Barnes Wallace armour-piercing bombs.

Of course we did not know at the time the real reasons for the movements of *Lützow* and *Scharnhorst* during the vital period. They were in fact very simple. *Lützow* was badly in need of repair, and had left her berth preparatory to going south through the Leads. This she achieved successfully, causing something of a furore in the Coastal Command and Naval aircraft world, because they failed to find and attack her. *Scharnhorst,* on the other hand, had gone down Alten Fjord for gunnery practice.

'Source' had been brilliantly conceived many months before, and was most carefully planned; not only for Alten Fjord but also for other possible heavily protected anchorages. The attack was skilfully executed by the midget submarines against the target, at the time, in the place, and with the supreme object for which it had been planned. We know now that the German High Command did not intend to use *Tirpitz* and *Scharnhorst* in the Atlantic; but, as I have said before in this book, the intentions of today can be reversed tomorrow. If *Tirpitz* had not been crippled, the Germans would still have possessed a force capable of challenging the Home Fleet at sea.

From now on, the influence of British submarines began to wane. This is not to say that we stopped fighting; but, because of the very nature of a successful war now being waged on all fronts, the British submarine was no longer in a position to exert decisive force at a vital point. Our operations continued, and even increased in volume with the larger number of operational submarines now available. The determination of officers and men in no way diminished and they achieved remarkable successes where targets now became scant.

The reader will have seen that our submarines exercised a powerful influence over the Far East in peacetime. In the Norwegian campaign, the effect of the British submarine could be seen by a

In the wardroom of *Unbroken* on the day of arrival at Gosport, autumn 1943. Left to right, the Coxswain, Chief Petty Officer Sizer DSM; Chief Petty Officer Lee DSM (torpedoes) and Chief Engine Room Artificer Manuel DSM and bar (the 'Chief').

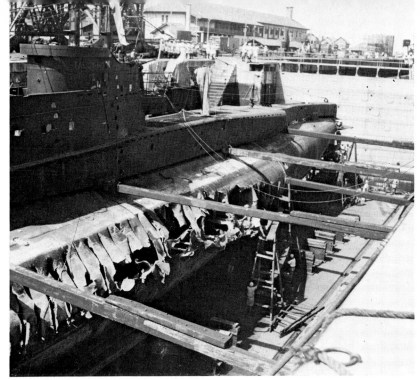

(Top) *Tally Ho* in dock at Colombo, 1944, showing chewed-up main ballast saddle tanks. The size of the submarine is indicated by man in white on dock's bottom. (Bottom) Admiral Sir James Somerville with crew of *Tally Ho* in Ceylon. Right front, Lt.-Cmdr. Bennington DSO DSC and, left front, the Coxswain, Chief Petty Officer C. Ridley DSM.

score of enemy ships sunk, although the unseen psychological effect on the German Naval High Command could not fully be appreciated until the end of the war.

Our signal contribution lay in the Mediterranean, dominated by enemy aircraft; and where, on paper, our surface forces were always inferior to those of the enemy and were actually, for the most part, inferior in armament, in numbers of ships, in speed and in the strategical position of bases, over which our enemies held all the aces. In the world above the sea, the indomitable will of British seamen, airmen, soldiers and Maltese civilians made a priceless attribute to our fighting ability and offensive spirit. Beneath the sea, our submarines played a vital role before, during and after the turning of the tide. This could be illustrated now, by taking the graphical record of our successes and laying it on the army's strategical maps of North Africa. These two pieces of paper would accord so perfectly that they would be almost interchangeable. When the submarines were winning the army was winning and vice versa. As at the pertinent times, neither our surface forces nor air forces could operate in the vital areas, the submarine effort was decisive. Mr. Winston Churchill had always maintained and great men such as Sir Archibald Wavell and Sir Andrew Cunningham had always known that the issue of the war in Europe would be decided in the Mediterranean—and indeed it was.

Before coming to British submarine activities during the remainder of the war, I think it worthwhile to dwell for a time upon that nerve centre and overall headquarters, Northways. We have seen much of Claud Barry in the earlier stages of the book and know what a good pair he and George Menzies made during those far off days in China. Unlike Sir Max Horton, Claud Barry was no tiger; nor did he possess his predecessor's enormous prestige and that, in itself, was something of a disadvantage. Nevertheless he was an able administrator and carried on Admiral Horton's work for two years, although in poor health.

Northways was continually beset by impossible demands for submarines to do fantastic things and, in this, Claud Barry had some difficulty in saying 'no'. Whilst Horton's word was normally accepted by most authorities, Barry had to give his reasons; and they had to be very good ones. As he knew me well and, I think, respected my opinions, he frequently asked them. This was a perfectly proper procedure for, although I was certainly very junior, my war experience at sea in operational submarines greatly exceeded that of all the other submariners at Northways put together.

The sad story of our chariots in the Mediterranean did not prevent a large number of these machines being built. Having them, we were expected to use them; particularly as they were one of Mr. Winston Churchill's pets. I was told one day that the Admiralty had proposed using chariots to attack any, or all, enemy ports between Calais and Bordeaux. "I wonder," I said to the Admiral, "whether any of these gentlemen know anything at all about this tide-swept coast; because to me the whole thing seems quite impossible."

"Exactly Mars," he replied. "But we have to convince them. So I want you to draw up full details of all the possibilities and, if we can find a good one, we'll use it. If we cannot, I want to be able to tell them why."

So I got down to the charts and tide-tables, and visited the Intelligence Centre at the Admiralty for all the photographic surveys I could obtain. I then marked in defences such as booms, nets, minefields, gun emplacements, the positions of airfields; spending an enormous amount of time. Fortunately I had spent much of my youth in Flanders and France and so was able to visualise the situation from the charts before me—an invaluable help. The chariots could only waddle along at a few knots, were limited in range; whilst the endurance of their gallant two-man crews also had carefully to be considered. Naturally all this took much time and, working about twenty hours a day, I was not wasting it. But, from the many enquiries about my progress, I began to feel that the Prime Minister was breathing down my neck.

I had been reminded, in view of chariot misfortunes in the Mediterranean, that the safety of the launching submarine must be of primary consideration, a precaution with which I heartily agreed. Although I tried hard to effect a penetration at some point, no weak enough spot could be found. The main difficulties were the dangers of heavily mined, closely guarded approaches and the strong tides, which even at neaps, the low-speed chariots could not combat. My written reasoning must have been effective; for I was thanked and the matter then dropped.

Already mentioned, are the difficulties we faced over bombing restrictions. This was a misnomer because the sanctuary area for a submarine precluded all forms of attack, including that of surface forces and even land fortifications. Also, the orders had continually been amended by signals, confidential Admiralty Fleet Orders and even the local orders of area flag officers. Deciding this to be unsatisfactory, I suggested that I should correlate all existing orders, discard non-essentials and condense the lot into a new book. This

was agreed; so, entitling my first book 'Submarine Attack Restrictions', I submitted it for the publisher's approval. To my amazement, it was accepted without alteration, set up, printed and distributed in less than a month.

Submarines have various methods of identifying themselves but, at night, this meant giving away one's position and, by day, the firing of coloured smoke candles from submerged could be equally dangerous. Therefore we took recourse to routeing, combined with the rapid but secret advance transmission of submarine movements to those concerned, particularly Coastal Command of the R.A.F.

One could establish a temporary submarine sanctuary, in the form of a circle or rectangle; but a more usual method was to put the submarine in the middle of a moving box which would allow for navigational errors. On the maps at Northways submarines would move along in their protected boxes, these being perhaps 20 miles across and 100 miles along, depending upon weather conditions and many other factors. 'Total' attack restrictions meant that a submarine was not to be attacked under any circumstances. 'Submerged' attack restrictions meant that the submarine would be immune on the surface between sunset and sunrise; but not by day. She only surfaced by day at her own peril and against orders.

During my regime there was only one incident, in *Rubis,* such a veteran that one would not have expected her to be caught in this manner. She was attacked when on the surface by day in the Bay of Biscay, by an R.A.F. Wellington, firing rockets. The aircraft's captain was perfectly right, and ceased fire when *Rubis* managed to establish her identity. But the submarine had been hit in the stern and had to return to Devonport. Here, she was visited by a highly delighted R.A.F. officer whose sole interest was to examine the damage. This he found somewhat disappointing; whilst his cavalier attitude offended Capitaine de Corvette Rousselot deeply, a matter of which the latter complained bitterly to me on his next visit to Northways. Sympathising with him, I did nothing further about it, because the episode had put me in a difficult position. I was always tearing into Coastal Command for making mistakes, and now they had a perfect comeback.

In those days, the navigation of aircraft over the sea was not easy and required an enormous amount of experience and training. There can be no doubt that the Fleet Air Arm were easily the best trained and by far the most experienced. The navigators in Coastal Command, largely through the Air Ministry's neglect in peacetime, lacked the opportunities for this extensive training.

Admiral Barry, feeling that submariners were running behind in the publicity stakes, asked me to write some newspaper articles which he felt desirable, mainly because the Royal Air Force were scooping the headlines. Of course, many submariners had been interviewed by the press but, until then, I do not think any had written of their own experiences or indeed had received permission to do so. Also in those days, there was a certain reticence about the Navy which affected even myself. As suggested, I wrote about *Unbroken* and delivered a file of typewritten foolscap to Douglas Reekie in Fleet Street. First using man-sized editorial scissors, Reekie added a few embellishments, and the result was published in a series. In this way the exploits of *Unbroken*, her crew and not least her captain, acquired a public image which was somewhat out of proportion and a little unfair on others.

About this time, and very much to my own relief, Lieutenant Andrew brought *Unbroken* safely home to Gosport. Wives and relatives had been assembled to meet her and I joined them. She arrived alongside to a great welcome and much publicity, all of which proved rather thrilling. My own conscience in the matter was a little salved by the knowledge that we had gained an Admiralty commendation for skill, an unusual accolade which was less frequently accorded than the award of decorations.

On one of his patrols, Andrew sank a tug and the 5,000-ton supply ship *Bologna,* in the Gulf of St. Eufemia. *Unbroken* also suffered a couple of misses and carried out a patrol blockading the Italian battleships in Taranto during the invasion of Sicily. I have always felt particularly indebted to Andrew for bringing her home safely. With the tempo of German and Italian anti-submarine activity then at its height, things could well have been otherwise.

At Northways we were lucky to have a score of cipher Wrens who worked very long hours and got through an enormous number of signals with great accuracy and competence. When worn out, as Duty Staff Officer, in the early hours of the morning the presentation of yet another bunch of recently deciphered and demanding signals could easily have led to invective. But these attractive young Wrens however tired themselves, always arrived so cheerfully, usually carrying the signals in one hand and a cup of tea in the other. It was a pleasure to work with them.

Frequently the Duty Captain at the Admiralty would ring up and ask us to do some cipher work. The request was a formality, for we could not very well have refused. The Admiralty was not allowed

Wrens, so civil servants were meant to do their ciphering. But, because of air raids, these had the right to go home at their usual time, thus leaving the Admiralty with only a handful of duty naval officers to cope with ciphers. As a result, all but emergency signals had to be left until the next day; unless Northways could deal with them.

I hope that, by now, all operational staff ciphering is done either by Wrens or by those who are willing to reduce bloodshed by doing their duty—whatever their 'rights'.

At the time of our bitter chariot operations in the Mediterranean, Admiral Barry had only recently relieved Sir Max Horton and could hardly be said to have been fully in the saddle. By the autumn of 1943, however, he was firmly established and greatly concerned over our Mediterranean losses. Therefore I was told to analyse them. The results showed that the main factor in the Mediterranean area lay in the size of the submarine. The bigger they were, the more likely their loss. Secondly, came the time element: more were lost in their first few patrols and more towards the end of their tour. Only thirdly seemed to come the experience of commanding officers and crews. Against Admiral Barry's advice, the Admiralty had twice extended the operational tour of our second last minelaying submarine, *Rorqual*, still under Napier's command. Together with *Severn* and four Italian submarines, *Rorqual* was engaged in running supplies to Leros which was under heavy German air attack in the fierce campaign for the Dodecanese Islands. She carried Bofors guns, ammunition, victuals and on one occasion a Jeep. *Rorqual* did invaluable work. However, she had had an arduous and most successful time in the Mediterranean, having first entered it (under Napier's command) in August of 1942. She was big, vulnerable and getting old. The Admiralty refused pointblank to recall her. Finally she got out in December 1943; but not before both Napier and his first lieutenant were suffering from jaundice. Although *Rorqual* was undoubtedly useful on these cargo runs and the army glad of her supplies, it cannot be maintained that the risk justified the benefits. Another factor about *Rorqual* was that many members of her crew had remained in her ever since those far off days in China, when she had first been indoctrinated into the rigours of that flotilla's exercises. During the lengthy refit in the United Kingdom, these men had been given their share of leave. Nevertheless it was unusual to find members of an old crew still together after so long, and so arduous, a time. To have lost her would have been criminal.

We now come to the height of folly, but I feel the story should be told, if only to prevent a repetition. This then is the tale of the 'Black Sea Fiasco'.

On the 28th November 1943, Mr. Winston Churchill, President Roosevelt and Stalin met at Teheran. Earlier in the month the Russians had retaken Kiev and now threatened the Crimea, from which Germans were evacuating in large numbers across the northern waters of the Black Sea to Odessa and other ports, still in German hands.

These waters are composed from the efflux of the great rivers Danube, Dniester, Bug and Dnieper and are muddy, badly charted because of shifting banks and, for the most part, shallow. Their salinity is next to non-existent; so for all diving purposes they may be considered fresh water.

This German evacuation, mainly from Sevastopol, was taking place in every craft they could lay their hands on; and these, of necessity, would mostly be small. The Russian Black Sea Fleet, including its submarines, were not successfully intercepting the evacuations which had reached the proportion of seaborne rout. It is most surprising that this should have been so; for the Soviet Navy was, at that time, almost a subsidiary of the Army and should have been acting vigorously on the latter's seaward flank.

The default annoyed Mr. Churchill who offered Stalin the services of British submarines, services which had been much appreciated by the Russians during early days in the Arctic, before they became jealous. I do not know whether or not Mr. Churchill consulted his naval advisers at Teheran, but it is unlikely that there would have been a submariner present. Before or upon Mr. Churchill's return, a requirement had been put before Northways for six 'S' class submarines, then based at Beirut, to proceed for operations in the northern waters of the Black Sea. This problem was put on my plate and since, on this occasion, I knew for certain who was the originator, it made me shudder.

The job was obviously one for motor gun and torpedo boats, backed up by aircraft. Submarines are vessels of comparatively deep draught, therefore the navigational difficulties were obvious. But the overriding problem lay in the fact that our submarines, without extensive re-ballasting, could not operate in conditions of fresh water.

Additionally, there existed a political problem of some magnitude. It was necessary to hoodwink the Turks by diving the submarines through the Dardanelles and Bosphorus, during which passage they were expected to remain undetected.

I was not helped by the naval constructor at Northways, a civil servant in uniform, who insisted that all British submarines were designed to operate in fresh water. Whilst this was true, he did not seem to appreciate the fact that all ships grow heavier with age, particularly when extra equipment is added. I knew from my own experience that no British submarine could operate successfully in a water density of less than 1017—this being about halfway between fresh and salt water.

Enormous pressure was now exerted on Admiral Barry, and I spent many hours with oceanographical surveys. My final report was that the submarines had a reasonable chance of getting through the Dardanelles, provided the Turkish mine-watchers for their controlled minefields were not alert. I did not consider there was much chance of any of them getting through the Bosphorus submerged, because of the strong out-running deep current.

These findings produced a three-dimensional 'flap' and a face-saving conference was hurriedly assembled at the Admiralty. Here a Foreign Office representative said that we might be able to get the Turks to turn a blind eye, if the submarines went through on the surface unobtrusively at night. With me was Captain 'Sammy' Raw, Chief of Staff at Northways, who said little; although he backed me up, at the crux.

This was the type of confrontation, that is to say Winston Churchill versus the experts, that could so easily lead to the rolling of heads; but it did not particularly affect me, because my head was of no consequence.

All the time at Northways, I had considered that one of my duties was to prevent unnecessary losses by a *bêtise* of this sort. So from the bottom of the long table, I found myself in direct conflict with the presiding Rear-Admiral—a situation not improved by the fact that he happened to be one of the very few naval officers I did not like. The antipathy was mutual and I have little doubt that my name was written in the book.

Nothing, it appeared, could convince them; so a signal was sent to Captain S/M.1., at Beirut, ordering him to prepare six 'S' class submarines for this purpose.

David Ingram replied that it would be necessary to dock and re-ballast all six submarines, a process which would take six weeks. Fortunately about this time, Stalin said he did not want our submarines, thereby pulling all chestnuts from the fire.

I have enlarged on this episode because, in this case, I knew for certain whence the directive had sprung. I knew also that, amongst

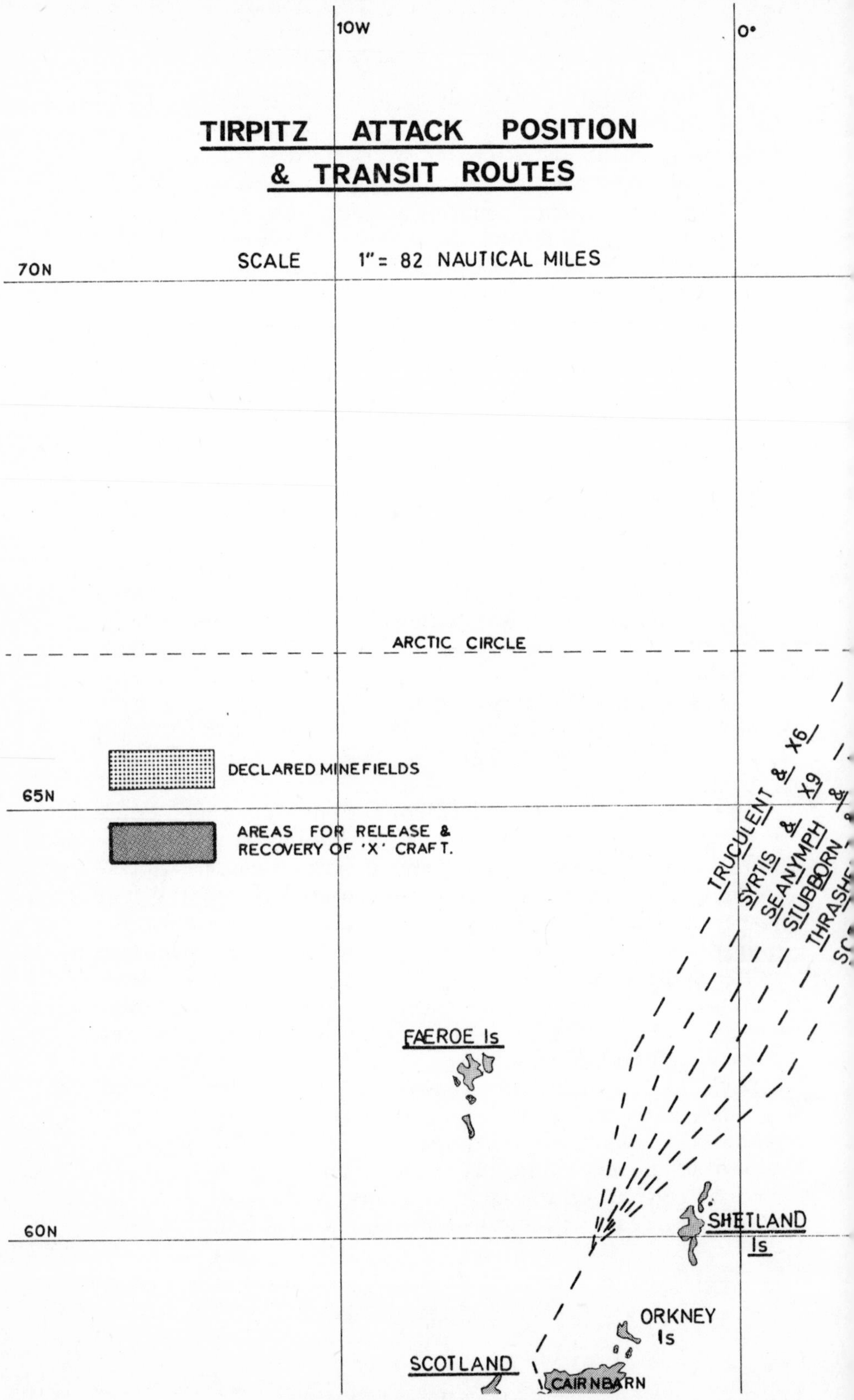

TIRPITZ ATTACK POSITION
& TRANSIT ROUTES

10W

0°

70N

SCALE   1" = 82 NAUTICAL MILES

ARCTIC CIRCLE

DECLARED MINEFIELDS

65N

AREAS FOR RELEASE &
RECOVERY OF 'X' CRAFT.

TRUCULENT & X6

SYRTIS & X9

SEANYMPH & STUBBORN

THRASHE

SC

FAEROE Is

SHETLAND
Is

60N

ORKNEY
Is

SCOTLAND

CAIRNBARN

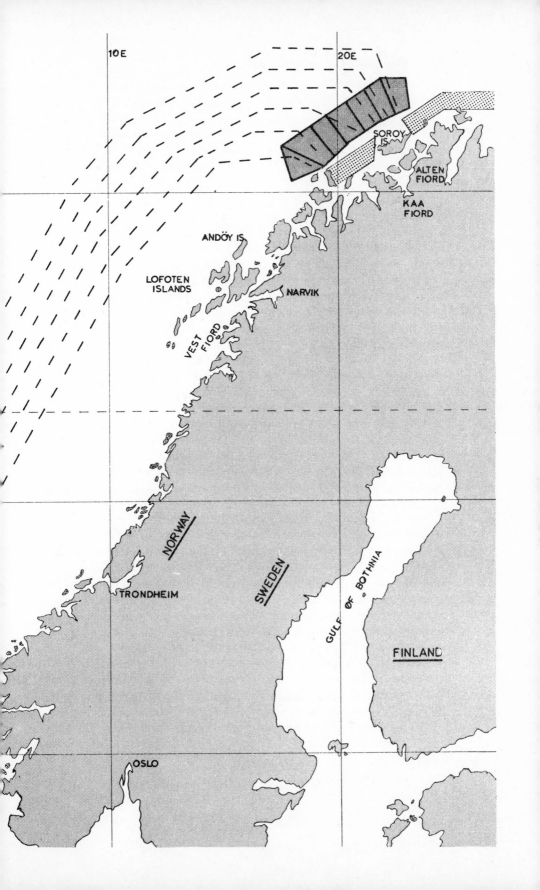

10 E

20 E

SOROY IS.

ALTEN FIORD

KAA FIORD

ANDÖY IS.

LOFOTEN ISLANDS

NARVIK

VEST FIORD

NORWAY

SWEDEN

GULF OF BOTHNIA

FINLAND

TRONDHEIM

OSLO

senior officers of the junior brigade—those who had been captains or rear-admirals at the commencement of hostilities—there was considerable resentment against political interference with the conduct of naval operations, not only in submarines but throughout the entire navy. It is interesting to me today, to read in Captain Menzie's diary that he and many of his contemporaries held similar opinions.

'Theirs not to reason why'.

In support, to the reader, of my contentions, with which the naval constructor disagreed, I would add this. If the density of pure fresh water is taken as 1,000 and that of normal sea water as 1,028, halfway works out at 1,014. When commanding *Thule* in 1945, we frequently operated in the Java Sea where low density water is sometimes encountered. On these occasions difficulty was experienced in keeping submerged control with a seawater density of 1,017 ... this despite the fact that, in anticipation of such a situation, I had already had 25 tons of ballast unofficially removed from the keel of H.M.S. *Thule*. The water density in the northwestern corner of the Black Sea is between 1,003 and 1,007.

Claud Barry, at the centre of these pressures, took things calmly and kept the machine running with well-oiled efficiency. I had of course known him in China and became to know him even better at Northways. It does not seem to me that he received full credit for the patience, hard work and cheerfulness with which he performed his many duties. Perhaps this is because he was not an ambitious man: rather did he have an eye to his family's future, knowing that his health was waning.

He invited me to accompany him to a nauseatingly splendid dinner party at Claridges in honour of high-ranking American and Allied naval officers. I was placed next to Admiral King, U.S.N., presumably in an effort to show him that the British were contributing their mite to the war at sea; but I found him cool and unprepossessing. Although to my mind revolting in war, I gorged myself on the 10-course, full-belly meal and was to suffer for it—perhaps because Claud Barry felt that we both needed cheering up after such a dull party, and took me to visit friends at the Ritz, where both the whisky and the conversation became animated.

I would like now to summarize the later operations in Home Waters and the Mediterranean, which continued with success and loss until the German surrender.

It has been a deliberate trend in this book to emphasise the fact that the difficulties of submariners were not always those imposed by the enemy; but, at least in part, by pre-war political blunders and wartime exigencies. Such problems beset the entire Navy and indeed all the Armed Forces, possibly to a slightly lesser extent, because their weapons were more readily understood than the antics of the obscure submarine. The reader will appreciate the enormous strain and responsibility imposed upon Admiral of the Fleet Sir Dudley Pound in his capacity as First Sea Lord and Chief of Naval Staff, from the beginning of the war until the autumn of 1943, a strain of which he died on Trafalgar Day of that year. Sir Dudley Pound was succeeded by Sir Andrew Cunningham, an appointment to which Mr. Churchill reluctantly agreed; for Sir Andrew was undoubtedly not only the most experienced but the strongest-willed high ranking officer in the Navy. The submarine 'Black Sea Fiasco' occurred shortly after Sir Andrew had taken over and it seems more than likely that the matter was thought too small to be brought to his notice. All were glad to see him inherit the post which he so richly deserved.

Although our two submarines in the area did not sight *Scharnhorst* and her destroyers during her last sortie, they were looking for her. *Scharnhorst's* sinking by Admiral Fraser's Home Fleet on 26th December 1943 released submarines for other duties.

A classic patrol, in February 1944, was that of a Dartmouth term-mate of mine, Arther Pitt. In *Taku,* he sank or wrecked three ships in five days off Skudesnes—a total of 14,000 tons! A large proportion of the submarine effort in Home Waters was now devoted to the training of ocean escorts and to the working-up of our own submarines destined for the Far East. Notwithstanding, many British and Allied operation were carried out, continuing the general trend in the Bay of Biscay, Norwegian and anti-U-boat patrols. Later, submarines were engaged in their now familiar duties aiding landing operations, particularly in Normandy. There are two unique episodes which I should mention before leaving the northern seas, the first being the most miraculous of the whole war; the second a success of the utmost significance for the future.

Lieutenant A.A. Duff in *Stubborn,* on patrol off Trondheim in mid-February 1944, sank two 2,000-ton ships with one remarkably accurate salvo. Two days later, in nearby Folda Fjord, *Stubborn* attacked an escorted convoy, but missed. This resulted in a sharp, heavy and accurate counter-attack which jammed her after hydroplanes hard a'dive, flooded an internal tank and damaged a propeller. *Stubborn* dropped to nearly 400 feet and had to blow main ballast tanks. She broke surface violently but plunged back to no less than 500 feet (200 feet below her designed depth) with a bow-down angle. In the deep water, there seemed no futher hope; but she hit bottom on an uncharted ledge or rock! The enemy held asdic contact and continued depth-charging. This put *Stubborn's* asdic set out of action, but did no further damage. (It would seem that the German charges were set too shallow. Indeed it is unlikely that the enemy thought a British submarine capable of such a great depth as 500 feet). Four hours after the commencement of their attack, the Germans left *Stubborn* unmolested; but she waited silently to ensure that they had gone. In the evening, Lieutenant Duff took action to get his submarine to the surface, when it was found that the after hydroplanes had freed themselves, probably by the violence of impact on the bottom. Lieutenant Duff, his officers and crew maintained the greatest calm, working hard now to get their submarine under way. But it was not for another three hours, and after having used up nearly all their compressed air, that *Stubborn* suddenly started to rise . . . and fast! Taking the unbelievable angle of 70° bow-up, she lunged to the surface where her bows 'fell over' with a mighty smash into the water and lay there—but for only a few seconds. Incredibly the crew had managed to make the engines workable and *Stubborn* made off at her best speed away from the land; although the damaged propeller proved a great hindrance and considerably reduced her progress. The sea became rough and, on the following evening, the rudder discon-nected itself. The submarine was now uncontrollable and, naturally, Duff did not wish to tempt providence by diving.

A signal was got through to base, and the destroyers *Swift* and *Meteor* were immediately sent to the rescue, later being covered by a fighter escort. Eventually *Stubborn* was towed into Lerwick and sent south to Devonport Dockyard for repairs.

I myself, then busy with the fitting-out of *Thule*, met Duff after arrival and examined *Stubborn* in the drydock. She gave the impression of a skeleton's chest; for her ribs protruded whilst, between them, her steel plates had been pressed inwards to form concave curves, this bizarre effect providing an unforgettable tribute to the workmanship of the men who built her.

We come more happily now to an event which is unique in the history of the world. Lieutenant J.S. Launders had, in wild November weather off the Lofoten Islands, already sunk the surfaced U-boat, *U.771*, in the traditional manner. But the venue of his unique success was when on patrol northwest of Bergen, as late as February 1945. *Venturer* had dived at dawn in the usual way, and was patrolling at periscope depth. During the forenoon, weak propeller noises were heard on the asdic set, being used as a hydrophone: these indicated a submerged U-boat. Twenty minutes later, a periscope was sighted on the correct bearing: now there was no doubt, so *Venturer* was brought round to an intercepting course. The U-boat was making a considerable amount of machinery clatter, something the Germans should have learnt to avoid long since. However, this did not appreciably affect the issue because *Venturer* was stalking the propeller noises. About twenty minutes after the first sighting, the U-boat's periscope was again seen; but Launders remained in some doubt as to her course, although having concluded that she was making for harbour. He therefore decided to track her for an hour. Judiciously using his asdic set as a destroyer would, Launders obtained bearings and ranges of his quarry, until her course and speed were established, assistance being given by the U-boat's unwary use of the periscope, which was again sighted. Now *Venturer* drew off, gradually increasing speed as she gained distance from the U-boat. In this way, she manoeuvred ahead and into a firing position. After another hour, *Venturer* was running towards the U-boat, ready to fire. After again establishing contact, Launders closed the range still further and unleashed his salvo, the torpedoes being set to run at 40 feet.

Thus was sunk *U.864,* so far the only known victim of torpedoes fired by one submarine at another when both were submerged throughout the encounter. The brilliantly successful attack, for which our equipment was really not then designed, is of supreme importance to the future existence of Great Britain, an island or group of islands which today is surrounded by hundreds of potentially aggressive Russian submarines.

Towards the end of the war, British and Allied submarine efforts along the Norwegian coast at last achieved considerable results, particularly against the vital enemy coal trade. But the culminating success was that of Lieutenant John Roxburgh, now in *Tapir,* who on 12th April 1945, sank *U.486* in a snap attack.

Previously, in the same area, Lieutenant H.P. Westmacott in the midget submarine *X.24,* after having been towed to the release position by Lieutenant I.S. McIntosh in *Sceptre,* penetrated through the Leads into Bergen harbour to drop his enormous charges under the big floating dock. The resultant explosion wrecked the target and damaged two vessels secured alongside. On that high note of midget submarine success, we must reluctantly leave Home Waters for a brief survey of the Mediterranean, before turning our attention to the Far East.

Our submarines' contribution towards the landings at Salerno was slight and comprised only a beach reconnaissance and the usual navigational beacon. The obsession with Italian battleships now of minimal war value in Taranto harbour still continued and, as late as 24th August 1943, *Ultor* and *Unrivalled* actually sailed from Malta for such a chariot attack. The operation was cancelled by the Commander-in-Chief—not surprisingly, since negotiations for a secret Italian surrender were already taking place in Madrid.

It is unfortunate that space precludes my mentioning more of our Mediterranean feats; but many must remain unrecorded in this book. Here, however, are a few such.

Unruffled, the appropriately named submarine of Lieutenant John Stevens, completed nineteen patrols in the Mediterranean during which she sank no less than ten enemy supply ships of some 35,000 tons, including a 10,000 ton tanker. In addition there were vessels damaged, and special operations.

Another, but later, stayer, was Lieutenant M.L.C. ('Tubby') Crawford in *Unseen,* who sank seven vessels of some 15,000 tons, apart from those damaged. It will be noticed that the average size of enemy ships in the Mediterranean was decreasing. They were thus more difficult to hit; but some compensation lay in the fact that a much larger proportion of ships sunk were now German. *Unseen* was to have a close shave on her sixteenth and last patrol, otherwise mainly uneventful. In rough weather off Nice in the south of France, she broke surface, immediately to be pounced on by an anti-submarine craft whose presence had been unsuspected. A very close pattern of charges followed immediately: because of this and the extra water taken to to keep the submarine down, 'Tubby' found himself at about 300 feet before *Unseen* pulled out of the dive. Fortunately internal damage was not too serious and an escape was made; albeit at a lesser depth, the submarine being designed for 200'

'Dicky' Gatehouse in *Sportsman* was another to survive a nasty attack, this time by an American aircraft. Altogether, it was an adventurous patrol. Having gunned and sunk two sailing vessels, *Sportsman* bombarded German forces escaping from Bastia in Corsica, and then picked up survivors from two Italian destroyers which had been sunk by the Luftwaffe—shortly after the Germans' discovery that Italy had surrendered. During *Sportsman's* return to base, she was bombed at night by an American Liberator (in an area of complete restriction against attack on submarines) having an officer seriously burned, and suffering much damage to her conning-tower and superstructure. However she made Algiers the following day. Before returning home, *Sportsman* had scored at least five ships sunk totalling some 20,000 tons, apart from those damaged.

The last three of this score fell to *Sportsman* in the Aegean, to which our submarines were, by the autumn of 1943, devoting most of their attention. Unfortunately the Italians in Rhodes had surrendered to a German garrison of inferior strength, thereby depriving us of that island's facilities and jeopardising our position in the Dodecanese. The Germans reinforced heavily, in order to protect their flank in Europe and a long drawn out battle ensued. In the period September 1943 until the end of Agean operations in November 1944, our submarines sank at least seventeen vessels of 40,000 tons, including a floating dock, with the usual proportion damaged. Additionally the Greek submarine *Pipinos* (Lieutenant C. Loundras) sank the ex-Italian destroyer *Calatafima* which had been taken over by the Germans. This success also serves to remind us that Greek submarines, although few in number, were with us all the way. Before finally leaving the Mediterranean area I would like to mention two exploits which gained Victoria Crosses, that highest of all awards for valour.

In late February and early March 1942, Lieutenant-Commander A.C.C. Miers commanding *Torbay,* after sinking a small coaster by gunfire, received a severe depth-charging whilst attempting to sink a destroyer off Corfu. Nevertheless he closed in towards the anchorage and sighted a distant troopship convoy entering Corfu Roads from the southward. Miers decided to follow the convoy, in an attempt to sink its ships in harbour. He therefore negotiated the narrow channel before moonrise, thus entering the enclosed roadstead. From this position he could keep the harbour entrance under observation whilst charging his batteries; but was forced to dive by an inshore patrol vessel.

Torbay dived in towards the harbour at dawn; but was badgered by another patrol vessel and had to shear off. She later approached the harbour in daylight and flat calm. To his annoyance, Tony Miers discovered that the troop convoy was not there, having presumably passed straight through the defended anchorage and left by the northern entrance. However, he attacked the *Maddalena,* a 5,200-ton supply ship which he damaged, probably also hitting another vessel in the harbour. For this achievement Lieutenant-Commander Miers was awarded the Victoria Cross, having spent some twenty hours inside an enemy defended anchorage.

In February 1942, Hugh Mackenzie, in his well-named *Thrasher,* attacked a supply ship off Heraklion (Crete) and was repaid by a sharp and accurate counter-attack from both A/S vessels and aircraft. After escaping from this, Hugh having decided the damage to be superficial, *Thrasher* came to the surface at night as usual. On the fore casing lay a 50-kilo bomb! This was lifted overboard without incident; but another was found to have crashed through the light plate around the gun-tower, and had remained lodged there. The casing, which ran along the top of the pressure-hull in all 'T' class submarines (having a great many small holes punched in it for free flooding when the submarine dived), was only about 3'6" high and full of obstructions such as frames. The only way to get rid of this second bomb was to drag it forward to the fore hatch recess, from which it could be lifted to the upper deck. This hair-raising job was accomplished by Lieutenant P.W.S. Roberts and Petty Officer T.W. Gould, a stint not helped by the fact that every time the bomb was moved, it made loud and fiendish noises. Both Lieutenant Roberts and Petty Officer Gould were awarded the Victoria Cross for this very gallant achievement.

It is interesting to note that Hugh Mackenzie was a little surprised at the efficient use of asdics and the general competence of enemy counter-attack. This dovetails with the conclusions of the German Staff in North Africa, previously mentioned, on the effects of our submarine campaign in the summer and autumn of 1941. It shows also that the Axis partners had taken immediate and successful steps to strengthen their anti-submarine prowess; for *Tempest* and *P.38* had just been lost in the central Mediterranean.

Quitting this high note of Victoria Crosses, I must regretfully record some further losses before returning to the Far East.

Summary of other losses September 1943 - end of War.
Home Waters:

It is at least partly true that the importance of the *effect* of submarine activity can be measured by one's own loss. This mercifully was to be small for the remainder of the war; and, in Home Waters, we lost only *Syrtis.* Commanded by Lieutenant M.H. Jupp, she sank a small ship by gunfire off Bodo in March 1944. It is of interest to note that only four enemy vessels are known to have been sunk by gunfire from our submarines in Home Waters: this was the last. *Syrtis* failed to arrive at Lerwick at the end of the month, and is presumed to have been mined on the same minefield which claimed Lieutenant Røren's *Uredd,* whose fine work was continued by Lieutenant R.M. Sars, in the new Norwegian submarine *Ula,* and Lieutenant S. Valvatne in *Utsira.*

Mediterranean

Lieutenant D.R.O. Mott failed to return from patrol with his *Usurper* in October 1944. She had recently arrived in the Mediterranean and may have been sunk by a German U.J. A/S craft. These were of shallow draught and highly efficient in anti-submarine work. *Usurper,* on the other hand, may have been mined; for there was an unknown enemy minefield in the vicinity of her patrol area.

Trooper, commanded by the most experienced 'Johnny' Wraith and with a battle-trained crew, failed to return from an Aegean patrol in the same month; having almost certainly been mined to the eastwards of Leros on a minefield which was then unknown.

In November 1943 we lost *Simoon.* Commanded by Lieutenant G.D.N. Milner, she had been ordered to patrol the Dardanelles' approaches, near Cape Helles, and failed to return. The circumstances of her loss are not known, but in view of very heavy German minelaying in the Northern Aegean, it seems that she must have hit a mine.

Our last Mediterranean tragedy took place in June of 1944 when *Sickle,* commanded by Lieutenant J.R. Drummond who had already sunk *U-303,* a 3,100 ton ship and had had other successes, carried out a most spirited patrol. On the 4th June she bombarded Mitylene, but was hit on the conning-tower by fire from enemy vessels and lost a man overboard who was, luckily, picked up by the Germans. *Sickle* dived her way out of this trouble to torpedo a German ship in the Doro Channel, getting two hits. She later attacked another ship which she missed, being sighted by German aircraft, although they do not appear to have attacked her. Three days later, *Sickle* reported an enemy convoy and that became her last signal.

The sinking of *Sickle,* presumed mined on her way southwards, closes the chapter of British Mediterranean losses, which amounted to 45 submarines sunk. Of these, 21 were mined or presumed mined. In this connection, it must be emphasised that Axis minelaying was prodigious. Rather than attempting to sum it up in figures, I would like to express it in the words of Captain G.C. Phillips, D.S.O., who was Captain S/M.10 at Malta when the Italian records were made available:

'Had we known of all these minefields, it is difficult to see how we could have operated our submarines in the Mediterranean at all'.

Even that statement does not allow for the renewed German mining effort in the Aegean after September of 1943.

Chapter 13

Far East

DECEMBER 1940 - AUGUST 1945

If, as we have seen in Chapter 3, the Japanese were prepared to strike at Singapore as early as 1932, it must follow that they were ready in September 1939 and thereafter. That they did not make a grab at Hong Kong and Singapore up to the end of 1939, I have attributed largely to the presence of the British 4th Submarine Flotilla. After that flotilla was withdrawn, the Japanese missed their two best opportunities, the first of which was when the Germans advanced into Holland, the second being in June 1940 when Italy entered the war. Had the Japanese acted at either of these times, it is highly probable they could have taken Hong Kong, Singapore and the Dutch East Indies without much difficulty and with no military interference from the United States. But they hesitated and were lost. This delay was obviously made in the hope that Great Britain would be beaten in Europe, an event which would have allowed British and Dutch colonies to fall into Japanese hands like ripe plums.

With one of the densest populations in the world, concentrated on a few small islands, Japan's position was—and remains—a most difficult one. Japan, like Britain, had to (and like Britain, still must) import food or starve. As healthy trade should always be balanced perfectly, Japan had to export industrial products and these could only be made with the raw materials she did not possess: nor did she possess oil.

Therefore Japan continually *demanded* trade concessions from all the Western powers; but, seeing the readiest supply of most she needed in the Dutch East Indies, concentrated her peremptory demands mainly on the Dutch. In retrospect one can say that, had Japan softened her requests and had the Western maritime nations been more conciliatory, the war might not have occurred when it did. However, with the Prussian trained and Prussian-minded

Imperial Japanese Army in political control of their country, war at some time was inevitable.

President Roosevelt and his advisers, who by now knew that the United States would be dragged into the war in Europe and rightly wished to crush Hitler, hardened their attitude towards Japan—no doubt realising that the American public needed shaking out of their complacency; and this was certainly achieved!

The Japanese Army overrode the carefully considered objections of the Imperial Japanese Navy, and the decision was made for war, in ignorance of the true industrial potential of the United States of America.

It seems incredible, in view of unprovoked Japanese aggressions in the past (treachery to us—although not to them), that their surprise attack on Pearl Harbour should have been so successful. But despite the paralytic strategical situation which this success evoked, it welded disparate American public opinion into solidarity of purpose.

As early as 1938 some rather vague and tentative talks had been held between the Americans, Dutch and British with regard to the common defence of the southeastern Asiatic area. These came to nothing concrete and even talks with the Dutch, in 1941, failed to produce a common naval signal book. The situation then was that, in the face of Japanese assault on all three Allies, there existed the will to cooperate, but scarcely any means of doing so. As a result, our naval forces were destroyed piecemeal by a highly efficient and well coordinated Japanese Imperial Navy with air support of the very best quality. After the disaster to *Prince of Wales* and *Repulse,* Allied naval activities degenerated into what is generally known as the 'Java Sea Campaign'. It is sufficient to say here that, with the sinking of the Dutch cruisers *Java* and *De Reuter, U.S.S. Houston, H.M.A.S. Perth* and the famous *Exeter* at the end of February 1942, the Japanese gained complete mastery at sea and were shortly to do so on land, by capturing Java and the remainder of Sumatra.

Thus in three months and against 15,000 Japanese killed or wounded, the British Commonwealth lost 166,500 men on land, at sea and in the air—of which well over 130,000 were prisoners of war. This colossal defeat, surely one of the worst in all history, not only created a massive strategical problem for the Allies, but rang down the curtain on Western predominance, throughout all Asiatic lands.

Allied submarines played very little part in this drama, mainly through absence. Of the two British submarines sent from the Mediterranean, Bill King in a somewhat defective *Trusty* arrived at

Singapore on 31st January, or fifteen days before the fall and suffered bomb damage. *Truant,* with which the reader will be familiar, still commanded by Hugh Haggard, was later sent direct to Batavia where she came under the orders of Admiral Helfrich, Royal Netherlands Navy.

One result of the Anglo-Dutch talks in 1941 was that the Dutch agreed to make some of their submarines available for the defence of Singapore—an obvious move which I believe the Americans should have followed. Consequently the Netherland's submarines *0.16* and *K.XVII* were placed under the command of Admiral Sir Geofrey Layton on the 1st December, *K.XI, K.XII* and *K.XIII* coming under command a week later—which was a week too late—and being followed by *0.19* and *0.20* four days after that.

The remaining eight Dutch submarines were either too old for operations or were refitting. It will be noted that none of these submarines were in intercepting positions when the Japanese initially landed at Singora, Patani and Kota Baru before dawn on 8th December. On the night of 12th December, Commander A.J. Bussemaker, in *0.16,* torpedoed and damaged four Japanese transports off Patani, near Singora. That was exactly five days too late and three dozen submarines too few!

Unfortunately the Japanese had, with great thoroughness, laid a minefield near Pulo Tioman, off the east coast of Johore, only two days beforehand. When coming south, *0.16* ran into this minefield and was lost with all hands except one, who managed to reach shore after nearly 36 hours in the water. It is thought that *K.XVII,* commanded by Lieutenant-Commander Besançon, was also lost on this minefield.

Lieutenant-Commander P.G.J. Snippe was detected and depth-charged by Japanese destroyers in the Gulf of Siam on the 19th December. After dark *0.20* surfaced in an effort to get away at her full speed of 20 knots*. But the Japanese were still there and a gun battle ensued, *0.20* being unable to dive owing to depth-charge damage. Whilst his gun's crew continued to engage the enemy, Snippe gave the order to abandon ship. Thus was lost the third Dutch submarine in a matter of twelve days or less. *K.XIII* under Lieutenant-Commander H.C.J. Coumou had better luck: she sank a 2,000-ton ship at anchor off Kota Baru and next day sank a 3,500-ton tanker. In January, Lieutenant-Commander H.F. Back Kolling in *0.19* sank a 4,000-ton vessel in the Gulf of Siam.

The loss of two Dutch submarines by mining was most

* American and Dutch submarines had that vital 4 knots extra speed.

unfortunate and does not reflect any great credit on the British staff who could, in my view, have routed submarines going to and from patrol into deeper waters further to the eastward. It also seems a pity that the few submarines available, in an area which should have had ample air reconnaissance, were not concentrated off Singora before 7th December. Although to the reader this may seem like being wise after the event, it was generally held in the China Fleet before the war that the most likely point of Japanese attack against the Malay Peninsula would be Singora. If one ignored the neutrality of Siam, as the Japanese could have been expected to do, this port and railhead was the obvious spot—a fact of which the Army were aware.

I have mentioned these gallant, but tragic and not too rewarding, activities of Netherlands' submarines in the very early days; because the results, slight as they were, point to the enormous damage that could have been done had the British been able to dispose the 38 submarines requested in 1937.

The Dutch submarines were now withdrawn to defend Java, in which they were assisted by *Trusty* and *Truant*. Before the fall of that rich island to the Japanese, three Dutch submarines under repair had to be destroyed and one was wrecked by air attack; the remainder falling back with *Trusty* and *Truant* to Colombo.

Of the 29 American submarines in the United States Asiatic Fleet, some were old and unfit for operations. They also suffered from a somewhat alarming disadvantage in that defective or badly designed pistols in their torpedoes' firing mechanism caused many a failure. If added to that is the previously mentioned 'early stage amorphism' which willy-nilly must have affected all American submarine commanding officers—a situation not improved by torpedo failures —one can perhaps understand the comparative ineffectiveness of United States submarines in early campaigns against the Japanese.

In the middle of 1941, the Americans had declined a suggestion that their Asiatic Fleet should operate under the command of the Commander-in-Chief British Eastern Fleet; because they were afraid their own Commander-in-Chief might lose identity and their ships be employed on objects of little strategical importance to the U.S.A. In the light of actual events, their decision seems to have been justified, although not perhaps their reasoning. In the event, American naval forces concentrated upon defending the Philippines whilst co-operating (as did the *Houston*, other American cruisers, destroyers and an aircraft-carrier) with the Dutch and British as far as possible. The Americans do not seem to have appreciated sufficiently rapidly that, after Pearl Harbour, the Philippines had little chance of survival against a determined Japanese assault; for the latter now had absolute command of the sea and most of the air. America's 29 submarines, not all of which were operational, sank only three Japanese ships bent on this invasion. They then withdrew from Cavite in Luzon to Surabaya where it was found impossible to cope with their many defects. The Americans then decided to base these submarines on Exmouth Gulf and Fremantle in Western Australia.

It is not within the compass of this book to elaborate upon the lack of cohesion between Allies nor upon the hopeless efforts of General Sir Archibald Wavell to establish unification of command and communications; his task had been rendered impossible by the lack of effective planning, at least a year beforehand.

It is now necessary to follow the British and Dutch submarines to Colombo and see how things shaped from there during the next two years. By March 1941, the Dutch had lost the majority of their valuable colonies; the Americans were hard put to defend the Pacific Islands and Northern Australia, both of which had now become strategically essential to them. The British were back at their beginnings, their main defence being *distance* at sea, and the protection of India and Ceylon on land. For part of this last purpose, Admiral Sir Geofrey Layton who had left Singapore before its fall, was appointed Commander-in-Chief, Ceylon. On the 26th March, Admiral Sir James Somerville hoisted his flag as Commander-in-Chief Eastern Fleet in the famous battleship *Warspite* at Trincomalee.

As Japanese surface forces were expected to attack Ceylon, using aircraft and perhaps landing troops, a submarine reconnaissance in the Malacca Strait became our main requirement and *Truant* was already there, sinking two ships on the 1st April. But the Japanese force did not come through the Malacca Strait; instead it took a circuitous route south of Java and made the middle of the Indian Ocean before attacking Colombo and Trincomalee, in the first week of that month. Happily Admiral Somerville had been forewarned by intelligence sources and was at sea, attempting to intercept the Japanese, which—perhaps fortunately—he was unable to do. Nevertheless an air attack from Japanese carriers sank the 10,000-ton 8" gun cruisers *Dorsetshire* and *Cornwall,* south of Ceylon on the 5th April and the aircraft-carrier *Hermes* on the 9th, east of that island.

There immediately ensued what might be called a paper and signal battle for submarines between the C-in-C Ceylon and the C-in-C Mediterranean Fleet, using the Admiralty as an adjudicatory link.

The latter won: to begin with, only the Dutch submarines *0.21, 0.23* and *0.24* were sent east; but most Dutch submarines were now suffering from a crop of defects and these did not get into their stride for some time.

The general situation in the Indian Ocean was such that Durban and Kilindini (Kenya) were now being used as main bases for battleships and as repair ports for submarines. Consequently there was a great deal of shuffling to and fro across the Indian Ocean, not only of submarines but of depot-ships: in this, the Dutch depot-ship *Colombia* was sunk in February 1943 whilst on passage from East London to Port Elizabeth, for docking.

Despite this, by April 1943 we had, in Ceylon, the fine depot-ship *Adamant* with the small passenger ship *Wuchang* and the Dutch *Plancius* as accommodation vessels; but so far, only three submarines were available. It was not unti October 1943 that the much delayed build-up even commenced. In the long meanwhile, the United States Navy had held the Japanese at the Battle of the Coral Sea (7th-9th May 1942) and had beaten superior forces of the Imperial Japanese Navy later in the same month at Midway Island—probably as important a victory of West over East as the Battle of Salamis, where, in 480 B.C., the Athenians and their Greek allies annihilated the Persian Fleet of Xerxes the Great. So what the Americans achieved by feats of arms, the British achieved more gradually by the effects of American action, in that the Japanese were no longer prepared to foray in strength across the vast expanse of the Indian Ocean.

But it was not until January 1944 that the *Adamant,* now under the command of Captain H.M.C. Ionides (known as 'Tin Sides') had collected a 4th Flotilla of six 'T' class and one 'S' class; to be reinforced by one of the former and four of the latter during February. The depot-ship *Maidstone* arrived at Trincomalee early in March, the 'S' class submarines being transferred to her as a new 8th Flotilla commanded by Captain L.M. Shadwell.

When I myself was at Northways in September 1943, the decision was taken that all new 'T' and 'S' class submarines would be sent to the Far East; for which they were adapted by improved air conditioning, refrigeration capacity and extra tanks for lubricating oil and fresh water. The most important alteration was the conversion of certain main ballast tanks to carry diesel fuel. This raised the range of the 'S' class to 6,500 miles and of the 'T' class to 11,000 miles, on paper. It meant carrying fuel externally (i.e.—outside the pressure hull but inside the the lightly constructed outer sheath which contains the main ballast tanks), which is a bad practice when liable to be depth-charged or attacked from the air, the reason being that an easily made oil leak will leave a surface slick, thus betraying not only the submarine, but her course and speed. Therefore it became usual, shortly before reaching the patrol area, to discharge the residue of external fuel and thoroughly to wash out the tanks, which were then used for ordinary salt water main ballast. Nevertheless the radius of action of British submarines was ample for their requirements.

British operational command in the Far East extended to the Bay of Bengal and down the Malacca Straight, almost to Singapore, and included the north-western coast of Sumatra to the equator*. American operational command embraced the whole East Indies area inside the Island Barrier. Outside, it covered a large section of ocean running from Sumatra right down the West Australian coast. In the British area, we were unlikely to find targets in deep water and became confined to operations in the extreme eastern part of the Bay of Bengal and Indian Ocean, our areas including the Andaman Islands, the Mergui Archipelago off the west coast of Siam, the Nicobar Islands, north-west Sumatra and the entire Malacca Strait. In this last, there was a chance of intercepting vessels and U-boats using Penang and, more important, tankers taking oil southwards from the refineries at Medan and Belawan in northeastern Sumatra. But, for the most part our targets were to be light craft, often extremely small, which the Japanese were using in ever increasing numbers for transporting supplies of rice, oil, rubber and even arms and ammunition. The enemy's reasons were twofold: firstly, that American submarines in the distant waters of the south-western Pacific had sunk so many of their merchant ships; secondly, only small vessels could use the shallows and so evade British and Dutch submarines which were the only allied warships capable of attacking them.

Periscope depth for the average American submarine was 60 feet and they usually preferred to avoid operations in less than 180 feet of water, whereas British submarines, with shorter periscopes, were capable of operating in only ten fathoms, or 60 feet. That does not mean to say that we enjoyed these restrictive shallows, in which one could so easily become trapped against an unfriendly shore. Also torpedoes, when fired, dive downwards before automatically recovering themselves and adjusting to the set depth: therefore one was likely to fire them into the mud.

As we have seen, from mention of the minefield so rapidly laid by

*See map page 57

the Japanese off Pulo Tioman, the enemy were capable of effective mining. As shallow water readily lends itself to this, we faced the reverse of the situation pertaining in the Mediterranean. In the latter, British submarines passed through many minefields of whose existence they were completely unaware. In the Far East, we sometimes credited the Japanese with minefields they had not laid. It is difficult to know just how much mining they carried out, because they deliberately destroyed as many records as possible when defeat and surrender became inevitable. For the same reason, it is impossible to establish beyond doubt the true record of enemy ships sunk, particularly as our targets were usually so small.

We operated then, mainly against small targets in the shoals, frequently using the gun, our efforts being effectively supplementary to American submarines' deep water activities. A great many patrols were carried out in the Far East; but when the reader considers that there are 120 volumes of British submarine patrol reports which cover a total of about 2,000 patrols throughout the war, he will readily understand that detail must be eschewed. Therefore in the remainder of this chapter I propose to mention only a few patrols which might be termed representative and some of special interest.

Before going into details it should be mentioned that, by early 1944, Sir James Somerville's fleet had also been painfully built up to a strength of four capital ships which included the aircraft-carrier *Illustrious*, with cruisers, destroyers and the submarines. Thus was composed the British Far Eastern Fleet, based mainly at Trincomalee with reasonably adequate repair facilities. A little later Sir James Somerville was relieved by Admiral Sir Arthur John Power as C-in-C British Far Eastern Fleet. This fleet should not be confused with the British Pacific Fleet which later operated under American command.

During 1943, our patrols in the areas previously described were carried out mainly by the Dutch submarines *0.21*, under Lieutenant-Commander J.F. van Dulm; *0.23*, Lieutenant-Commander A.M. Valkenburg and particularly *0.24* under Lieutenant-Commander W.J. de Vries. Their patrols included many special operations, these being a most important part of all Allied submarine activities amongst the thousands of islands which stretch between the Coral Sea and the Bay of Bengal, and in the Malayan Peninsula.

I will start with 'Jolly Jack' Hopkins who arrived at Northways one day in the autumn of 1943, full of affability and charm, went in to see the Admiral and came out announcing that he was to command *Thorough*. As this submarine, then building at Vickers Barrow, had been promised to me, my feelings can be imagined! But Jack, being a ball of fire, was an asset in any flotilla and a raconteur of indescribable imagination. He did not have a great deal of opportunity at sea and was, in this way, representative of many who suffered from target dearth. On his first patrol in the Far East, he was somewhat inaccurately depth-charged by an anti-submarine trawler off Port Blair. On the second, *Thorough* carried out brief reconnaissance and landed agents; but unfortunately had only a glimpse of a U-boat in bad visibility, without time to attack. However, a coaster was sunk by gunfire. On her third patrol, *Thorough* laid mines off the Sumatran coast. ('T' class submarines could lay a dozen mines from the six internal tubes and then reload with torpedoes). Then, junks and coasters were destroyed by gunfire; prisoners being brought back to Ceylon. On the fourth patrol, *Thorough* again laid mines near Penang, sank some more junks and acted as air sea rescue vessel.

These operations seem dull and unrewarding: nevertheless they all required a considerable amount of skill. For instance, the sinking of a coaster, close inshore where the water is too shallow for diving and in the face of complete enemy air control, requires fine judgement. Not only could a Japanese aircraft attack, but could also summon up nearby A/S vessels whose keels might be scraping the tops of the submarine's periscope standards during the subsequent depth-charging. An indication of the skill and judgment used is portrayed by the fact that the British lost only one, perhaps two, submarines to Japanese depth-charge attack during over 250 patrols in all Far Eastern and Pacific areas. Of these, *Thorough's* experiences are reasonably representative.

There were highlights however, one of them being Mervyn Wingfield's patrol in *Taurus* during November 1943. Wingfield had recently had his periscopes repaired; for these had been damaged on his last patrol in the distant Aegean. This time *Taurus* was off Penang. Captain S/M.4 radioed an intelligence report indicating that a U-boat might be approaching the Penang base. Wingfield dived *Taurus* well before dawn in a likely position, which proved correct. A large U-boat, on the surface, was sighted through the periscope on the port quarter of *Taurus*, steering a parallel course. Even though rain squalls often blotted out his target, Wingfield managed to attain a broad firing track, and got his salvo off, at long range. An explosion was heard which gave a running range of about 6,000 yards—this was correct, as *Taurus* had fired from the enemy's quarter. Thus was lost the enormous Japanese U-boat *I.34* of 2,200 tons. Mervyn Wing-field, in *Taurus,* had a most distinguished career in Far Easter waters, finding more targets than most and causing great destruction.

Now we come to another tiger in that area, and another called 'Ben'. Lieutenant-Commander L.W.A. Bennington, whom we have already seen with *Porpoise* in the Mediterranean, now had the delightfully named submarine *Tally Ho.* In February 1944, again at night and near Penang, Bennington carried out a snap surface attack on a U-boat, diving immediately because a second U-boat had been reported. *Tally Ho's* torpedoes sank the German *U.I.T.23,* the ex-Italian *Giulani* of 1,100 tons. As was so often the case in the Malacca Strait, the second 'enemy' turned out to be a junk. Next, this dead-eyed Dick carried out a submerged attack on a very small Japanese ship of only 500 tons, and scored a torpedo hit from a range of 1,300 yards, sinking his quarry.

Now was to take place an amazing night encounter with a Japanese torpedo boat which resulted in another extraordinary submarine escape. In poor visibility, the two vessels suddenly met, too close for *Tally Ho* to dive and too close for the enemy to ram, although she tried. On the torpedo boat's second attempt, the two vessels met practically head on and passed each other on opposite courses in direct physical contact; for the torpedo boat's propeller gouged through the light plating of *Tally Ho's* port main ballast tanks, each successive propeller blade slashing slices along the submarine's side. *Tally Ho,* by diving, escaped her enemy which must also have been damaged. As there were no serious leaks through the pressure hull, Bennington was left in the position that he could manage submerged; but had only his starboard main ballast tanks upon which to surface. As their use might roll the submarine over, the starboard tanks were of little service. The only means of proceeding on the surface was to empty all internal tanks and generally lighten the ship as much as possible, thereby gaining the positive buoyancy of a water-sodden log. Bennington's position was most unenviable; for *Tally Ho* had become crippled in restricted enemy waters over which the Japanese had complete control of the air. But by patience, skill and determination Bennington and his crew managed to creep sluggishly back to Ceylon, 1,200 miles away.

After repairs at Colombo, *Tally Ho* was back in the fray within ten weeks, next having two of those dullish patrols more normally associated with the area. But Bennington went on to gun and sink a 300-ton ship, 13 junks and the Japanese submarine chaser *No.2,* in a fierce gun action where unfortunately his gunnery officer was mortally wounded. In *Tally Ho's* case, it seemed that the fox came to the hounds for, in her last few days before returning to the United Kingdom, Bennington scored no less than three torpedo hits on the wretched Japanese minelayer *No.4* of only 600 tons. Thus *Tally Ho* passes out of the picture on her way home, carrying a captain of tremendous record; both in the Mediterranean and Far East.

Storm, one of the 8th Flotilla's submarines, was commanded by Teddy Young who had a reputation for creating havoc with his gun. Space precludes mention of more than one of *Storm's* patrols; but this one gives the reader some idea of what our submarines could achieve, provided the targets were found. By October 1944, the 8th Flotilla and *Maidstone* had moved down to Fremantle in Western Australia whence the submarines operated inside the Island Barrier, under American operational command. Nickel ore, a commodity of immeasurable value to the Japanese, was exported from Pomelaa in South Celebes and, there being no large ships, the enemy were using schooners or any bottoms available. These vessels carried about 30 tons, a valuable amount of nickel ore. Having arrived in the area from Fremantle by way of the Ombai Strait—west of Timor—*Storm* had a somewhat dull patrol and, when due to return, Teddy Young asked permission to remain another three days in the area. This was granted: on the 29th October and 1st November, four nickel traders were sunk, the crews being placed on board other native craft, some of which, such as a gaff-rigged schooner, were beautiful and a pity to destroy. The 2nd November proved a busy day; for a total of seven nickel ore ships were sunk. *Storm* took the crews prisoner and at one time had 38 on board. At this point, Teddy Young had to co-opt them to help jettison the cargo of yet another schooner, in order that she could be used as a rescue ship. In this way, about 300 tons of nickel ore were sent to the bottom, and the enemy deprived of 11 small vessels. Such were the distances, that *Storm* covered over 6,200 miles in this 34-day period.

In September 1944, Rear-Admiral Barry became ill and was relieved by Rear-Admiral G.E. Creasy. When it was realised that the build-up of British submarines in the Far East would now out-run the requirement in our own areas, the Commander-in-Chief of the United States Navy, Admiral King, was informed that we wanted to operate some of them from Fremantle and wished to know how they could best be employed. Admiral King welcomed the proposal and a scheme was worked out whereby the 8th Flotilla would be based at Fremantle, moving up to Subic Bay when the Philippines were recaptured, and being succeeded at Fremantle by the 4th Flotilla. In the meanwhile a new Second Flotilla was being formed at Trincomalee, based on *H.M.S. Wolfe,* a large liner converted to submarine depot-ship. The British were now rapidly approaching the figure of 40 operational submarines in the Far East, twice the number we had ever had in the Mediterranean, up to the height of the struggle—i.e. before the battle of El Alamein.

The paucity of torpedo targets had caused our submarines to turn themselves into submersible gunboats. In what would have been (had they known it) a constructors' nightmare from the topweight viewpoint, we 'won' as much hardware as possible from the Army or any other likely source, until our bridges bristled with machine-guns, in additon to the 4" and Oerlikon normally carried. Half-inch armour plate was added wherever possible until we could, if need be, take on a Japanese submarine chaser with good hope of success—as Bennington had proved. Nevertheless such action was normally avoided because the chance of an enemy shell puncturing the pressure-hull could so easily produce a case of valour before discretion leading to disaster. One ambition, never fulfilled to my knowledge, was to 'nick' a 40mm. Bofors gun to replace the 20mm. Oerlikon. In dealing with all these small craft, ammunition became a problem which some resolved by boarding, then sinking their quarry with demolition charges. The Japanese retaliated by laying traps, making such a procedure dangerous. They also armed their small, and frequently modern, coasters with batteries of heavy automatic guns (similar to Bofors) which could make things uncomfortable at even 5,000 yards.

After my own arrival in *Thule,* about October 1944, I developed a policy, which was to ram wooden vessels, thus sparing their crews who could be picked up. That left the heavily armed coasters. These could be engaged by a very short range surprise attack from submerged (emulating the pre-war submarine gunnery tactics previously described): or they could be attacked from long range at which their multiple 'fall of shot' would be scattered, whilst the more accurate British 4" gun could pick them off with high explosive shell.

Unfortunately *Thule* had little opportunity of putting these theories into practice; because, of our six patrols, four were special operations during which we were allowed to attack nothing. On the first of our offensive patrols, *Thule* carried out a submerged attack on a Japanese U-boat entering Penang by daylight. Our estimation of enemy course and speed were accurate for I saw one of the three torpedoes fired explode in line with the enemy's conning-tower; but was not happy with the noise of the explosion. I later learnt that, in this way, I had suffered the mortifying experience of seeing a torpedo (of which the warhead was actuated on an electro-magnetic principle) explode prematurely. A local intelligence report later suggested that this U-boat had been damaged, although there was no evidence of her sinking.

Thule then had a furious time during which she acted as beacon for a Fleet Air Arm strike on Sumatran oil, destroyed two lighters by gunfire, rammed 13 large junks and was depth-charged with about 70 Chinese on board! Twenty prisoners who wanted to go to 'India', as they called it, were taken to Trincomalee, the remainder being disembarked into sampans and sent ashore.

Commander Bill King, who had conducted his first Far Eastern war patrols in *Trusty* at the time of our early disasters (on one occasion spending 56 days at sea in appalling conditions), was now back on the station in *Telemachus*. In October 1944, he carried out a large special operation on the east coast of Johore not far from Mersing, landing a party and a large quantity of stores. A combination of engine defects and enemy activity prevented further contact with the shore. Thus some members of operation 'Carpenter' had to be left unsatisfactorily stranded. Further, it was thought the operation might be compromised.

But in February 1945, *Thule* made contact at a beach which was largely cut off from the mainland by swamps, and only twenty miles from Singapore Naval Base. Here we brought many vital supplies to the newly-named Carpenter-Mint operation, which was in contact with guerrillas controlling the area. Our men ashore also had powerful radio sets through which they sent information of great value to the projected British invasion of Malaya.

It proved one of the most important British special operations and, in May, *Thule* was again sent, this time with a minor invasion force. A platoon of Royal Marines were to take control of the beach, whilst no less than four tons of arms, ammunition, radio equipment and victuals were to be landed. For the purpose we had fourteen rubber landing craft with several spare outboard engines in case of defects previously experienced. *Thule* was brought close inshore to expedite the replenishment; thus lying stopped, 1,000 yards from the coast and about five miles from divable water. It made a very odd feeling to be waiting there; armed to the teeth, like an old-fashioned gunboat, whilst the Royal Marines took complete charge of an enemy beach.

Everything went smoothly and we were able to bring out men

who had long been in the jungle, some of whom were thought dead, including a few American airmen shot down over Singapore. Many were sick or wounded but all these were watched over by Chief Petty Officer Nicholson, D.S.M., my excellent coxwain. Running southwards down the Carimata Strait, we passed into the Indian Ocean through the Sunda Strait by the reverse of our inward route, this time proceeding to Fremantle where we arrived on 4th June.

It is pertinent here to make some general comments upon special operations which can be said to fall into four categories—

Firstly, and most popular with submariners, is the case where operators are carried as part armament of the submarine, to be used when opportunity offers, after the previous careful consideration of possibilities. This type of attack proved highly effective against the vulnerable Italian railways, one chief exponent having been the army's Captain R. Wilson, D.S.O. with his assistants.

The second category arises from a direct military requirement such as the destruction of an important bridge on an enemy army's line of communication.

Thirdly, and heavily developed against the Japanese by both British and Americans, is the Carpenter-Mint type of clandestine minor invasion in which enemy territory is held by guerrillas who are landed, supplied, reinforced and evacuated by submarine.

The foregoing may be considered as military operations in which, during the last war, the submarine commanding officer knew the objectives and could evaluate risks. They were therefore reasonably popular with submariners.

The last category, in which the submarine is the carrier for spys and saboteurs, is dangerous from the submariners' viewpoint because the commanding officer does not know (and cannot know) the final objectives, nor their likelyhood of fulfillment. It is in this type of landing that the submarine runs the greatest danger of betrayal; for those ashore, who know of her imminent arrival including time and place, are usually unaware of her utter vulnerability throughout the landing process. Also, 'cloak and dagger' operators are not Secret Service and frequently have contacts who learn too much. This is illustrated by the fact that Baron d'Astier de la Vigerie was waiting at Antibes for *Unbroken*, when it had been a condition of the submarine's use that none ashore should know.

Clandestine warfare remains a submarine capability and, in view of a modern submarine's great value, it is important to reiterate that her captain must be in complete command of the entire operation at times of danger to his vessel—as I was in control of the beach during the landing part of Carpenter—Mint II, being represented ashore by Captain Onslow, Royal Marines.

To complete *Thule's* activities: we were given an offensive patrol in July 1945. This time, we made the Java Sea, through the Lombok Strait, on the surface by night, and closed the coast; there to attack from long range a heavily armed coaster which was driven ashore and destroyed on the rocks. In a close range surprise gun attack from submerged *Thule* sank a similar coaster, which had no time to retaliate. She was laden with drums of oil. Proceeding westwards along the Javanese coast, we destroyed a third coaster which was drawn up in a slipway, damaging the latter. In a further burst of activity, *Thule* ran into a bay, there to sink a 400-ton vessel which seemed warlike, but did not open fire, perhaps at surprise to see us sweeping into this little bay of sanctuary. Here we, in our turn, were surprised by a Japanese aircraft zooming over the hills to attack with bombs which missed 50 feet astern, as we were diving into the mud. Having been missed 50 feet ahead, also when diving, after our attack on the first coaster six days beforehand, I began to feel that perhaps we were chancing our arm too far. However *Thule* was now recalled to carry out Carpenter Mint III, which never took place; for the war ended. We again passed through the Sunda Strait, at 20 knots on the surface by moonlight, being helped by a 4 knot current. Thus my last sight of the enemy in war was that of two patrol vessels prowling around Thwartaway Island which, as its name indicates, blocks a part of the Sunda. Fortunately they did not see us for, having fired 450 rounds of 4" ammunition during the past week, we were down to a few practice shell, with which the gun was loaded.

In the meanwhile, the famous Ben Bryant had assumed command of the 4th Submarine Flotilla from the depot-ship *Adamant,* now at Fremantle. The *Maidstone* and 8th Flotilla had, for some months, been operating from Subic Bay in Manila—not a very desirable base, since shore facilities were still under construction and an annoying swell often prevented more than two submarines lying alongside *Maidstone* at the same time. The 'S' boats of the 8th Flotilla sometimes carried out long patrols, as much as 35 days; and to be obliged to live in the submarine after this time at sea is an unpleasant experience, particularly in sweltering heat. Nevertheless these 'S' class submarines continually conducted patrols in the shallow inshore waters of the Seven Seas, frequently being given enemy reports by United States submarines which could not themselves operate amongst the shoals.

The brothers Joe and Kenneth Martin were then in *Solent* and *Sleuth,* being operated by Admiral Fife, U.S.N., in a team known as the 'Martin Bros.' which gained much credit. Being together produced better gunnery results; and the practice was extended to other pairs.

By this time, American submarines had almost annihilated the Japanese merchant fleet and such was the success of British submarines' activities in inshore waters that coastal traffic had virtually ceased to move, by the end of July 1945. Even Admiral Sir Bruce Fraser, whose successes with the British Pacific Fleet and particularly its aircraft-carriers (under Sir Philip Vian) are well-known, found it difficult to employ the improved midget submarines of the X.E. Class, now on the station. But ingenuity prevailed and, on 31st July, Lieutenant M.H. Shean, R.A.N.V.R., in *X.E.4,* cut both the Singapore—Saigon and the Hong Kong—Saigon submerged telegraphic cables, not far from Cape St. Jacques in French Indo China.

About the same time, *X.E.1* under the command of Lieutenant J.E. Smart, R.N.V.R., and *X.E.3* commanded by Lieutenant I.E. Fraser, R.N.R., were towed by *Spark* and *Stygian* to the Horsburgh Lighthouse whence they penetrated the Johore Strait to attack and severely damage the Japanese heavy cruiser *Takao,* which was only saved from sinking by the shallow water. Lieutenant Fraser and Leading Seaman Magennis were both awarded the Victoria Cross for this most gallant attack.

Whilst again omitting names and many deeds, I hope I have been able to convey an impression of the type of operations conducted by our submarines in Far Eastern waters. Although the total tonnage sunk amounted to only 3% of that sunk by American submarines, the results of these operations greatly exceeded anything this figure might suggest. The effect was to tighten the American's throttling blockade to a stranglehold which the Japanese could not loosen.

Although losses are always so sad, ours were few.

Lieutenant C.R. Pelly in *Stratagem,* after sinking an enemy ship of 2,000 tons by torpedo in November 1943, near One Fathom Bank—a very restricted part of the southern Malacca Strait—and being ineffectively counter-attacked was later found by a Japanese destroyers off Malacca. A severe depth-charging in shallow water ensued which caused considerable flooding and put the submarine completely out of action. Lieutenant D.C. Douglas escaped from forward, with nine men. The enemy destroyer rescued Douglas and seven others: these were subsequently split up, those left at

Singapore either dying or being executed—nauseating in the circumstances, for these men could not be accused of spying. Douglas himself and two of the men were luckier; for they were sent to Japan and survived the war, after very unpleasant experiences.

Lieutenant D.S. McN. Verschoyle-Campbell, commanding *Stonehenge,* after an eminently successful first patrol off Penang, was next sent to the north coast of Sumatra, leaving Trincomalee on 25th February 1944. Three weeks later *Stonehenge* was overdue. The incomplete Japanese records give no indication of how she was lost, so her fate remains unknown. However, to my mind, in view of the consummate skill of her commanding officer during his first patrol, it seems likely that *Stonehenge* struck a floating mine.

Early in 1945, Lieutenant-Commander H.B. Turner, a term mate of mine at Dartmouth, had taken over *Porpoise* from Hubert Marsham and, having completed one successful minelaying patrol, was on his second, when another minefield was laid off Penang. This lay was reported by radio; but nothing further was heard from *Porpoise.* This ageing minelaying submarine had been the first of her class of six; but had some essential differences, the main one being that her oil fuel was carried in external tanks, somewhat similarly to the method by which extra fuel was loaded into 'T' and 'S' class submarines. Whilst no official cause of loss has been given, there was a very strong report circulating at the time, that she had been bombed by Japanese aircraft near Penang, and had subsequently dived but leaked oil. The report continued that Japanese A/S vessels, summoned from Penang, had traced the oil slick, thus sinking the 74th and last British submarine lost in World War II.

Of these six minelayers, *Rorqual,* having left the Mediterranean and been refitted, had returned to the Far East for yet another tour of operational duty which, after six years of active war, must be a record. Fortunately that battle-worn submarine was spared.

Before finishing this chapter, I feel it fitting to close on a description of the most successful British submarine attack of all time, a feat rivalled only by Commander Joe Enright, captain of the United States submarine *Archerfish,* who obtained six torpedo hits upon the new 68,000 ton Japanese aircraft-carrier *Shinano,* thus sinking the biggest ship so far to be destroyed by a submarine.

Commander, 'Baldy', A.R. Hezlet, D.S.O., D.S.C., whom we have already seen in the Mediterranean, after an already successful Far Eastern tour in *Trenchant,* was now to achieve a signal success; furthermore a success for which I know he had planned, being out to get a Nachi class heavy cruiser.

Early in June 1945, when *Thule* was coming southwards through the Carimata Strait, we sighted *Trenchant* northbound by night. *Thule* dived and closed to an attacking position. Of course *Trenchant* was inviolate, because submarines were not allowed to attack each other in this area; but it made good practice. With *Thule's* eight forward torpedo tubes set to 'safe', and having gained the advantage of the moon, I watched *Trenchant* slide past at 500 or 600 yards distance and on an ideal firing track. Through the periscope, it was possible even to identify her officer of the watch.

There goes 'Baldy', I thought, quite unwary; lucky hound to have an offensive patrol. "I'll bet," I remarked to my first lieutenant, "he goes off and sinks a fat cruiser."

And that is exactly what 'Baldy' Hezlet did. Having been ordered north to cover the Australian landings at Brunei and finding that he could not reach the ordered position in time, Hezlet asked Commander Submarines 7th Fleet for permission to reconnoitre the Banka Strait from the northwards, appreciating that an enemy cruiser at Batavia might pass through this strait northbound for Singapore.

Admiral Fife granted permission and *Trenchant* made towards the shallow and tide-ridden waters, in which the Dutch submarine *0.19* had laid a minefield only six weeks previously. In darkness on 7th June, *Trenchant* fell in with *Stygian,* commanded by Lieutenant G.S. Clarabut, on normal patrol outside the Dutch minefield. In true Nelsonic style, Hezlet had *Stygian* come alongside for a conference, where it was decided that Clarabut should patrol outside the minefield whilst *Trenchant* penetrated into the more dangerous waters; both having a good chance of interception, should this Japanese cruiser come north. Accordingly, they parted and proceeded on their business.

The northern entrance to the strait lies between Banka Island and Sumatra, being only seven miles in width between ten fathom lines. At the western side of this comparative narrows lies the Klippen Shoal; immediately west of this runs a one-mile-wide north-south channel which is flanked by an enormous expanse of shallows and mud. Stretching from the Klippen Shoal to the eastwards, *0.19's* minefield blocked the main entrance to the Banka Strait except for a 1½-mile gap at the eastern side, between the last mine and the shallows off Banka Island. The entire area is flat, muddy, foetid and uninspiring; but visibility remained good throughout the action.

About noon on 7th June, *Trenchant* dived between the minefield and Banka Island to patrol in the narrows' centre, finding all quiet;

except for an unsuspecting guard vessel to the south-east. *Stygian* patrolled five miles north of Klippen Shoal, along the 10-fathom line. So the day passed: with two British submarines in ambush, rather more than halfway between Batavia and Singapore.

In the dark early hours, when both submarines were on the surface, they received an enemy report from the American submarine *Blueback* which told them that a heavy cruiser and a destroyer had left Batavia northbound. This report must have been delayed in transit; because *Trenchant* sighted a Kamikaze class destroyer very shortly after its receipt.

Expecting the cruiser to be following, Hezlet remained on the surface, keeping bows-on to his enemy which passed nearby. When all seemed well, the destroyer sighted *Trenchant*, made a violent alteration of course towards and opened fire. The two vessels were so close that each was inside the turning circle of the other. *Trenchant* went ahead at full speed and fired one of her stern tubes at the enemy; but the range was too short for the torpedo to recover from its initial dive and pick up its depth, thus it ran under the target. Still expecting the cruiser, Hezlet doggedly remained on the surface and skilfully slipped into the night. After the destroyer had disappeared to the southwards, *Trenchant* radioed news of the incident to *Stygian*. Clarabut steered southwards to give assistance; but hearing no more, resumed his patrol position.

Both submarines dived as usual at dawn. About ten o'clock in the forenoon, *Trenchant* sighted the same, or a similar, destroyer coming up from the south and going between the Klippen Shoal and the Sumatran shallows. A little later *Stygian* sighted this destroyer which was searching for a submarine, perhaps aided by an aircraft, also seen. Sighting no cruiser, Clarabut decided to get rid of the destroyer and attacked her. But the latter spotted the discharge or the torpedo tracks, avoided the torpedoes, and depth-charged *Stygian*. The submarine suffered some damage; but, as a result of holding the destroyer's attention, Clarabut had given *Trenchant* a free hand,

Hezlet in the meanwhile, deciding that any enemy cruiser would also use the narrow channel west of the Klippen Shoal, closed in towards the latter. Shortly before noon a heavy cruiser was sighted about six miles to the southward, on the expected course. Incredibly, this target was not zig-zagging nor did she have any escort, either surface or air. The cruiser, whose speed was only 15 knots, did exactly as Hezlet had anticipated, even to making a navigational change of course around the shoal at the proper time.

From about 3,000 yards, Commander Hezlet carried out a truly expert attack, firing eight torpedoes spaced along the cruiser's side with a little overlap to allow for errors. At optimum efficiency, five torpedoes could be expected to hit . . . and five did!

Thus ended the war career of Japan's most famous cruiser, the 13,000-ton *Ashigara;* although the drama had yet to run out. For *Trenchant* was now turned, in order to bring her stern tubes to bear, and fired two torpedoes from them; but these missed because the *Ashigara* altered course towards the Klippen Shoal in an effort to beach herself. During her turn, *Trenchant* was using a lot of periscope and the crew were allowed to look at their stricken enemy. Despite colossal damage, the Japanese cruiser maintained its morale and discipline. She still steamed at a very slow speed and her secondary armament opened fire on *Trenchant's* periscope. But she could not last and, waterlogged and ablaze, she rolled over and sank about half an hour after being hit. On board her were a great many troops, being transported north to reinforce Singapore, about 5,000 by some estimates.

The Kamikaze class detroyer had now returned to the scene where she dropped some perfunctory depth-charges, zig-zagging madly. Whilst *Trenchant* crept away to the eastwards, the previously mentioned guard vessel picked up some survivors; but the loss of life must have been heavy indeed.

For this early conceived and brilliantly executed attack, 'Baldy' Hezlet received the Distinguished Service Order and was further decorated by Admiral Fife with the United States Legion of Merit, degree of Commander.

On this summit of British submarine achievement, and with my own inadequate tribute to whose who died, I end the story.

It can truthfully be said that never in the long history of war has any armed force been subjected to such destruction, year after year, and yet survived to inflict upon its enemies losses out of all proportion to the size of this small band of British submariners and their friends.

Brief Summary

It is possible rapidly to dispose of submarine effort from the Russians, Japanese and Italians; these three navies having commenced hostilities with a very high proportion of submarines. It seems odd therefore that they achieved so little.

As regards the Russians, their submarines, in common with the remainder of their navy, were split between the Arctic, the Baltic, the Black Sea and the Pacific coast of Siberia. We have already seen that both their methods and equipment were dated, a situation not improved by a command divided between the captain and a commissar. All Russian naval activity fell largely under control of the Soviet Army, to which it was ancillary. One can say that, in the Second World War, Soviet submarine achievement was negligible. The Russians have however learnt their lessons well and now truly understand the value of sea power which they are exploiting to the full. The Russians are a brave people of whose great technical achievements we are well aware: it would therefore be folly to underestimate the enormous power of the four hundred or so submarines they now possess.

In view of the marked efficiency displayed by Japanese naval and air forces, it is difficult to explain their failure in the submarine world. Many Japanese submarines were used on supply runs, reinforcing the vast numbers of islands which they conquered, this role again being ancillary to army requirements. They also devoted much attention to midget submarines, carried by large parent vessels; but most of these efforts failed. Japanese submarine losses were heavy: however it seems improbable that this would have affected their fighting spirit, which is well known. Their soldiers, even when isolated, displayed amazing courage; yet I think there must be a psychological explanation for their underwater failures. As mentioned early in the book, a submarine commanding officer is not only alone; but long alone with great responsibility. In a squadron of aircraft or in a flotilla of destroyers, there are others who encourage and inspire. It may be that a combination of heavy responsibility and the necessity for individual initiative somehow inhibited Japanese submarine captains in their decisions. But whatever the cause, Japanese submarine results were not compatible with the effort expended.

The Italians were not too successful either; although they operated well in the Atlantic when under German overall command. Perhaps the Italians tended to overrate, in the Mediterranean, dangers of air detection, arising from too intimate a knowledge of the conditions. They were inclined to remain deep, relying on hydrophones to detect approaching vessels. In those days, this was not the best way of finding targets.

German U-boat activities have been mentioned previously; but it should be added that they over-expanded. In the later stages of the war, U-boats went on patrol with comparatively untrained officers and men: frequently mechanical teething troubles had not been ironed out. Under the Nazi system, U-boat captains were expected to obey orders implicitly, no matter what the shortcomings of men and material. They knew also that their families would be maltreated should they object. Such influences resulted in a deterioration of morale which, combined with Hitler's scuttling notions, led to many a U-boat too easily blowing herself to the surface and abandoning ship. This is a reflection on the system, rather than the men, and also reflects the grave damage done to German shipyards as soon as Allied bombing became accurate.

After the early failures, American submarines quickly got into their stride and, from the Allied viewpoint, sank much more than all others combined. Of 8½ million tons of Japanese shipping sunk, United States submarines accounted for nearly 5 million, or about twice the score of American naval and military aircraft. In this, they were aided in the earlier days by Japanese delay in instituting convoy systems; for our Far Eastern enemy underestimated the value of his merchant shipping in relation to the enormously extended lines of sea communications which came about through his own conquests. American submarines also sank some 200 Japanese warships, nearly one-third of the entire Imperial Japanese Navy. Some American submarine attacks, particularly against destroyers, were of unparalled high audacity, resulting in the staggering total of 42 such craft being sunk. In addition they claimed a total of 25 U-boats, including two German ones.

From a grand total of 288 submarines, the Americans lost 52, 41 of these in the Pacific and (to them) south-west Pacific areas. The greater size of American submarines increased vulnerability when actually under submerged attack; but, on the other hand, superior surface speed proved an asset, not only in attack but in escape.

When the achievements of British submarines and Allied submarines operating under British control are related to those of the Americans, the result of some two million tons may seem disappointing. This is not really so because, although we were at war for two years longer, our numbers of operational submarines were at all times below half those of the Americans and, on most occasions, considerably less than that. For instance, at their peak, the Americans had more than 160 submarines operating in the Pacific Ocean. If, in this vast area, targets were more thinly spread; so also were their escorts and defending aircraft.

There is no doubt that the Germans faced the most efficient anti-submarine forces; although these were usually extenuated. In the Mediterranean, the combination of German and Italian anti-submarine effort proved equally formidable; yet it was here that our submarines played a vital part at the fateful time.

If all submarine operations, on both sides, are considered over the two world wars, it is an inescapable conclusion that the Anglo-Saxon races predominate in this form of warfare; even if Scottish names are most prominent in the British lists! Because of their low running costs, nuclear submarines are economical; at the same time being the most effective weapon-carriers on earth. It would therefore seem logical that British Islanders, including Little Englanders, should pay more attention to them.

Epilogue

The most fitting tribute we can pay to those who died in two world wars for Western freedom is that we should remember not only their sacrifice but the causes of it. I sincerely hope that the reader will now have a mental picture of the submariners' struggle which is of course only a small part of the whole.

Violence has always been a facet of human nature and the present signs are that it will continue to be so; for, since the demise of the British Empire and Commonwealth, there has been more widespread conflict, in the absence of major declared warfare, than since the European dark age which followed the fall of Rome.

Apart from the age old failings of vanity, greed, fear and ambition; we suffer today from the mass propagation of political dogmas which inculcate a general malaise, particularly noticeable in the young. Demagogy is universal, a situation exacerbated by the colossal vanity of some politicians and others who set themselves above God and nature, denying the First whilst attempting to reduce human passions to a formula and mankind to a computerised antheap. The media of mass propagation are so influential that, when fed with misrepresentations and half-truths, they become overwhelmingly convincing. As this practice is universal; it is not surprising that the peoples of all the world are continually misled.

Today Great Britain is over-populated in that she can feed only about half the 60,000,000 people who live in these islands, a situation which is now bound to worsen every year. None will suggest that Britain will wage war on that account; but there is a much more dangerous population explosion in China, a country which is rapidly improving her nuclear weapons and has announced that she is prepared to fight the world. The neo-Marxist sophisms of Chinese leaders readily lend themselves to bloodshed for which even little children are being indoctrinated.

Waves of invasions spreading from the East have often sprung from the border areas of China, as the Russians know only too well. The Soviet Union, allowing for the ruggedness of its Siberian territories, is considerably under-populated and does not produce from its land even one half of the agricultural potential. In these circumstances, it is understandable that the Kremlin fears and expects invasion when China is ready to act. A head-on collision between the two powers in Siberia could well result in Russian defeat; for they would be fighting at odds of one to three.

From long study of history, war and revolution, my own belief is that, in order to thwart such an invasion, the Russians seek to encircle China by way of the Indian Ocean. Success in this could divert Chinese ambitions towards Australia, a country potentially capable of supporting at least 50,000,000 people and probably a great many more. It would be despicable for the British to desert Australia and New Zealand after all their sacrifices in two world wars.

Ever since the seventeenth century when Peter the Great studied shipbuilding in Holland and England, subsequently returning to Russia with large numbers of shipwrights, mechanics and engineers, Russian ambition has never ceased to look oceanwards. That their success across the seas has only been recent, was attributable mainly to the ice which blocks their ports and the confinement of some of the latter in the inland waters of the Baltic and Black Sea. Many seafaring nations, such as the British and Japanese, have added to this containment in various wars.

The much criticised Crimean campaign was one of these wars, proving brilliantly successful by keeping the Russians out of the Mediterranean for exactly one hndred years. But since the Second World War, wherever Britain has withdrawn or allowed her influence to weaken, the Soviet Union has filled the gap. Their Navy now controls the Eastern Mediterranean and only little Israel prevents (but for how long?) their strategic access to the Suez Canal and aggressive use of the Indian Ocean. This advance will at the same time give the Russians complete economic domination over Western Europe which depends upon the irreplaceable supply of North African and Middle Eastern oil. As we should know, the Kremlin is a governing body which plans every move well in advance and, being comparatively unaffected by public opinion either inside or outside the Soviet Union, can implement its carefully laid plans.

It is not my view that the Russians wish to conquer Western Europe; but rather to cripple it, thus sealing their flank and rear whilst advancing eastwards by sea across the Indian Ocean and at the same time gaining and consolidating places of strategic importance (i.e. Ceylon) as they progress. As an adjunct to their conquests, they will continue to foment rebellion in their path and in their rear; for an insurrection as far away as South America at least embarrasses the United States and adds to a general war of attrition which is designed to paralyse the West.

As the Washington Conference of 1922-23 gave Japan undisputed mastery over the Western Pacific, so has the British Government's abject and unnecessary surrender of Aden given the Russians control of the Indian Ocean, across which run some of Europe's most vital trade routes. Almost at the same time this government announced that our aircraft-carriers were to be faded out and immediately encouraged experienced personnel to quit the Fleet Air Arm earlier than necessary, in order that it could never be reconstituted. In my opinion, these acts are tantamount to treason.

It is a popular misconception, deliberately put about, that because Britain no longer has an empire she does not need a Navy. The then First Sea Lord, Admiral Sir David Luce, resigned on the issue of aircraft-carriers and the abolition of all Naval fixed-wing aircraft, whilst persuading the remaining Naval Members of the Board not to resign with him, in order that continuity of work could be maintained. Although such resignations are almost unknown, this one passed practically unnoticed, an indication of the terrifying ignorance of British public opinion in maritime affairs.

For too long have we lived under the protective shield of the United States Navy and the American Army and Air forces, a protection which has burdened the United States of America to a point beyond further endurance. A similar argument applies to all the countries of the West; but I confine myself to Britain. We are a maritime trading nation, dependent for our life-blood upon ocean trading routes, at present menaced by hundreds of Russian submarines.

War is an extension of political policy and its primary object is to subject another nation to one's will. Should the Russians at any time wish to do this to Britain, their submarines could starve and destroy us in six weeks, without firing a single shot above the surface of the oceans. Although the United States might wish to help us, I doubt that American public opinion would allow it; for Americans feel, with perfect justice, that they have paid too much for too long for too little. Also, the United States has horrifying internal problems which could easily vitiate her European obligations.

N.A.T.O. has overcome staff and communication difficulties

which were so evident in the early days of the war against the Japanese; but there are suicidal political schisms within N.A.T.O. and its entire future is in the melting pot.

In view of the Russians' tremendous loss of manpower during the Second World War, they have not, in the more recent past, been in a position to enter any major conflict. That situation is now reversed: the Russian Empire is one of the most powerful the world has ever seen, on land, at sea and in the air. Their recent invasion of Czechoslovakia, an act at least partly brought about by irresponsible Western propaganda, not only sealed a gap in their defences but made their future intentions crystal clear.

Britain is the weakest link in N.A.T.O. because of her utter dependence upon seaborne trade, whilst she has virtually no Navy to protect it. I quote the recent words of the late Admiral of the Fleet Sir Michael Le Fanu, made on relinquishing the post of First Sea Lord: 'The Navy is barely able to defend itself, let alone the country.'

That then is your Navy today; although Sir Michael Le Fanu fought hard to retain a tiny balanced force, just capable of expansion. If the Navy is not given a potent injection of money and encouragement, it stands, despite its present excellence, in grave danger of dying. There is a level below which no viable armed force can fall; and that level has long since been reached. If Britain discards her 'Sure Shield,' she will be struck down.

The best way to avoid war is to make one's country strong, as Sweden has done for 150 years. The reader may have wondered why I devoted so much attention to the influence of British submarines in the Far East. Although not a shot was fired, this influence was exerted in peacetime *for peace;* and retained its effect until the submarines were removed. A similar influence has always been exercised in the years of peace by the entire Navy and all our Armed Forces. These forces must be maintained to prevent the Western position being ferreted away from under a nuclear deterrent of decreasing effect and almost impossible use.

The burning by Caesar of his boats was not such a desperate move as it may seem. For, in those days, a new fleet could be built in a few weeks by the wielding of many axes. Today, with the increasing sophistication of modern warships and the many years required for their construction; if called upon, the Navy must fight with what it has.

The Navy should be not only balanced; but planned in conjunction with other forces, particularly those of the air. Therefore in a call for more submarines, I am not trying to advance their claim above that of other ships. For instance, although the fleet aircraft-carrier is a vulnerable ship in war, it remains of the utmost value for peace-keeping purposes and, in my view, replacements should be laid down for the two fleet-carriers we have. Other ships should be built proportionately, particularly anti-submarine vessels; and the Navy must retain its own fixed-wing aircraft, such as Phantoms, whilst every sizeable warship should be armed with improved Harriers or other vertical take-off aircraft.

Under the sea, more diesel-electric submarines are necessary, if only for training purposes. These can however be armed with torpedoes and missiles carrying either conventional or tactical nuclear warheads. For its great power and unlimited range, the nuclear submarine also remains a most economical proposition.

From *Venturer's* 1945 success against *U.864,* recent technology has developed the smaller fast submarine into a formidable U-boat killer. Therefore I believe we should build many nuclear submarines of this type, designed to work in underwater wolfpacks against enemy U-boats in the same way that the old mobile patrol tactics were planned for attack on enemy heavy warships and convoys. In suggesting that our submarines' torpedoes and ship-to-ship missiles should be capable of carrying tactical nuclear warheads, I am not giving anything away; for the Soviet Admiral Gorshkov made a similar suggestion long ago, which has probably been enforced.

Since the last war, successive British governments have failed to encourage either the shipbuilding industry or our Merchant Navy. As a result, much of our trade is now carried in foreign-built ships flying alien flags; but these equally need protection, if we are to receive their cargoes and maintain our exports.

The question of money inevitably arises where any proposals for re-armament are made. Some will remember that Stanley Baldwin of the 'sealed lips' successfully and deliberately misled the British people over the armaments and intentions of Germany; despite Mr. Winston Churchill's loud and constant warnings with regard to the true situation.

Notwithstanding my criticisms of our great leader, bedevilled as he was by the sins of his predecessors, few would now deny that without Churchill's indomitable spirit we would have lost the war. Stanley Baldwin's government saved money at the expense of armament. Since the war, Britain has squandered money at the expense of armament.

Any great island trading nation which can spend (1969-1970)

nine *thousand* million pounds on functional social security and only six hundred million pounds on its Navy is living in a state of psychedelic stupor. Without security in defence, there is no security whatsoever. If the British do not re-learn this lesson, and quickly, they will lose even those small beginnings to which they are now reduced. This country lacks, not money, but willpower.

Although no Themistocles, I know that my submariner friends, both dead and alive, would wish me to exhort Englishmen to look to their ditch, Britons to the revival of oceanic trade, merchants to their fleets and governments to their duty.

SI VIS PACEM PARA BELLUM

London 1st June 1971

APPENDIX I
WAR GAME AND MOBILE PATROL TACTICS.

When hostilities with Germany commenced, in the Far East we were taking only precautionary measures against Japan. Had Whitehall believed that Japan would make war simultaneously with Germany, the naval disposition would have been different; perhaps something like that given below. As many of the submarines in the real 4th Flotilla were lost in the war, I have used numbers for this game which starts on the afternoon of 3rd September 1939. All times are Zone minus eight, or Hong Kong time, which is 8 hours ahead of G.M.T.

NAVAL FORCES—GENERAL.
At Hong Kong. (Commodore in Charge)
5 local defence destroyers, 10 gunboats, 1 flotilla of M.T.B.s and 5 Sunderland flying boats—lent from R.A.F. Seletar, Singapore—these last having an advanced fuelling base at Pratus Island which is some 240 miles southeast of Hong Kong.

At Singapore. (C-in-C, China Fleet)
Depot-ship *Medway,* flying flag of C-in-C; local defence craft, half a squadron of Sunderlands and other reconnaissance aircraft. Straits and the approaches to harbours heavily mined.

At Penang.
2 cruisers southbound to reinforce China Fleet.

Arabian Gulf.
1 minelaying submarine eastbound at utmost despatch.

Red Sea.
The crack 1st Cruiser Squadron southbound at 30 knots. 2 fast River-class, 3 minelaying, 3 'O' class and 4 'S' class submarines southbound at utmost despatch. There would have been other reinforcements; but the point here is that we could have had 13 fresh submarines available for patrol from Singapore by 22nd September, and some before that.

OPERATIONAL AT SEA ON CHINA STATION.

140 miles nor'east of Cam Ranh Bay, French Indo-China.
Force 'Q' (Rear-Admiral in Command). 5 heavy cruisers, 2 aircraft-carriers and 8 fleet destroyers. Course N.E., speed of advance 20 knots.

Between Luzon and Formosa.
1st Division of 5 submarines—11, 12, 13, 14 and 15.
2nd Division of 5 submarines—21, 22, 23, 24 and 25.
3rd Division of 5 submarines—31, 32, 33, 34 and 35.

The above dispositions are based upon an appreciation that the Japanese will commence hostilities without declaration of war, that Hong Kong can be taken from the landwards and that although enemy troop convoys may use the Formosa Strait, their heavy naval units will not. Intelligence about Japanese activities is not good; but enough is known to believe that troop convoys are at sea. The situation is tense, but let us come to the game timetable for 3rd September 1939—Hong Kong times.

Over Formosa Strait and Bashi Channel (south of Formosa).
AIR PATROL— 3 Sunderlands of the 5 based upon Hong Kong and Pratus.

1600   Sunderland 006 reports: 'Large convoy 90 miles eastsou'east of South Cape (Formosa), course sou'west, speed 12 knots.'

1603   Sunderland 006 reports: 'Under attack from Japanese aircraft.' (No more is heard from 006).

1700   Sunderland 007 reports: 'Japanese convoy Zebra 1, previously reported by 006, positon 87 miles sou'east of South Cape, course sou'west zigzagging. Speed of advance 10 knots, entering Bashi Channel. Close escort of 1 light cruiser, 8 destroyers and small seaplane or aircraft-carrier. Was attacked by, and have shot down, Jap A/S aircraft. Land based fighters now gunning . . . .'

1710   From Military H.Q. on Hong Kong border: 'Japanese very active. No attack yet.'

1712   From Captain S/M 4. (in *Medway* at Singapore) to Submarines on Patrol: 'Anticipate heavy signal traffic. Coding staffs are therefore to deal with ciphers, under careful supervision of Engineer Officers.'

1715   C-in-C China Fleet to Admiralty: 'In view of unprovoked Japanese attacks and their obvious intentions, previously reported, request permission to commence hostilities against Japan.'

1754   Admiralty to C-in-C China Fleet: 'Your 1715, not repeat not yet. Japanese intentions have been damanded.'

1755   British ship, S.S. *Wysang:* 'S.O.S. Am under gunfire from 4 Japanese heavy cruisers. Two battleships and large aircraft-carrier just over horizon. My position 25° 20' north, 129° 20' east. Am on fire and sinking.'

NOTE- The Japanese received immediate intelligence of British Force "Q" sailing before dawn on 3rd September from Cam Ranh Bay and therefore ordered their convoy covering force to sail from Amami Oshima in the Ryukyu Islands were it had assembled for this very purpose. The two forces are now set to meet in the southwestern part of the Bashi Channel (between Luzon and Formosa) shortly before dawn on 5th September. (S.S. *Wysang* was sunk by this Japanese covering force about 100 miles southeast of Okinawa).

1800   Captain S/M 4. to Submarines on Patrol: 'First Division take up extended 15-miles interval mobile patrol on path of convoy reported by Sunderland 007, datum position Apples Apples 20° 10′ N., 121° 10′ E. at 2000. Course north, speed of advance 8 knots. Second Division adopt similar line with datum position Beer Beer 100 miles west of Apples Apples, course east, speed of advance 8 knots. Third Division datum position Charlie Charlie 90 miles southwest of Apples Apples; course north, speed of advance 8 knots, patrol interval not to exceed 5 miles. All submarines to take maximum precautions against Japanese U-boats or aircraft and are to remain unsighted. Strict wireless silence to be maintained except for convoy and heavy unit reports which are to be made by usual mobile patrol procedure. Keep H/F transmissions to minimum compatible with these objects. Hostilities have not yet repeat not yet commenced against any nation. Summary of incidents with Japanese and reports of their warships and convoy Zebra follow.'

1907   Commodore Hong Kong to C-in-C repeated to China Fleet: 'Japanese have attacked across border and are being resisted.'

1918   C-in-C to Commodore Hong Kong: 'You are authorised to take all warlike measures necessary for the defence of the Colony. Good luck.'

1920   C-in-C to China Fleet: 'Commence hostilities against Germany only repeat Germany only. In view of situation vis-a-vis Japan, upon which country an ultimatum has been served, German ships are not to be allowed to interfere with potentially more important operations.'

2045   C-in-C to China Fleet: 'At sunset Japanese slow convoy Yorker was reported southbound in Molucca Passage, escorted by 2 battleships, 1 fleet-carrier, 5 heavy and 2 light cruisers and 16 destroyers. Composition—35 troop and supply ships and 4 tankers. Appreciation is that this convoy will approach Malaya through the Java Sea, being the support force for fast convoy Zebra now in Bashi Channel. The British ultimatum to Japan expires at midnight. Hostilities against Japan are not repeat not to be commenced until ordered.'

2130   C-in-C to Rear-Admiral Commanding Force "Q": 'In event of war with Japan, your main object will be the destruction of slow convoy Yorker with cooperation of R.A.F. Malaya—the northern Carimata Strait before dawn on 12th September being the most likely place and time of interception. It is therefore important that your force should remain intact in any brush with convoy Zebra or the Japanese heavy force reported by S.S. *Wysang*. Our submarines will be ordered to attack this latter convoy and its remote covering force, in that order of priority. Force "Q" is limited to a single dawn air torpedo attack provided a suitable opportunity arises, which now seems likely. After dawn on 5th September and in the absence of further orders Force "Q" is to proceed at utmost despatch to Labuan there to re-fuel. Submarines are not repeat not to be attacked east of 118° East.'

2210   Captain S/M 4. to Submarines on Patrol: 'In the event of war with Japan, your target priority is—troopships, tankers, transports, fleet-carriers, battleships, heavy and light cruisers in that order. Submarines are not repeat not to be attacked east of 118° East.'

2247   MANILA RADIO NEWSFLASH: 'The United States has made a swingeing protest against Japanese violation of international law on Hong Kong border and atrocities at sea. All American Asiatic forces alerted. President has ordered United States Pacific Fleet to sail from Pearl Harbour—destination unknown.'

2327   C-in-C to China Fleet: 'Main Japanese Fleet sailed from Inland Sea after dark. Composition believed to be 4 battleships, 2 fleet-carriers 2 light carriers, 2 cruiser squadrons and at least 16 destroyers. Staff appreciation is that this fleet will not enter South China Sea until American intentions are clear. Japanese U-boats have been detected by local A/S craft off both Hong Kong and Singapore.

4th September.

0007   *Submarine 15* to First Division (by H/F): 'EMERGENCY. Hudrophone effect from convoy of large vessels 10 miles to sou'west. Enemy speed about 12 knots, approximate course south. Consider this to be convoy Zebra.'

0013   *Submarine II* (First Divisional Leader) to *Submarine 15* (by H/F): 'Close convoy, shadow and report. When hostilities commence, you are not, repeat not, to attack.'

0016   *Submarine II* to *Submarine 13* (by H/F): 'Make convoy enemy report on full power.'

0017   C-in-C to China Fleet: 'Commence hostilities against Japan.'

0019   *Submarine 13* to C-in-C, Captain S/M 4., repeated Force "Q", Submarines on Patrol: 'EMERGENCY. At 0007 *Submarine 15* obtained hydrophone effect from heavy southbound convoy in position 87 miles 185 degrees from South Cape Formosa. *Submarine 15* ordered to shadow, not attack.'

0049   Captain S/M 4. to First Division repeated Second Division and Submarines on Patrol: 'Your 0007 enemy report received. Withdraw sou'westwards at 16 knots maintaining good H/F reception distance. *Submarine 13* is to continue repeating *Submarine 15*'s enemy reports on full power. Second Division is approaching you from westwards."

0053   Captain S/M 4. to Submarines on Patrol: 'No submarine is to attack another submarine, not even a suspected Japanese U-boat, anywhere east of 118° East.'

0107   *Submarine 13* to C-in-C, Captain S/M 4., repeated Force "Q" and Submarines on Patrol: '*Submarine 15* reports sighting convoy at 0045, enemy course now westerly.'

0110   Captain S/M 4. to Second Division repeated Submarines on Patrol: 'If necessary adjust your division's course and speed for dawn attack from submerged. Maintain 5-mile intervals.'

0131   Captain S/M 4. to Third Division repeated Submarines on Patrol: "Concentrate to 2½-mile intervals and position your division for submerged attack after Second Division, allowing the latter until noon today.'

0147   Captain S/M 4. to First Division repeated Submarines on Patrol: 'Convoy Zebra's anticipated mean course is sou'west; but both zigzagging and longer tactical alterations of course must be expected. First Division close to 10-mile intervals on *Submarine 15* maintaining present line of bearing, reducing speed as necessary.'

The stage is set for atacks on convoy Zebra by the Second Division at dawn and by the Third Division about noon on 4th September; but there are some complications which are now being considered by the C-in-C, his staff and Captain S/M 4., on board *Medway*.

Firstly, it is appreciated that the Japanese convoy commander is aware of a British submarine transmitting on high power about 60 miles away and probably realises that there is H/F chatter closer to him. In the darkness, he has therefore altered course to west; but will not wish to maintain this direction for too long, as it takes him towards Pratus and Hong Kong from either of which he may expect dawn aerial reconnaissance. It is therefore considered that convoy Zebra will alter course to the south before daybreak, thus regaining its proper line of advance.

Secondly, if the First Division remains in contact with the enemy convoy and, at the same time, maintains its H/F communications down the line, it will run into the Second Division during darkness.

Thirdly, no submarines are yet deployed against the strong Japanese covering force headed sou'westwards at 20 knots; although this is yet a long way off.

The decision is therefore taken to clear the First Division out of the combat area, even though this means losing contact with convoy Zebra for three hours.

4th September Timetable, continued.

0201   Captain S/M 4. to First Division repeated Submarines on Patrol: 'At 0230 break off contact with convoy Zebra and return at 18 knots to position Apples Apples forming mobile patrol on line of bearing 135°-315° at 10-mile intervals. Course northeast dived by day from 0600 at 3 knots, your datum position and initial pivotal point being Apples Apples.'

0213   C-in-C China Fleet to R.A.F. Kaitak (Hong Kong): 'Request Sunderland dawn reconnaissance from Pratus, based on last report of convoy Zebra from *Submarine 13*.'

At 0530 the convoy is, in fact, sighted by *Submarine 21* of the Second Division; but further westwards than expected, and this necessitates a surface run by *Submarine 24* and *Submarine 25* in order to gain their submerged firing positions.

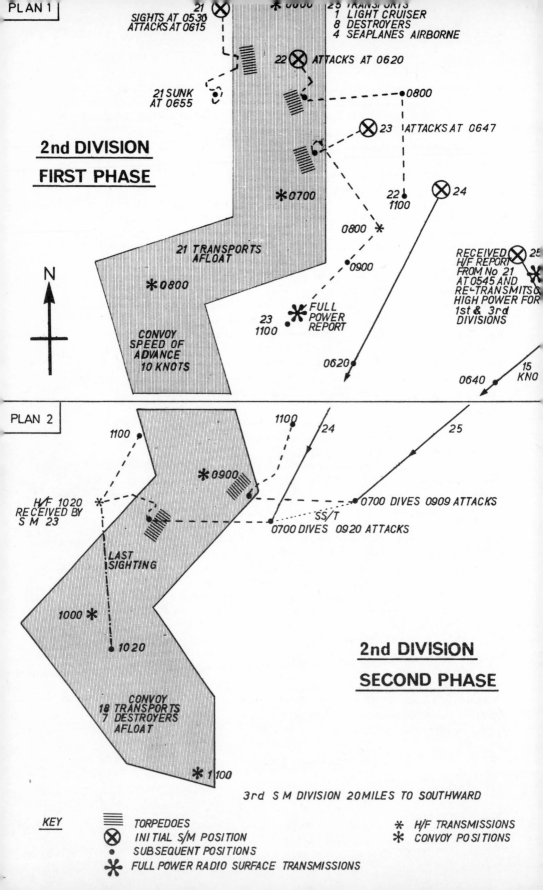

PLAN 1

21
SIGHTS AT 0530
ATTACKS AT 0615

25 TRANSPORTS
1 LIGHT CRUISER
8 DESTROYERS
4 SEAPLANES AIRBORNE

22 ⊗ ATTACKS AT 0620

21 SUNK
AT 0655

2nd DIVISION
FIRST PHASE

⊗ 23   ATTACKS AT 0647

•0800

✳0700

22
1100

⊗ 24

0800 ✳

21 TRANSPORTS
AFLOAT

0800

N

✳0800

•0900

RECEIVED
H/F REPORT
FROM No 21
AT 0545 AND
RE-TRANSMITS ON
HIGH POWER FOR
1st & 3rd
DIVISIONS

⊗ 25
✳

CONVOY
SPEED OF
ADVANCE
10 KNOTS

23
1100

✳ FULL
POWER
REPORT

0620

0640

15
KNO

Plan 2

1100

1100

24

25

✳0900

H/F 1020
RECEIVED BY
S M 23

✳

0700 DIVES 0909 ATTACKS

SS/T

0700 DIVES 0920 ATTACKS

LAST
SIGHTING

2nd DIVISION

SECOND PHASE

1000 ✳

•1020

CONVOY
18 TRANSPORTS
7 DESTROYERS
AFLOAT

✳ 1100

3rd S M DIVISION 20 MILES TO SOUTHWARD

KEY

▤ TORPEDOES
⊗ INITIAL S/M POSITION
• SUBSEQUENT POSITIONS
✳ FULL POWER RADIO SURFACE TRANSMISSIONS

✳ H/F TRANSMISSIONS
✳ CONVOY POSITIONS

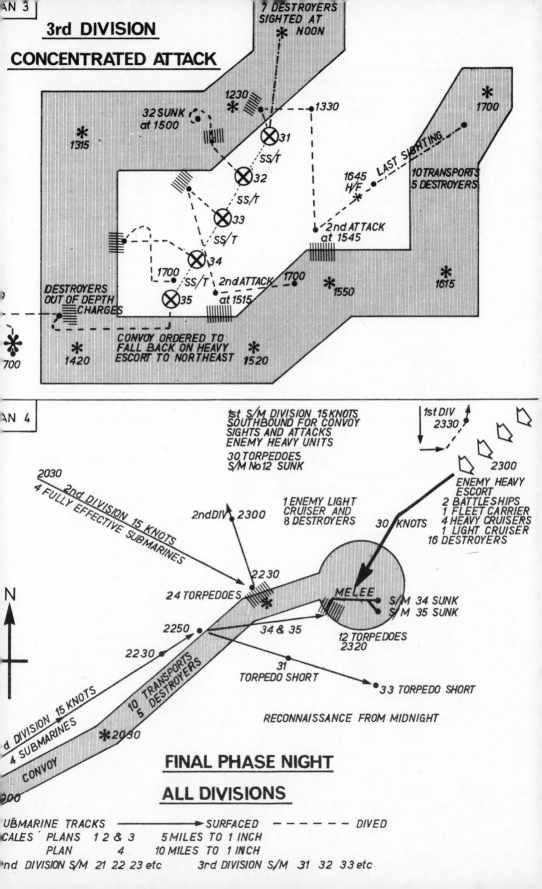

3rd DIVISION
CONCENTRATED ATTACK

7 DESTROYERS
SIGHTED AT
NOON

1230

1330

32 SUNK
at 1500

31
ss/t

32
ss/t

33
SS/T

34
SS/T

1700

35

1700

1315

1645
H/F

LAST SIGHTING

1700

10 TRANSPORTS
5 DESTROYERS

2nd ATTACK
at 1545

2nd ATTACK
at 1515

1550

1615

DESTROYERS
OUT OF DEPTH
CHARGES

CONVOY ORDERED TO
FALL BACK ON HEAVY
ESCORT TO NORTHEAST

1420

1520

700

1st S/M DIVISION 15 KNOTS
SOUTHBOUND FOR CONVOY
SIGHTS AND ATTACKS
ENEMY HEAVY UNITS

30 TORPEDOES
S/M No 12 SUNK

1st DIV
2330

2300

2030
2nd DIVISION 15 KNOTS
4 FULLY EFFECTIVE SUBMARINES

2nd DIV 2300

1 ENEMY LIGHT
CRUISER AND
8 DESTROYERS

ENEMY HEAVY
ESCORT
2 BATTLESHIPS
1 FLEET CARRIER
4 HEAVY CRUISERS
1 LIGHT CRUISER
16 DESTROYERS

30 KNOTS

2230

24 TORPEDOES

MELEE

S/M 34 SUNK
S/M 35 SUNK

2250

34 & 35

12 TORPEDOES
2320

2230

10 TRANSPORTS
5 DESTROYERS

31
TORPEDO SHORT

33 TORPEDO SHORT

3rd DIVISION 15 KNOTS
4 SUBMARINES

2030

CONVOY

RECONNAISSANCE FROM MIDNIGHT

N

200

FINAL PHASE NIGHT
ALL DIVISIONS

SUBMARINE TRACKS ——————→ SURFACED – – – – – – DIVED
SCALES PLANS 1 2 & 3   5 MILES TO 1 INCH
        PLAN   4   10 MILES TO 1 INCH
2nd DIVISION S/M 21 22 23 etc   3rd DIVISION S/M 31 32 33 etc

If the reader will kindly study Plans 1, 2 and 3 in this Appendix, it will be seen that the submarines do not only attack; but also report on H/F and S.S/T to others in their own division and by high power, on selected occasions, to all ships and authorities outside their division.

From Plan 3, it can be seen that the convoy was last sighted in daylight from *Submarine 31* at 1645. Her H/F signal is received by *Submarine 33* and passed through *Submarine 34* to *Submarine 35*. This last, being 30 miles astern of the convoy, half-surfaces (to get her main aerials out of the water) and transmits the convoy's position, course and speed on full power.

Acting on this information, Captain S/M 4. orders the Second and Third Divisions to chase the convoy, attacking by night from the surface. This order results in the melee shown on Plan 4. The First Division, which has sighted nothing all day, is ordered to intercept and polish off convoy Zebra, with the heavy Japanese covering force as an additional target—if met.

When convoy Zebra is attacked by the Second Division at 2230, the Japanese Admiral of the covering force (constantly beset by a fuel problem) detaches a light cruiser and 8 fresh destroyers to forge ahead at 30 knots, and these arrive in time to sink *Submarine 34* and *Submarine 35* after the Third Division's 2320 attack.

But the Japanese Admiral himself now runs into trouble; for the First Division, concentrated and southbound at speed, fires 30 torpedoes at his heavy ships from a range of 3,000 yards. The First Division wheels and escapes into the night at 18 knots before even its presence is suspected by the enemy. All five submarines have fired to hit the fleet carrier, a most conspicuous target which is sunk by six hits. In addition a heavy cruiser is sunk by 'overs' and one of the battleships is severely damaged by two hits. But *Submarine 12* fails to receive the retirement signal and continues towards the convoy whilst re-loading, when a screening destroyer rams and sinks her.

To sum up. British submarines have sunk 21 transports or troopships, 1 fleet-carrier, 1 heavy and 1 light cruiser and 5 destroyers, these last only because they crossed lines of fire. Five British submarines have been sunk. In all, 144 torpedoes have been fired and 52 hits obtained. Further, the First Division is active, each of its four remaining submarines still having eight torpedoes now (with rapid power loading) ready for firing.

At midnight the leader of the Second Division, who has four torpedoless submarines, reports convoy Zebra down to 7 transports at 2230 and retiring northeastwards. At 0115 on 5th September the First Division's leader reports the results of his atack upon the enemy heavy force and emphasises that a big fleet-carrier has certainly been sunk. No report is made by either of the two remaining submarines of the Third Division because they have lost touch.

Whilst the C-in-C realises that Force "Q" now has a good opportunity for a dawn torpedo bombing attack, he reflects that this force has already played its part by drawing the enemy heavy units into a trap. He also estimates that the arrival of the 1st Cruiser Squadron at Singapore by 10th September will give him ten 8" gun cruisers to attack enemy convoy Yorker in the Carimata Strait. In addition he has two aircraft-carriers and can rake up 15 destroyers. These, with the submarines and R.A.F. bombers should be capable of savaging convoy Yorker and turning it back. The C-in-C therefore orders Force "Q" and the First Submarine Division to Labuan for re-fuelling and instructs the remaining submarines to proceed to Singapore for fuel and torpedoes.

Thus ends the battle that never was. So I feel the Japanese were wise not to attack Singapore without first gaining vitally important bases and airfields in French Indo-China.

CRITIQUE

It is my view that the Fourth Submarine Flotilla was capable of such a success in September of 1939; because it had been highly trained for this very purpose. Six months later, it would probably not have been even one half as good; for its splitting-up had broken the teamwork, cohesion and tactical communication efficiency essential to wolfpack assault. The one third proportion of torpedo hits allowed in this War Game was substantiated during the war itself. My loss rate of five submarines from fifteen, is probably excessive; but here I have allowed for 'early state amorphism;' although this would have been minimal in a flotilla still inspired by the verve, willpower and energy of Captain George Menzies.

The reader will recall the two Italian convoys which I have described in some detail, those of September 1941 and October 1942. In the first case, four very small and very slow submarines sank 66% of the convoy which comprised large troopships. In the second case, four similar submarines, with the addition of *Safari*, sank 50% of the convoy, plus a destroyer and probably severely damaged a ship which put into Lampedusa. In neither of these cases were inter-submarine communications good, nor were proper mobile patrol tactics employed. I therefore think it reasonable to believe that with thrice the number of much faster, doubly-armed and highly coordinated submarines in the War Game, the result of 84% of the transport sunk is realistic.

Some may think that I have not given sufficient credit to the Japanese for ingenuity; but it should be remembered that they were heavily committed in China and would have been uncertain about American reaction. That, in this game, the Japanese managed to get their convoys undetected as far as Formosa and the Molucca Passage reflects devious and effective routeing. They may not have acted as I have suggested. but the fact remains, that in order to invade Malaya, their convoys would have had to cover great distances and they possessed only a few large merchant ships capable of over 12 knots.

With modern underwater communications and weapons, I feel strongly that nuclear submarine wolfpack tactics—although greatly different from those I have described—can provide Great Britain with a large proportion of the naval power she so urgently needs against all commers, whether upon, below or above the sea.

APPENDIX II—NAVAL APPOINTMENTS HELD BY AUTHOR

YEAR & RANK.	SHIP OR ESTABLISHMENT & SENIOR OFFICERS.	DISTINCTIONS.
1928-1932 Cadet	Royal Naval College, Dartmouth, Captain S.J. Meyrick and Captain Wodehouse.	Boxing
1932 Cadet	Eight Inch Gun Cruiser *Norfolk*, Home Fleet. Captain J.F. Somerville.	
1932-1934 Midshipman	H.M.S. *Norfolk*, Flagship, Americas & West Indies Station Vice-Admiral the Hon. Sir R.A.R. Plunkett-Ernle-Erle-Drax KCB DSO. Captain H.E.C. Blagrove.	Rifle & Pistol shooting
1935 Midshipman	H.M.S. *Orion*, Flagship, Second Cruiser Squadron, Home Fleet. Rear-Admiral S.J. Meyrick. Captain E de F. Renouf.	Commendation from C-in-C for High Angle (Ack-Ack) fire control.
1935-1936 Acting Sub-Lieutenant	Royal Naval College, Greenwich and Sub-Lieutenants' Courses at Portsmouth. *(Selected for Gunnery specialisation after three years in submarines)*	Naval History. Commendation for Junior Staff Course. Athletics (¼ mile) Rugby—United Services. Hockey—Navy
1937 Sub-Lieutenant	Submarine Course, Fort Blockhouse. Short Air Course, H.M.S. *Courageous* H.M. Submarines *Grampus* and *Swordfish*.	Equal top. Commendation from C-in-C for paper on the role of Fleet Air Arm in War. Hockey—Navy

Lieutenant	In command of 100-strong naval draft to China	Rugby—Home Fleet. First independent command, at age 22.
1938 Lieutenant	Submarine depot-ship *Medway*, China Fleet. (Sick list and 'Light Duty') Captain Claude Barry DSO.	Commendation from C-in-C for re-organisation of Fleet Mail to overcome chaotic condition on mainland
1938-1940 Lieutenant	Navigator & Armament Officer, H.M. Submarine *Regulus*. Captain G.C.P. Menzies & Commander John Money.	of China.
1940 Lieutenant	First Lieutenant, H.M. Submarine *Perseus,* arriving in Mediterranean on 8th August. Lieutenant-Commander Peter Bartlett.	
1941 Lieutenant	Submarines Commanding Officers' Qualifying Course. Staff Officer Operations, 7th Submarine Flotilla, Captain R.M. Edwards. Commanding Officer, H.M. Submarine *H.44* - Training flotilla.	
1942-1943 Lieutenant	Commanding Officer, H.M. Submarine *Unbroken*, 8th S/M Flotilla (Capt: G.A.W. Voelcker) and 10th S/M Flotilla Captains G.W.G. Simpson & G.C. Phillips.	D.S.O., D.S.C. Awarded 6 months' seniority *Admiralty commendation for skill.*
1943 Lieutenant	Assistant Staff Officer Operations to Flag Officer Submarines —Rear-Admiral Claude Barry, CB DSO.	
1944 Lieutenant	Commanding Officer, H.M. Submarine *Thule*, 3rd S/M Flotilla, Home Waters, Captain R.S. Warne.	
1944-1945 Lieutenant-Commander	Commanding Officer, H.M. Submarine *Thule*, 4th S/M Flotilla, Far East. Captains H.M.C. Ionides CBE and B. Bryant,DSO DSC.	Bar to D.S.C.
1946 Lieutenant-Commander	Selected for first post-war Naval Staff Course. Naval Tactical Course.	

250

1946-1949 Lieutenant- Commander	First Lieutenant and Training Officer, H.M. New Zealand cruiser *Bellona,* Captains M.B. Laing and D. Hammersley-Johnson. (Recommended for promotion to Commander by the latter)	Commendations from New Zealand Navy Board - i) For services in command of Naval Training Camp. ii) For conduct of a month long Board of Inquiry.
1949 Lieutenant- Commander	Assistant Staff Officer Intelligence, Hong Kong.	
1950 Lieutenant- Commander	Unemployed Time in order to stand for Parliament at Windsor.	
1950-1952 Lieutenant- Commander	Commanding Officer, Escort Maintenance Vessel *Duncansby Head* and Minesweeper Group, Reserve Fleet, Sheerness - some 15 ships, 25 officers and 350 men.	Last independent command.

SHORT BIBLIOGRAPHY.

Admiralty Charts. The Hydrographer of the Navy.
Battle for the Mediterranean, The
    Captain Donald Macintyre DSO** DSC*
British Admiralty, The, Leslie Gardiner.
Columbia Encyclopedia, The, Columbia University.
Far and the Deep, The, Edward P. Stafford.
Italian Navy in World War II, The, Commander M.A. Bragadin.
London Gazette, The, Offical Despatches.
Navy at War, The, Captain S.W. Roskill DSC.
Navy Lists, Admiralty.
One of Our Submarines, Commander Edward Young DSO DSC*,
    R.N.V.R.
Second World War, The, Winston S. Churchill.
War Against Japan, The (Official History),
    Major-General S. Woodburn Kirby CB CMG OBE MC.
War at Sea, The (Official History), Captain S.W. Roskill DSC.

INDEX